An Overview of the Pre-Suppression Society of Jesus in Spain

Brill Research Perspectives in Jesuit Studies

Editor

Robert A. Maryks (*Independent Scholar*)

Editorial Board

Ariane Boltanski (*Université Rennes 2*)
Carlos Eire (*Yale University*)
Alison Fleming (*Winston-Salem State University*)
Paul Grendler (*University of Toronto, emeritus*)
Stephen Schloesser, S.J. (*Loyola University Chicago*)

Volumes published in this Brill Research Perspectives title are listed at *brill.com/rpjs*

An Overview of the Pre-Suppression Society of Jesus in Spain

By

Patricia W. Manning

BRILL

LEIDEN | BOSTON

This is an open access title distributed under the terms of the CC BY-NC-ND 4.0 license, which permits any non-commercial use, distribution, and reproduction in any medium, provided no alterations are made and the original author(s) and source are credited. Further information and the complete license text can be found at https://creativecommons.org/licenses/by-nc-nd/4.0/

The terms of the CC license apply only to the original material. The use of material from other sources (indicated by a reference) such as diagrams, illustrations, photos and text samples may require further permission from the respective copyright holder.

This publication is also available in Open Access at www.brill.com/rpjs thanks to generous support from the following institutions:
– College of the Holy Cross, Worcester (MA)
– Le Moyne College, Syracuse (NY)
– Santa Clara University (CA)
– Saint Louis University (MO)
– Ateneo de Manila University (Philippines)
– Georgia Southern University (GA)

This paperback book edition is simultaneously published as issue 2.3 (2020) of *Brill Research Perspectives in Jesuit Studies*, DOI:10.1163/25897454-12340007.

Library of Congress Control Number: 2020946476

Typeface for the Latin, Greek, and Cyrillic scripts: "Brill". See and download: brill.com/brill-typeface.

ISBN 978-90-04-43430-1 (paperback)
ISBN 978-90-04-43431-8 (e-book)

Copyright 2021 by Patricia W. Manning. Published by Koninklijke Brill NV, Leiden, The Netherlands. Koninklijke Brill NV incorporates the imprints Brill, Brill Hes & De Graaf, Brill Nijhoff, Brill Rodopi, Brill Sense, Hotei Publishing, mentis Verlag, Verlag Ferdinand Schöningh and Wilhelm Fink Verlag. Koninklijke Brill NV reserves the right to protect this publication against unauthorized use. Requests for re-use and/or translations must be addressed to Koninklijke Brill NV via brill.com or copyright.com.

This book is printed on acid-free paper and produced in a sustainable manner.

Contents

An Overview of the Pre-Suppression Society of Jesus in Spain   1
    Patricia W. Manning
    Abstract   1
    Keywords   1
    Glossary of Frequently Used Terms   1
1   Introduction   4
2   Ignatius of Loyola   8
3   The Early Years of the Society of Jesus in Spain   16
4   Borja and Mercurian's Generalates   31
5   Encounters with the Inquisition   37
6   Admission Redux: Excluding *Conversos* from the Society   45
7   Aiding Catholics under Siege   50
8   The Question of Religiously Minded Women   54
9   Theological Debates   58
10   Jesuits' Roles in the Inquisition in the Seventeenth Century   75
11   Jesuit *Aprobación* Writers   77
12   Pedagogy   79
13   Preaching   85
14   Publications by Jesuits   90
15   Jesuit Celebrations   114
16   Domestic Life in the Society   118
17   Seventeenth-Century Crises   119
18   Controlling Chocolate and Tobacco Usage in the Society   126
19   The Immaculate Conception, Part 2: The Seventeenth and Eighteenth Centuries   127
20   Publications Unfavorable to the Order   131
21   The Expulsion   134
22   The Aftermath   135
23   Conclusion   139
    Bibliography   141

An Overview of the Pre-Suppression Society of Jesus in Spain

Patricia W. Manning
University of Kansas, USA
pwmannin@ku.edu

Abstract

In *An Overview of the Pre-Suppression Society of Jesus in Spain*, Patricia W. Manning offers a survey of the Society of Jesus in Spain from its origins in Ignatius of Loyola's early preaching to the aftereffects of its expulsion. Rather than nurture the nascent order, Loyola's homeland was often ambivalent. His pre-Jesuit freelance sermonizing prompted investigations. The young Society confronted indifference and interference from the Spanish monarchy and outright opposition from other religious orders. This essay outlines the order's ministerial and pedagogical activities, its relationship with women and with royal institutions, including the Spanish Inquisition, and Spanish members' roles in theological debates concerning casuistry, free will, and the immaculate conception. It also considers the impact of Jesuits' non-religious writings.

Keywords

Society of Jesus – Jesuits – Spain, 1521–1772 – immaculate conception – probabilism – Ignatius of Loyola – *Spiritual Exercises* – Francisco de Borja – Baltasar Gracián – Juan Bautista Poza – Mateo de Moya – Luisa de Carvajal y Mendoza – women's spirituality

Glossary of Frequently Used Terms

Affective spirituality	Devotional practices that involve the emotions in prayer life.
Alumbradismo	From the Inquisition's point of view, this movement's meditative practices were more passive than orthodox ones. Practices often varied from one individual

---

© PATRICIA W. MANNING, 2021 | DOI:10.1163/9789004434318_002

This is an open access chapter distributed under the terms of the CC BY-NC-ND 4.0 license.

	to another and from group to group within the movement, so it is difficult to pinpoint a system of beliefs for all practitioners, but *alumbradismo* generally favored mystical contact with the divine over formal religious ceremonies.
Alumbrado or *alumbrada*	A person who practices *alumbradismo*. An *alumbrada* is a woman who practices *alumbradismo*.
Aprobación	Literally, approbation. This is one of the terms used for official approvals of printed texts by the Consejo de Castilla (Council of Castile).
Auto de fe	Literally, act of faith. An often public ceremony in which the sentences of those found guilty by the Inquisition were read.
Beata	A devout laywoman who led a religiously motivated lifestyle. Some *beatas* were renowned for their visionary capacities; some took vows as tertiaries.
Calificadores	Assessors who were charged with evaluating the doctrinal soundness of texts or ideas expressed by defendants of the Inquisition.
Casuistry	The study of cases of conscience, which is to say sacramental confession cases, in order to consider both the individual's circumstances and decision-making process in addition to more broad concepts of morality.
Cátedra	A chaired teaching position at a university.
Censura	Literally, censorship. This is one of the terms used for official approvals of printed texts by the Consejo de Castilla (Council of Castile); *calificadores* for the Spanish Inquisition also sometimes titled their assessments in this fashion.
Colegio	Outside of the Society of Jesus's usage, either a school or college, including a residential college at a university. In Jesuit usage and in this narrative, a *colegio* is any Jesuit institution that houses Jesuits who have completed their formations along with those who are still in the process of formation.
Converso	Initially, a person whose family had converted from Judaism. The term also later came to be applied to those whose families had converted from Islam.
De auxiliis	Literally, on help; the debate concerning the role of grace and free will in the Catholic Church.

AN OVERVIEW OF THE PRE-SUPPRESSION SOCIETY OF JESUS IN SPAIN

Holy Office
: The Holy Office of the Inquisition. The unqualified term references the Spanish Holy Office. I will specify when I refer to the Roman body.

Illuminism
: The translation of *alumbradismo*.

Immaculate conception
: The theological concept that Mary, the mother of Jesus, was free from original sin from the moment of her conception.

Immaculist
: The point of view that favored the idea that the Virgin Mary was free from original sin from the moment of her conception.

Ilusa
: Literally, dreamer or naïve in contemporary Spanish. The term was used by the Inquisition for mystics whose visions were not considered authentic.

Infused contemplation
: The concept that the mind becomes totally centered on God after being given this ability from the divine.

Inquisition
: At times, I employ the unmodified term to reference the Spanish Inquisition. A 1478 papal bull authorized the Spanish monarchs to appoint inquisitors. The Spanish Inquisition was abolished for the final time in 1834. I will add the adjective Roman when I refer to that body.

Junta
: A temporary royal council. Several Spanish monarchs formed *juntas* to promote the immaculate conception.

Limpieza de sangre
: Literally, purity of blood. Statutes were enacted to make people demonstrate that their lineages were free from Jewish (and eventually Muslim) ancestors in order to obtain certain positions in Spanish society.

Maculist
: The point of view that believed that the Virgin Mary was cleansed of original sin at some point after her conception.

Memoriales
: Documents that make a request or ask for a favor from an authority. This was a common practice in early modern Spain; many people wrote *memoriales* to officials.

Memorialistas
: People who write *memoriales*.

Morisco
: A term for a person of Muslim lineage.

Motín de Esquilache
: The Esquilache riots. A series of protests in 1766 that began in Madrid and became the pretext for the expulsion of the Society of Jesus from Spain.

Portada
: The frontispiece of a printed book. This initial page generally contains information about the dedicatee in addition to the title, author, and publication details.

Probabilism	A moral theory that allows an individual to choose an option that favors free will even if another option is more probable in deciding whether a course of action is permissible or not.
Probabiliorism	This moral theory limits the degree of choice in probabilism. According to probabiliorism, one must follow the option one believes is more probable.
Reales Estudios	Literally, royal studies. A program of university-level courses at the Colegio Imperial in Madrid.
Relación	An account, often made to inform a person in authority.
Suprema	The Supreme Council of the Spanish Inquisition.
Visitador	A Jesuit sent by the superior general to inspect a particular province. (This same position is referred to as *comisario* in the *Constitutions*.)
Vita	Literally, life. In the context of this narrative, the term refers to the life stories of confessees or fellow Jesuits written by members of the Society.

1 Introduction

The Society of Jesus began in Spain. It was the birthplace not only of Ignatius of Loyola (*c*.1491–1556) but also of a number of the early Jesuits. Counting Ignatius, five of the seven initial members of the order, the "co-founders" as they are termed, were from Spain.[1] The other four were Diego Laínez (1512–65), Nicolás de Bobadilla (*c*.1509–90), Francis Xavier (1506–52), and Alfonso

---

1 Manuel Revuelta González, "Ignacio de Loyola: El fundador de la Compañía," *Historia* 16, no. 191 (1992): 37–48, here 44–45. Capitalization follows Brill's Jesuit Studies house style, rather than the rules for capitalization in Spanish and other romance languages. House-style rules concerning capitalization and their divergence from romance-language usage are apparent in the representation of titles of articles and books, the names of journals, and terms relating to Catholic liturgy.

I do not identify which men are members of the Society of Jesus in the notes or bibliography, but on occasion I will do so in my text when this information is relevant. I also generally eschew the courtesy title of father; however, I employ it occasionally when an individual's status as a priest is important to my argument.

I gratefully acknowledge the support of the staff of the Interlibrary Loan Department at the University of Kansas for obtaining the research materials necessary for this essay. General research fund allocations 2166082 and 2301038 from the University of Kansas funded the archival research cited here. The intellectual companionship of my colleagues Isidro J. Rivera and Luis R. Corteguera always enriches my work. In this case, Luis provided valuable insight on the Chicago method for an inveterate MLA user and Isidro helped with thorny translation issues. Elspeth Healey and Kivilcim Yavuz helped decipher the meaning of an abbreviation. I

Salmerón (1515–85).[2] Beyond the first members, the Jesuits classified as "the inner circle of first Jesuits" were also Spanish. In addition to the aforementioned Laínez, Juan Alfonso de Polanco (1517–76), Jerónimo Nadal (1507–80), and Francisco de Borja (1510–72) all shared this nationality.[3] After the death of Superior General Francisco de Borja (in office 1565–72) in 1572, the Spanish monarch King Philip II (1527–98, r.1556–98) tried unsuccessfully to lobby for the election of another Spanish superior general and subsequently attempted to discredit the order's governance after his plan failed.[4]

Some scholars, particularly those interested in a pro-Catholic perspective, such as Marcelino Menéndez Pelayo (1856–1912), laud Spain for its adherence to Catholicism, including its status as "the cradle of St. Ignatius."[5] It is true that the concerns of the home country of the founder and a number of early members were crucial to the young order's decisions concerning the admission, and eventual exclusion, of descendants of non-Christians (*conversos*, literally, converts), as well as the exclusion of women—with one notable Spanish exception in the person of Princess Juana de Austria (1535–73). However, such propagandistic views of history imply unrealistic levels of support for the nascent Society in Spain.

---

also thank Robert A. Maryks, for inviting me to write this piece and for his patience, and Tim Page for his careful editorial eye. Finally, I thank the reader for Brill for his or her suggestions.

2 Javier Burrieza Sánchez, "Establecimiento, fundación y oposición de la Compañía de Jesús en España (siglo XVI)," in Teófanes Egido, Javier Burrieza Sánchez, and Manuel Revuelta González, *Los jesuitas en España y en el mundo hispánico* (Madrid: Fundación Carolina, Centro de Estudios Hispánicos e Iberamericanos, Marcial Pons, 2004), 49–106, here 49. When house style does not have a preference, if historical figures are best known in the English-speaking world by Anglicized versions of their names, I use them in my text. If this is not the case, I use the most common version of individuals' names as determined by house style, the electronic edition of the Real Academia de la Historia's *Diccionario biográfico español* (hereafter *DB~e*), and Jesuit sources.

3 John W. O'Malley, *The First Jesuits* (Cambridge, MA: Harvard University Press, 1993), 13. The relatively short length of this essay means that it is not possible to include an exhaustive bibliography. The works referenced are those most salient to my argument and should be treated as the starting point for the reader's own research about the Society. Since this piece is written for an English-speaking audience, I make every effort to cite resources in English. However, as will become evident, much of the research about the Society of Jesus in Spain is written in Spanish. For readers of Spanish, see Egido, Burrieza Sánchez, and Revuelta González, *Jesuitas en España*, for a history of the order in the Hispanic world.

4 See Javier Burrieza Sánchez, "La Compañía de Jesús y la defensa de la monarquía hispánica," *Hispania sacra* 60 (2008): 181–229, here 206 for a summary of Philip II's endeavors in this matter.

5 Marcelino Menéndez Pelayo, *Historia de los heterodoxos españoles* (Madrid: Librería Católica de San José, 1881), 3:834. All unattributed translations are my own.

Nonetheless, some continue to maintain a view of the Society of Jesus in Spain informed by opinions like that of Menéndez Pelayo. For example, Dale K. Van Kley asserts that, in contrast to more widespread opposition to the Jesuit community in France, "Spain [...] largely escaped such concentrated doses of anti-Jesuitism, in part because of the Society's largely Spanish origin." Moreover, Van Kley opines: "[Benito] Arias Montano and [Melchor] Cano did not an anti-Jesuit school of opinion make."[6] While it is true that the Spanish situation differed from that of France, there was opposition to the Society of Jesus in Spain beyond Melchor Cano (1507/9–60). (Arias Montano's [1527–98] opposition to the order is largely a subsequent invention).[7] Following Antonio Astrain's (1857–1928) research, Henry Kamen asserts that Cano and the archbishop of Toledo Juan Martínez Guijarro (1477–1557), who Latinized his name as Silíceo, "were only part of a wider campaign to discredit the Jesuit order."[8] As the Society in Spain established schools and members taught in them, ministered, and wrote, rumors and negative texts, often handwritten works, began to circulate about the community. Yet, when compared with a number of other European countries, the appearance of anti-Jesuit sentiment in Spain is admittedly different. Before the mid-eighteenth century, overtly anti-Jesuit texts that circulated in printed form in Spain were generally prohibited in short order. As negative sentiments toward the community intensified, printed publications reanimated critiques of the order from previous centuries. These helped fuel the tensions that led to the Jesuits' expulsion from Spain.

The relationship between the Jesuit order and Spain is complex and often characterized by conflicts with authorities, including Spanish monarchs and the Spanish Inquisition. Tensions between superiors general, Spanish monarchs, and popes arose over questions of loyalty, sovereignty, and internationalism.

---

6   Dale K. Van Kley, *Reform Catholicism and the International Suppression of the Jesuits in Enlightenment Europe* (New Haven: Yale University Press, 2018), 59, 61.

7   See Antonio Pérez Goyena, "Arias Montano y los jesuítas," *Estudios eclesiásticos* 7 (1928): 273–317, for details.

8   Henry Kamen, *The Spanish Inquisition: A Historical Revision*, 4th ed. (New Haven: Yale University Press, 2014), 207, 434n105. The initial volumes of Antonio Astrain's seven-volume *Historia* detail the early opposition to the Society. See especially Astrain, *Historia de la Compañía de Jesús en la asistencia de España* (Madrid: Administración de Razón y Fe, 1912–25), 1:321–40, 1:341–65, Biblioteca Nacional de España, herefater BNE, Biblioteca Digital Hispánica, hereafter BDH; http://bdh-rd.bne.es/viewer.vm?id=0000010528&page=1 (accessed April 28, 2020). In representing the names of modern Spanish authors, I follow the orthography used in the BNE's catalog. In the cases of non-Jesuit historical figures whose surnames have variants, when house style does not have a preference, I use the forms employed by the Real Academia de la Historia in the *DB~e*.

Disputes also arose in Spain with other Catholic religious orders over several theological points, including grace versus free will and the immaculate conception. Religious orders also jockeyed for position in the Spanish Inquisition, for designations as royal preachers, and for positions as confessors to the king and queen. As regalism and other ideological currents like the reform of Catholic institutions gained ground, the Society was increasingly attacked. In Spain, the Jesuits' supposed role in instigating the 1766 protests in Madrid known as the *motín de Esquilache* (the Esquilache riots) became a crucial justification for the order's expulsion in 1767. A thorough examination of the motives for the expulsion would require more space than is available in an overview, but this narrative deliberately avoids presenting a continuous thread that leads from the order's early years to the expulsion of the Society from Spain and the Spanish Empire. This decision was not "philosophically or politically inevitable," as Jonathan Wright and Jeffrey D. Burson maintain about the suppression.[9]

In order to tease out the complicated relationship between the Society and the home country of many notable Jesuits, this essay references a range of evidence, including historical, theological, and literary details.[10] Unfortunately, due to space limitations, music, science, and art in the Society cannot be given the attention these topics deserve. Considering the prominent role that writing played in the order itself and in the scholarly lives of individual members, texts produced by Jesuits—and in some cases the polemics that surrounded these works—play a prominent role in this essay. Texts critical of the order were diligently followed by Jesuits. Even the most cursory foray into the vast amount of correspondence left behind by Jesuits demonstrates that the order closely followed the publication of polemical texts about it.[11] Their efforts to respond to them—through written responses or lobbying for the prohibition of critiques—usually only provoked more ire from their detractors.

---

9   Jonathan Wright and Jeffrey D. Burson, "Introduction: Towards A New History of the Eighteenth-Century Suppression in Global Context," in *The Jesuit Suppression in Global Context: Causes, Events, and Consequences*, ed. Jeffrey D. Burson and Jonathan Wright (Cambridge: Cambridge University Press, 2015), 1–10, here 2. Wright and Burson describe the inevitability point of view as an "exaggeration" (2).

10 This interdisciplinarity reflects the research approach of the field of Jesuit studies in the twenty-first century as the most logical means to study an order with connections to a variety of scholarly disciplines.

11 See, e.g., *Cartas de algunos PP. de la Compañía de Jesús: Sobre los sucesos de la monarquía entre los años 1634 y 1648*, ed. Pascual de Gayangos (Madrid: Imprenta Nacional, 1861–65), for correspondence now housed in the Real Academia de la Historia in Madrid.

2   Ignatius of Loyola

From classical literature to celebrity gossip websites, stories of dramatic life changes attract interest. In this context, it is not surprising that the transformation that Ignatius underwent following leg wounds sustained in a 1521 battle with the French in Pamplona has been the subject of much attention, ranging from scholarly analyses such as that of W. [William] W. Meissner (1931–2010) to fictionalized treatments such as John L'Heureux's (1934–2019) poem.[12] Ignatius was born around 1491. Relatively little is known about his early life, including the years he spent at noble courts in Arévalo and Nájera.[13] Confined to bed as he recovered from surgery to repair his injuries, and without his preferred chivalric novels, Loyola turned to the only available reading material: devotional books. According to Ignatius's account, "un Vita Christi y un libro de la vida de los Santos en romance" (a life of Christ and a book about the lives of saints in the vernacular [Spanish]) accompanied him as he convalesced.[14] Since the late 1800s, scholars have attempted to ascertain precisely which works Ignatius consumed, both in order to clarify this very salient detail of the founder's life and to consider the impact of these works on his writing and religious practices.[15]

2.1   *Concerns over Ignatius's Religious Orthodoxy*

As Ignatius transitioned from courtier to religious seeker, he came to the attention of religious authorities because he shared communalities with groups of people that were already being subjected to scrutiny because of their beliefs.

---

12   W. [William] W. Meissner, *Ignatius of Loyola: The Psychology of a Saint* (New Haven: Yale University Press, 1992); John L'Heureux, "From St. Ignatius Loyola, Founder of the Jesuits: His Autobiography," in *No Place for Hiding: New Poems* (Garden City, NY: Doubleday, 1971), 35–43.

13   Enrique García Hernán, *Ignacio de Loyola* (Madrid: Taurus, Fundación Juan March, 2013), 15. I will alternate between Ignatius's first name and Loyola in my text. In the course of his conversion, Íñigo began to use the name Ignacio (Ignatius).

When the names of towns and regions in Spain do not have distinct spellings in English, I maintain the Spanish form, with one exception. I use Aragon instead of Aragón because this place name appears frequently in the phrase province of Aragon.

14   Ignatius of Loyola, *Fontes narrativi de S. Ignatio de Loyola et de Societatis Iesu initiis*, vol. 1, Monumenta Historica Societatis Iesu 66 (Rome: Apud Monumenta Historica Societatis Iesu, 1943), hereafter *FN* 1:370.

House style requires modern English-language names for places of publication.

15   See Terence O'Reilly, "Early Printed Books in Spain and the *Exercicios* of Ignatius of Loyola," *Bulletin of Spanish Studies* 89, no. 4 (2012): 635–64, here 638 for the state of this research.

AN OVERVIEW OF THE PRE-SUPPRESSION SOCIETY OF JESUS IN SPAIN 9

As a result, Ignatius's practices were examined by diocesan and inquisitorial tribunals.

In the first two decades of the sixteenth century, members of a meditative school called *alumbradismo* (illuminism) passively waited for enlightenment from the spirit in their meditative relationship with the divine. This passivity differentiated illuminism from the more orthodox Franciscan meditation methods from which it derived. Moreover, many of illuminism's earliest practitioners were *conversos*. Beyond the Inquisition's concerns with potential backsliding among those who had converted to Catholicism (and their descendants), it is not at all incidental that investigations of private, more personal spiritual practices, which did not need the intervention of the clergy, became an area of greater concern once Martin Luther (1483–1546) broke with the Catholic Church.[16] Indeed, some ecclesiastical authorities found similarities with Ignatius's meditative methodology and the *alumbrados'* techniques.

Ignatius also had connections to Spanish humanism. Although Pedro de Ribadeneyra's (1526–1611) biography of Ignatius relates that the founder developed a negative opinion about Erasmus (1466/69–1536) in Barcelona, this account has been questioned by scholars. Ribadeneyra's version seems to derive from an already existing account by Luís Gonçalves da Câmara (*c*.1519–75), which placed the incident in a different temporal moment. In Câmara's version, during Ignatius's 1526–27 stay in Alcalá de Henares his confessor suggested that he read Erasmus's *Enchiridion militis christiani* (Handbook of a Christian knight [1503/4]), but Ignatius instead read a more traditional text. Terence O'Reilly posits "that Ribadeneira, writing in the late sixteenth century when Erasmus was a *persona non grata*, altered da Câmara's account in order to safeguard Ignatius' orthodoxy."[17] The 1559 prohibitions of Erasmus in the Indices of Prohibited Books in Spain and Rome meant that many subsequent Catholics were unlikely to acknowledge debts to Erasmus; this tendency in Catholic historiography continued for a significant period of time.[18]

Regardless of whether Ignatius might first have encountered the *Enchiridion* in Alcalá, then the heart of Spanish Erasmianism, both Loyola and Manuel de

---

16 Kamen, *Spanish Inquisition*, 94–97. The beliefs of *alumbradismo* are too complex to be summarized adequately here. For the Inquisition's principal concerns with the movement, see the 1557 Edict of Toledo in Antonio Márquez, *Los alumbrados: Orígenes y filosofía (1525–1559)*, 2nd ed. (Madrid: Taurus, 1980), 229–38.

17 O'Reilly, "Early Printed," 660–61.

18 John W. O'Malley, "Renaissance Humanism and the Religious Culture of the First Jesuits," reprinted in O'Malley, *Saints or Devils Incarnate? Studies in Jesuit History* (Leiden: Brill, 2013), 181–98, here 182. See 182–98 for an exploration of the Jesuits' relationship with humanism.

Miona (c.1477–1567), his confessor in that city, had a number of connections to members of the Erasmian movement. And such contacts indubitably aroused concerns about Loyola's orthodoxy on the part of the Spanish Inquisition. In Alcalá, Ignatius was friendly with several members of the Eguía family, including Diego (c.1488–1556) and his brother Miguel (c.1495–1546), the printer of Erasmus's *Enchiridion* in Spain. (Diego de Eguía and another sibling, Esteban [c.1485–1551], eventually became Jesuits.)[19]

Between 1531 and 1533, after Ignatius left Spain, Miguel de Eguía was imprisoned by the Inquisition after Francisca Hernández (*fl.* late fifteenth century to early sixteenth century) denounced him as a *luterano* (Lutheran, the term the Inquisition used for all those accused of having Protestant sympathies). Hernández was a *beata* (a devout laywoman) in Valladolid who was arrested by the Inquisition in 1529; she denounced many individuals in the course of her trial.[20]

Barring the discovery of additional documentation that currently is not known to us, our knowledge about the concerns on the part of ecclesiastical authorities, including the Spanish Inquisition, about Ignatius is imperfect. The surviving paperwork from Alcalá in 1526 is incomplete: records from Salamanca in 1527, Paris in 1536, Venice in 1537, and also Vicenza in 1537 are missing, as is documentation on the allegations made in Rome in 1538.[21] Whereas Kamen believes that the Inquisition detained Loyola in Alcalá and Salamanca because of preoccupations over his possible connections to *alumbrados* and *conversos*, Javier Burrieza Sánchez believes that Loyola's role as spiritual advisor to "mujeres, y de dudosa reputación" (women, particularly those with doubtful reputations) was the reason for the Inquisition's interest in Ignatius's

---

19   Marcel Bataillon, *Les jésuites dans l'Espagne du XVIe siècle* (Paris: Les Belles Lettres, 2009), 147–50, cited in O'Reilly, "Early Printed," 660, and O'Reilly, "Early Printed," 661. See 661n125–26 for Ignatius's references to the Eguía brothers.

20   See Kamen, *Spanish Inquisition*, 93–99 for an overview of the Eguía and Fernández cases. See Stefania Pastore, "Unwise Paths: Ignatius of Loyola and the Years of Alcalá de Henares," trans. John Tedeschi, in *A Companion to Ignatius of Loyola: Life, Writings, Spirituality, Influence*, ed. Robert Aleksander Maryks (Leiden: Brill, 2014), 25–44, here 38–44, and Luis Fernández, "Íñigo de Loyola y los alumbrados," *Hispania sacra* 35 (1983): 585–680, here 592–656—and also referenced in note 30—for more details about people with ties to *alumbrado* ideas in Ignatius's circle.
      The broad spectrum of practices and behaviors encompassed by the term *beata* makes it difficult to define, but Mary E. Giles (1934–2003) offers a functional definition: "A woman who dedicated herself to God, living by herself or with other women in a community, sometimes attached to a religious order" ("Glossary," in *Women in the Inquisition: Spain and the New World*, ed. Mary E. Giles [Baltimore: Johns Hopkins University Press, 1999], 377–79, here 377).

21   García Hernán, *Ignacio de Loyola*, 17–18. See Meissner, *Ignatius of Loyola*, 127–38 for an English summary of Ignatius's encounters with religious authorities in Spain.

AN OVERVIEW OF THE PRE-SUPPRESSION SOCIETY OF JESUS IN SPAIN 11

behavior in Alcalá.[22] From surviving evidence, both the diocese of Alcalá and the Inquisition seemed concerned that Ignatius's practices were rooted in Judaism; since many *alumbrados* were of *converso* lineage, this might have been the origin of this line of questioning.[23]

A theme emerges from the early investigations of Ignatius in Spain: the Inquisition was apprehensive about Ignatius instructing others in religious matters without the benefit of formal training in theology. For this reason, in Alcalá, the Inquisition forbade him from teaching on religious matters for three years. The Inquisition in Salamanca suggested that Ignatius pursue further studies before attempting to develop and disseminate new spiritual practices.[24] In the estimation of Kamen and many other scholars, it was Ignatius's desire to avoid further interrogations by the Inquisition, combined with that body's request that he obtain formal training, which motivated him to leave Spain to study in Paris.[25] (The investigations outside of Spain lie outside of the scope of this essay, but in scholars' estimation, the inquiries made in Paris did not rise to the level of formal judicial cases.)[26]

After these experiences, Ignatius attempted to distance himself from the more heterodox elements in the Spanish milieu. In 1545, in writing to King John III of Portugal (1502–57, r.1521–57), Loyola assured the monarch of his orthodoxy. Ignatius listed the various legal investigations that had been carried out concerning his practices and declared that he had never been ordered to abjure any of his ideas, nor had he received any penitences or been forcibly exiled. In Loyola's estimation, he had been forced to undergo such rigorous examination because of his lack of formal education. He assured the king that this attention was entirely unrelated to "cosa alguna de cismáticos, de lutheranos ni de alumbrados, que á estos nunca los conuersé ni los conocí" (anything about schismatics, about "Lutherans" or about illuminists; I never conversed with them or met them).[27] In a technical sense, this statement is true, in that certain individuals had not yet been classified as heterodox by the Inquisition

---

22   Kamen, *Spanish Inquisition*, 138–39; Javier Burrieza Sánchez, "La percepción jesuítica de la mujer," *Investigaciones históricas, época moderna y contemporánea* 25 (2005): 85–116, here 89.

23   See Robert A. Maryks, *The Jesuit Order as a Synagogue of Jews: Jesuits of Jewish Ancestry and Purity-of-Blood Laws in the Early Society of Jesus* (Leiden: Brill, 2010), 46–48 for the sources that document these concerns.

24   José Luis González Novalín, "La Inquisición y la Compañía de Jesús," *Anthologica annua* 37 (1990): 11–56, here 15, 16.

25   Kamen, *Spanish Inquisition*, 138–39.

26   González Novalín, "Inquisición," 17.

27   Ignatius of Loyola, *Epistolae et instructiones*, vol. 1, Monumenta Historica Societatis Iesu 22 (Madrid: Typis Gabrielis Lopez de Horno, 1903), *Epp. Ign.*, Joanni III regi lusitaniae, 15 martii 1545, epist. 81, 1:296–97.

when Ignatius interacted with them. In Luis Fernández's (1908–2003) estimation, the judicial context is significant for the interpretation of Ignatius's statement: Loyola did not know anyone who had been formally condemned by the Holy Office on these charges.[28]

But there were such profound links between all of these movements and the university in Alcalá that it seems implausible that Ignatius truly did not know anyone with connections to "Lutheran" or *alumbrado* movements or humanists who strayed from orthodoxy. Several prominent intellectuals in Alcalá, including Juan de Valdés (c.1505–41), departed as the Inquisition started to conduct trials.[29] A number of people in Ignatius's circle or their close friends either were mentioned in others' statements to the Inquisition or investigated themselves by that body.[30] From the Inquisition's point of view, it was especially concerning that many of those associated with the university in Alcalá were *conversos*.[31] The link between Jewish ethnicity and *alumbradismo* reappears later in the sixteenth century in accusations against the Society.

There were also a number of women interested in spiritual matters who resided in Alcalá and its environs. For many, the mere mention of *beatas* erroneously conjures up heterodox behavior to the point that this idea is labeled "a cliché."[32] Some *beatas'* practices were orthodox. For example, a number of laywomen interested in religion clustered around Archbishop of Toledo Francisco Jiménez de Cisneros (c.1436–1517), the founder of the university at Alcalá de Henares.[33] Women formed an important part of Loyola's early spiritual trajectory from the moment he picked up his sister-in-law's devotional texts during his recovery. Ignatius mentions the importance of a *beata*, whom he does not name, as an important spiritual influence during his time in Manresa; Enrique García Hernán identifies her as the nun María de Santo Domingo (1486–1524).[34] Many of Ignatius's early followers were female. Such gender inclusiveness was radical in the 1400s.[35]

---

28 Fernández, "Íñigo de Loyola," 591.

29 Pastore, "Unwise Paths," 27; Kamen, *Spanish Inquisition*, 98. When sources differ as to the life dates of Spaniards, I prefer the dates listed in the *DB~e*.

30 Fernández, "Íñigo de Loyola," 592–656; Pastore, "Unwise Paths," especially 38–44.

31 Fernández, "Íñigo de Loyola," 586.

32 Ángela Atienza López, "De beaterios a conventos: Nuevas perspectivas sobre el mundo de las beatas en la España moderna," *Historia social* 57 (2007): 145–68, here 146.

33 Pastore, "Unwise Paths," 28–29.

34 García Hernán, *Ignacio de Loyola*, 120.

35 Darcy Donahue, "The Mysticism of Saint Ignatius of Loyola," in *A New Companion to Hispanic Mysticism*, ed. Hilaire Kallendorf (Leiden: Brill, 2010), 201–29, here 219; Elizabeth Rhodes, "Ignatius, Women, and the *Leyenda de los santos*," in *Companion to Ignatius of Loyola*, ed. Maryks, 7–23, here 19.

AN OVERVIEW OF THE PRE-SUPPRESSION SOCIETY OF JESUS IN SPAIN 13

Beyond the gender politics of the era, the context in which Loyola developed a circle of female followers is significant. There were a number of women who had prominent roles in *alumbrado* circles, so this characteristic would have been particularly suspicious in the Spain of that moment in time.[36] Since the presence of women among Ignatius's followers was likely a point of concern for the authorities who examined Ignatius and his beliefs, his religious community started to become more circumspect about its direct interactions with women, particularly those not from the higher social strata.[37]

For many of the Society's early detractors, the question of the Jesuits' orthodoxy was settled when Pope Paul III (1468–1549, r.1534–49) sanctioned the creation of the Society of Jesus in 1540. But the Dominicans were not satisfied. To mention only the most prominent Dominican critic of the Society, Cano continued to denounce what he perceived to be the order's heretical practices. As John W. O'Malley observes, the manuscript Cano composed between 1552 and 1556, *Censura y parecer que dio contra el instituto de los padres jesuitas* (Censure and opinion that was given against the Institute of the Jesuit fathers), detailed his misgivings that the Jesuits' practices shared similarities with those of the *alumbrados*.[38] Cano had other objections to the Society of Jesus. In 1557, when corresponding with Charles V's (1500–58, r.1516–56 as king of Spain) royal confessor, Cano mentioned that he believed the Jesuits to be *alumbrados*, but this letter focused on the dangers posed by the *Ejercicios espirituales* (Spiritual exercises, hereafter *Exercises*). According to Cano, meditation would distract workers from their tasks.[39]

2.2 Hagiography versus Historiography

The type of scholarship that O'Malley characterized in 1993 as "not always free of hagiographical vestiges, especially when dealing with Ignatius" still lingers.[40] For those reverentially interested in the life of Ignatius, coming to terms with biographers' descriptions of Íñigo as a young, single man with an active sex life could no doubt prove difficult.[41] Yet, Ignatius himself does not seem to have

---

36   Fernández, "Íñigo de Loyola," 662.
37   Donahue, "Mysticism of Saint Ignatius," 225.
38   O'Malley, *First Jesuits*, 294, 292. *Censura y parecer que dio contra el Instituto de los PP jesuitas* is the non-modernized title of the manuscript. When original orthography is helpful in locating rare books and handwritten texts in search engines, I provide it in footnotes. In my text, I modernize spelling and punctuation of titles.
39   Astrain, *Historia de la Compañía de Jesús*, 2:78, 77.
40   O'Malley, *First Jesuits*, 2.
41   See, e.g., Meissner, *Ignatius of Loyola*, 23; García Hernán, *Ignacio de Loyola*, 53–54.

14 MANNING

been especially reticent about his past to his brethren in the Society of Jesus. Early Jesuits, like Laínez and Polanco, refer to Ignatius's youthful "misconduct," particularly with women. Câmara references the misbehavior of young men in the prologue to the biography that Ignatius dictated to Câmara.[42] Since Câmara mediated the text that was dictated to him, the label of autobiography is not entirely accurate. For this reason, O'Malley terms the work "Ignatius's so-called *Autobiography*."[43]

Although the dictated text that came to be known as Ignatius's autobiography was not printed, handwritten copies circulated in the Society.[44] In the ensuing decades, Nadal frequently referenced this work to present Ignatius as the model of what a Jesuit should be for both members of the order and potential ones.[45] Once Borja became superior general, he stopped the circulation of Loyola's autobiography. In its place, Borja tasked Ribadeneyra with writing a version of the founder's life, a work characterized as "the life of a saintly founder of a religious order."[46] This biography is more circumspect about Loyola's youthful behavior. Scholars wonder whether Borja might have expurgated the more colorful anecdotes from Ignatius's early years from texts.[47]

Ignatius's sexual conduct, however, was not the only issue that was elided in the transition from the dictated autobiography to biographies about the founder. The early Society expunged references that could connect Ignatius to figures in the illuminist movement from versions of his life story. In fact, García Hernán posits that Ignatius's autobiography was taken out of circulation for this motive.[48]

This tension between omitting and recording certain aspects of Loyola's life was already evident in Ignatius's description of his connections with

---

42   Burrieza Sánchez, "Percepción jesuítica," 88.

43   John W. O'Malley, "Some Distinctive Characteristics of Jesuit Spirituality in the Sixteenth Century," reprinted in O'Malley, *Saints or Devils Incarnate?*, 165–80, here 166.

44   John W. O'Malley, "The Historiography of the Society of Jesus: Where Does It Stand Today?," in *The Jesuits: Cultures, Sciences, and the Arts, 1540–1773*, ed. John W. O'Malley et al. (Toronto: University of Toronto Press, 1999), 3–37, here 4.

45   O'Malley, "Historiography of the Society of Jesus," 5; Ulrike Strasser, "'The First Form and Grace': Ignatius of Loyola and the Reformation of Masculinity," in *Masculinity in the Reformation Era*, ed. Scott H. Hendrix and Susan C. Karant-Nunn (Kirksville, MO: Truman State University Press, 2008), 45–70, here 50.

46   O'Malley, "Historiography of the Society of Jesus," 6–7.

47   Burrieza Sánchez, "Percepción jesuítica," 88, and Wenceslao Soto Artuñedo, "Ignacio de Loyola y la mujer," *Proyección: Teología y mundo actual* 187 (1997): 299–318, here 302, cited in Burrieza Sánchez, "Percepción jesuítica," 88.

48   Pastore, "Unwise Paths," 27–28; García Hernán, *Ignacio de Loyola*, 20.

heterodox movements in corresponding with this king of Portugal. Such deliberate overlooking, or at least attempting to overlook, potentially problematic issues emerges in other aspects of the historiography of the early Society, such as the question of whether Ignatius fathered a child. (Like other scholars who discuss this issue, I do not intend to resolve the matter, but rather to suggest that it is a valid point of inquiry.) Scholars familiar with the Society of Jesus note that Hugo Rahner's (1900–68) study of the founder of the Jesuits omitted any reference to a document then in the Roman Archives of the Society of Jesus (Archivum Romanum Societatis Iesu, hereafter ARSI) that referenced Loyola's daughter. In an apparent effort to protect Ignatius's reputation, the document was subsequently taken out of the ARSI collection. Romeo de Maio maintains that certain correspondence sent to Ignatius by women has also disappeared.[49]

By the same token, Ignatius's sexual conduct as a young man should not be overly emphasized. In Elizabeth Rhodes's estimation, scholars' interest in Loyola's pre-Jesuit sexual life, without consideration of "his failings in other areas," reveals a great deal about our expectations of men, namely that there exists a "traditional preference that the heroic man—even the religious man—be virile, in the model of Augustine's *Confessions*."[50] Since the mores of sixteenth-century Spain tacitly expected sexual activity on the part of males, children born out of wedlock were common, even in the Loyola family. Both Ignatius's father and siblings, one of whom was of the cloth, acknowledged their illegitimate offspring.[51] In point of fact, as Amanda L. Scott demonstrates, in 1511, Martín García de Óñez de Loyola (1548/49–98), one of Ignatius's brothers, appointed María Beltrán de Loyola (*fl.* early to mid-sixteenth century; married 1516), their illegitimate half-sister, as *serora* for the church of San Miguel,

---

49   Rhodes, "Ignatius, Women, and the *Leyenda de los santos*," 17, 17n34, and Romeo de Maio, "Ignazio di Loyola e la donna," in *Ignacio de Loyola en la gran crisis del siglo XVI. Congreso internacional de historia, Madrid 19–20 noviembre 1991*, ed. Quintín Aldea (Bilbao: Mensajero and Santander: Sal Terrae, 1992), 283–86, here 283, 284, cited in Rhodes, "Ignatius, Women, and the *Leyenda de los santos*," 17.

50   Rhodes, "Ignatius, Women, and the *Leyenda de los santos*," 17n31.

51   José Martínez de Toda, "María Villarreal de Loyola, ¿presunta hija de Íñigo de Loyola? (Los Loyola de la Rioja del siglo XIV)," *Archivum historicum Societatis Iesu* 75 (2006): 325–60, here 358, cited in Rhodes, "Ignatius, Women, and the *Leyenda de los santos*," 18.

16   MANNING

located in Azpeitia.[52] (*Seroras* were laywomen who were licensed to take care
of churches and shrines in Navarre and the Basque country.)[53]

This tendency to want to present the Society in a positive light did not apply
solely to Loyola. In addition to the aforementioned examples concerning the
life of the founder, Robert Aleksander Maryks details the seventeenth-century
Jesuits' desires to remove references to Laínez's and Polanco's *converso* roots
from Francesco Sacchini's (1570–1625) history of the order. Maryks also observes that several more recent historians decided not to mention Benedetto
Palmio's (1523–98) anti-*converso* writings.[54]

3   The Early Years of the Society of Jesus in Spain

3.1   *Admission*

At a moment in Spanish history when many institutions were imposing *limpieza de sangre* (purity-of-blood) statutes to exclude those of *converso* ancestry, the Jesuit order chose not to do so. Moreover, a number of prominent early
Jesuits, such as Laínez, the order's second superior general (in office 1558–65),
came from *converso* families. According to Ribadeneyra, who recounted a
mealtime conversation between Ignatius and the early Jesuits, the founder
would have been pleased to have had a Jewish lineage because such origins
would give him the same ethnicity as Jesus and Mary.[55] As Maryks notes,

---

52   Amanda L. Scott, "St. Ignatius of Loyola, María Beltrán de Loyola, and the Seroras
      of Azpeitia," talk at the Sixteenth Century Society Conference, Albuquerque, NM,
      November 3, 2018. See https://www.academia.edu/37756345/_St._Ignatius_of_Loyola
      _Mar%C3%ADa_Beltran_de_Loyola_and_the_Seroras_of_Azpeitia._Sixteenth_Century
      _Society_Conference._Albuquerque_NM._2018 (accessed April 29, 2020) for the abstract
      of this talk. Juan Garmendia Larrañaga (1926–2015) transcribes a document and inven-
      tory list that seems to have been prepared at the start of Beltrán de Loyola's time as *serora*
      in Garmendia Larrañaga, "El Señor de Loyola, patrono de la iglesia de San Sebastián de
      Soreasu y sus filiales: Las seroras S. XVI," *Boletín de la Real Sociedad Bascongada de los
      Amigos del País* 63, no. 2 (2007): 471–81 (reproduced with different pagination from Eusko
      Ikaskuntza, 2010; http://www.euskomedia.org/PDFAnlt/jgl/70223232.pdf [accessed
      April 28, 2020], here 224–25).
53   See Amanda L. Scott, "*Seroras* and Local Religious Life in the Basque Country and Navarre,
      1550–1769," *Church History* 85, no. 1 (March 2016): 40–64, for an overview of *seroras*' roles.
54   Maryks, *Jesuit Order as a Synagogue of Jews*, 94, 97, xxix–xxx.
55   *Patris Petri de Ribadeneira* (Madrid: Editorial Ibérica, 1923), 2:375–77, cited in Jean
      Lacouture, *Jésuites: Une multibiographie*, vol. 1, *Les conquérants* (Paris: Seuil, 1991),
      1:199–200.

AN OVERVIEW OF THE PRE-SUPPRESSION SOCIETY OF JESUS IN SPAIN   17

Ribadeneyra's "closet-*converso*" identity undoubtedly informed his recording of this and other positive comments by Loyola about those of Jewish origins.[56]

While the early Jesuits would admit those whose ancestors were of the Jewish faith or *moriscos* (whose ancestors were Muslims), they had other criteria for those whom they admitted. In O'Malley's estimation, the Jesuit community was "much concerned with the character, talents, and health of the candidate, what his interests were, and how well suited he was to the style of life in the Society and the character of its ministries—to 'our manner of proceeding.'"[57] Also, the *Constitutions* specify that admitted men should "have a good appearance."[58] This requirement was not purely an aesthetic one. It was informed by Galenic theories, which believed that one's outward "appearance" reflected one's "character."[59]

In contrast to other religious communities that drew members from the highest echelons of society or obliged entrants to pay fees in the forms of dowries or other contributions, the Jesuits imposed no such lineage or financial requirements.[60] But the order also wanted to make certain that candidates' families would be able to survive without the income their sons would otherwise provide for them. Therefore, according to the *General Examen*, men whose parents "are in present and extreme need of the candidate's aid" should not be admitted. At the same time, the text cautions, "rarely, however, do such necessities occur."[61] This criterion (along with available information about Jesuits' backgrounds) attests that the Society drew members from the lower ranks of the nobility and from families of educated professionals or successful businesspeople.[62]

Beginning in 1593, the order became less welcoming to those of *converso* heritage. And it was unease on the part of Spanish and Portuguese Jesuits that ended the policy of *converso* admissions.

---

56 Maryks, *Jesuit Order as a Synagogue of Jews*, 42, 45.

57 O'Malley, *First Jesuits*, 81.

58 Ignatius of Loyola, *The Constitutions of the Society of Jesus and Their Complementary Norms*, trans. George E. Ganss (St. Louis, MO: Institute of Jesuit Sources, 1996), [151], [158]. The *Constitutions* are referenced by bracketed paragraph number.

59 Cristiano Casalini, "Discerning Skills: Psychological Insight at the Core of Jesuit Identity," in *Exploring Jesuit Distinctiveness: Interdisciplinary Perspectives on Ways of Proceeding within the Society of Jesus*, ed. Robert Aleksander Maryks (Leiden: Brill, 2016), 189–211, here 195.

60 Jodi Bilinkoff, *The Avila of Saint Teresa: Religious Reform in a Sixteenth-Century City* (Ithaca, NY: Cornell University Press, 1989), 88–89.

61 *Constitutions*, [37].

62 A. Lynn Martin, "Jesuits and Their Families: The Experience in Sixteenth-Century France," *Sixteenth Century Journal* 13, no. 1 (1982): 3–24, here 6–7.

3.2 Exclusion: The Lack of a Female Branch

Although initially open to *conversos*, the order was not open to women. Unlike a number of other Catholic religious orders, such as the Order of Friars Minor (Franciscans) and the Order of Preachers (Dominicans), the Society of Jesus lacks a female branch. As a number of scholars explain, the increasing claustration of female religious in the wake of the Council of Trent (1545–63) could not be reconciled with the Jesuits' active ministry. Furthermore, Ignatius was concerned that Jesuits' potential commitment to minister to nuns in hypothetical Jesuit convents would necessitate removing men from the itinerant missionary work that was an important hallmark of the order.[63] After all, the *Constitutions* specify that Jesuits should be "ready at any hour to go to any part of the world" at the behest of their superiors or the pope. In point of fact, the prohibition against Jesuits' supervision of women of the cloth in the *Constitutions* follows this reference to the need for Jesuits to be available to travel for evangelization.[64] (This restriction has been modified in the modern Society.)

Despite his misgivings, in 1545 Ignatius acceded to Pope Paul III's request that some women "live in obedience" to Loyola; however, this arrangement did not even last for two years.[65] (By the latter 1540s, rather than continue Jesuits' direct involvement in charitable outreach efforts directed toward sex workers or those in danger of turning to sex work, Ignatius instead advised members to delegate this task to noblewomen who were connected to the order.)[66] So when Isabel Roser (*fl.* mid-sixteenth century) and her companions arrived in Rome, they were sent to help in the institution that would eventually come to be known as the House of St. Martha.[67] Although Roser was an important benefactor of the Society in Barcelona, after the pope granted her petition to join the Society, her presence in the Jesuit community in Rome proved problematic. The manner in which Roser tended to Ignatius during an illness disquieted Palmio. In addition to this behavior, the visit of Roser's two nephews disrupted life in the community.[68] After the order parted ways with Roser

---

63 Gemma Simmonds, "Women Jesuits?," in *The Cambridge Companion to the Jesuits*, ed. Thomas Worcester (Cambridge: Cambridge University Press, 2008), 120–35, here 120–21; Lisa Fullam, "Juana, S.J.: The Past (and Future?) Status of Women in the Society of Jesus," *Studies in the Spirituality of Jesuits* 31 (November 1999): 1–39, here 4, 21–22.

64 *Constitutions*, [588].

65 O'Malley, *First Jesuits*, 75.

66 Alison Weber, "Jesuit Apologias for Laywomen's Spirituality," in *Devout Laywomen in the Early Modern World*, ed. Alison Weber (London: Routledge, 2016), 331–52, here 332.

67 Elizabeth A. Lehfeldt, *Religious Women in Golden Age Spain: The Permeable Cloister* (Aldershot, England: Ashgate, 2005), 190.

68 Fullam, "Juana," 18.

AN OVERVIEW OF THE PRE-SUPPRESSION SOCIETY OF JESUS IN SPAIN   19

and her two female companions, the Roser family sued over the Jesuits' actions concerning her possessions.[69] Even though the Society won the lawsuit, Dr. Francisco Ferrer (*fl.* mid-sixteenth century), one of Roser's nephews, testified that Loyola's actions were motivated by Roser's wealth.[70] This accusation would prove damaging to the community in the long term, as the image of Jesuits plotting to inherit the property of their devotees would become a commonplace critique. For example, in Burgos in 1572 the Augustinian friar Bernardino de Castro (*fl.* mid- to latter sixteenth century) accused the order of scheming for financial benefits by targeting the women to whom it ministered.[71] The *Monita privata Societatis Jesu* (Private instructions of the Society of Jesus), better known as the *Monita secreta* (Secret instructions), a text first published in Poland in the early seventeenth century, spuriously purports to circulate the Society's secret guidance to members, including the cultivation of wealthy devout widows for the financial gain of the Jesuit community.[72]

As Rhodes notes, the episode with Roser is frequently analyzed in highly gendered terms. Although Roser is portrayed as an overly demanding, well-to-do woman who wanted too much time and attention from the busy man occupied with the work of establishing his religious order, factors beyond gender, such as the dispositions and expectations of all those involved, also played a role in this situation.[73] However, moving beyond the individuals in question, the incident also reveals Ignatius's broader views on gender and the role of women in the Catholic Church. In advising Roser on how she should spend her widowhood, Ignatius suggested an enclosed convent. Roser followed his

---

69   Simmonds, "Women Jesuits?," 122.

70   Fullam, "Juana," 19.

71   Anthony D. Wright, "The Jesuits and the Older Religious Orders in Spain," in *The Mercurian Project: Forming Jesuit Culture 1573–1580*, ed. Thomas M. McCoog (St. Louis, MO: Institute of Jesuit Sources, 2004), 913–44, here 926.

72   See Sabina Pavone, *The Wily Jesuits and the* Monita secreta: *The Forged Secret Instructions of the Jesuits; Myth and Reality*, trans. John P. Murphy (St. Louis, MO: Institute of Jesuit Sources, 2005), 225–26. The text was composed by Hieronim Zahorowski (1582–1634), a former Jesuit (O'Malley, "Historiography of the Society of Jesus," 8). See Gauvin Alexander Bailey, "'Le style jésuite n'existe pas': Jesuit Corporate Culture and the Visual Arts," in *Jesuits: Cultures, Sciences, and the Arts, 1540–1773*, ed. O'Malley et al., 38–89, here 40 for a seventeenth-century French anti-Jesuit satire that suggested that the order used its elaborate artwork to inveigle such women.

73   Elizabeth Rhodes, "Join the Jesuits, See the World: Early Modern Women in Spain and the Society of Jesus," in *The Jesuits II: Cultures, Sciences, and the Arts, 1540–1773*, ed. John W. O'Malley et al. (Toronto: University of Toronto Press, 2006), 33–49, here 38, 40–41, 45–46n4.

suggestion: at the end of her life, she was claustrated in a Franciscan convent in her home city of Barcelona.[74]

Moreover, the decisive terms in which the Society disavowed the possibility of a female community excluded—and still excludes—women. As Lisa Fullam observes, if Loyola had only wanted to sever the order's relationship with Roser and her companions, he had a number of possible arguments to make to the pope; however, Ignatius made a broader argument concerning the need for Jesuits' freedom of movement, which led the pope to decree that the order would not have a female branch.[75]

3.3   Early Jesuit Foundations in Spain

When Antonio de Araoz (1515–73) became provincial of Spain in 1547, the Jesuits' membership and footprint in Spain. was quite small—the order's presence was limited to the cities of Alcalá de Henares, Valladolid, Valencia, Gandía, and Barcelona.[76] Although Jesuits in Portugal could have lent personnel to Spain, they did not do so.[77] In contrast to Spain, the Society of Jesus in Portugal benefited from strong support from the monarchy, and therefore its membership was more robust.[78] Despite a relative lack of personnel in Spain, the order established a number of new institutions, including Gandía in 1545 and Córdoba in 1554.

As the married duke of Gandía, Borja, along with his wife, underwrote the Jesuit *colegio* at Gandía. Borja was especially interested in this establishment as a source of education for the *morisco* population of his duchy.[79]

This was not the only ministry to the *morisco*s on the part of the order. In Granada, the order established a special school to instruct *morisco*s in the 1550s. Juan de Albotodo (1527–78), the Jesuit who ran it, was from a *morisco* family and delivered sermons in Arabic. Farther to the north in Ávila, another Jesuit of *morisco* lineage, Ignacio de las Casas (1550–1608), also instructed the population in matters of doctrine.[80]

---

74   Lehfeldt, *Religious Women*, 190.

75   Fullam, "Juana," 18–19.

76   Astrain, *Historia de la Compañía de Jesús*, 1:259–78.

77   María del Pilar Ryan, *El jesuita secreto: San Francisco de Borja* (Valencia: Biblioteca Valenciana, Generalitat Valenciana, 2008), 143.

78   See Julián J. Lozano Navarro, *La Compañía de Jesús y el poder en la España de los Austrias* (Madrid: Cátedra, 2005), 89–91 and 93 concerning Charles V, and Nuno da Silva Gonçalves, "Jesuits in Portugal," in *Mercurian Project*, ed. McCoog, 705–44, here 707–8 for a brief summary of the support for the Society of Jesus on the part of the Portuguese kings.

79   Ryan, *Jesuita secreto*, 83.

80   Patrick J. O'Banion, *The Sacrament of Penance and Religious Life in Golden Age Spain* (University Park, PA: Pennsylvania State University Press, 2012), 161.

AN OVERVIEW OF THE PRE-SUPPRESSION SOCIETY OF JESUS IN SPAIN   21

Yet, opposition prevented expansion into some areas. In Granada, for instance, rumors that the Jesuits did not maintain the seal of the confessional dogged the order. In Seville, the Society was denounced in sermons.[81] In relating details of the province of Toledo between 1540 and 1580, Bartolomé de Alcázar's (1648–1721) *Chrono-historia de la Compañía de Jesús en la provincia de Toledo y elogios de sus varones ilustres* [...] (Chronological history of the Society of Jesus in the province of Toledo and praise for its illustrious men [...]), which was published in 1710, notes a number of incidents in which members were forced to flee after hostile receptions.[82]

Nonetheless, the order continued to establish new Jesuit institutions. The scholarship about this expansion suggests a strategic motive for some of the Jesuit building boom between 1548 and 1551. During these years, Borja was a secret member of the Society of Jesus. In contrast to the order's standard practice, Borja did not renounce his temporal goods until he joined the community publicly. In the interim, he used his significant economic resources to become an important patron of several Jesuit institutions. Not only did Borja continue supporting the order's *colegio* (either a school or college, including a residential college at a university; see page 22 for more details) in Gandía that he began as the duke of Gandía but he also financed the construction of the Collegio Romano. This intensive building phase was motivated by the fact that Borja's membership would remain secret for a limited period of time and then control of his finances would pass to the son who succeeded him as duke. Moreover, these building projects, and therefore the training that took place at these institutions, would not have been financially possible for the

---

81   Doris Moreno, "Francisco de Borja y la Inquisición," in *Francesc de Borja (1510–1572), home del Renaixement, sant del barroc: Actes del Simposi Internacional (Gandia, 25–27 d'oct.– València, 4–5 nov. de 2010)*, ed. Santiago La Parra (Gandía: CEIC Alfons el Vell, 2012), 351–75, here 359. House style prefers Gandía over Gandia.

82   Bartolomé de Alcázar [Bartholome Alcazar], *Chrono-historia de la Compañia de Jesvs, en la provincia de Toledo: Y elogios de sus varones illustres, fundadores, bienhechores, [f]autores, é hijos espirituales* (Madrid: Juan Garcia Infançon, 1710), 1:253, 255–59, for example. BNE. I indicate the library where I consulted the text because rare books and manuscripts are organized by library in the bibliography. While the BNE's catalog lists the title as "autores," the text reads "fautores." This imprint is reproduced in the BNE's BDH. See http://bdh-rd.bne.es/viewer.vm?id=0000016699&page=1 (accessed April 29, 2020).

    In citing rare books, manuscripts, and historical documents, I maintain the original orthography in any citations as well as in the title and printer in my notes and bibliography; but house style governs the capitalization and punctuation of these titles. If the representation of the author's name in a rare book or manuscript differs from the manner in which he or she is cataloged today, I include the original form in brackets in the footnotes and bibliography. In my narrative, I use modern orthography for authors' names and book titles.

early Society without Borja's monetary assistance.[83] Amid this growth, there were parts of Spain, like La Mancha, where it appears that a Jesuit presence did not appeal to inhabitants.[84]

While the term *colegio* suggests a school in contemporary usage, the employment of the term by early Spanish Jesuits was more complex. Any Jesuit institution that housed both Jesuits who had finished their formations and those still in formation was called a *colegio*.[85] To mention one example of this usage, in 1633 Antonio Perdiguer (d.1640), a misbehaving Jesuit, was to be sent to "un colegio pequeño donde no aya estudiantes" (a small *colegio* where there are no students). The stipulation that he was not to hear confessions from women or visit them while there suggests the nature of his transgressions.[86] As a rule, I maintain the term *colegio* in Spanish because, in most cases, it is the most precise descriptor possible. Some *colegios* eventually became universities themselves, as was the case in Gandía, or affiliated, either formally or informally, with already existing universities.

In considering religious art, one tends to think of public displays in churches, but art was also displayed in *colegios*. Although the notion of a "Jesuit style" consisting of expensive and elaborate aesthetics has been discredited in favor of acknowledging that the order's artistic production was in tune with the local community, Gauvin Alexander Bailey notes several trends in Jesuit religious art. Certain themes were of particular interest to the Society, such as depictions of martyrdoms and of Jesuit saints.[87] It is in this context that we can

---

83   Ryan, *Jesuita secreto*, 104, 114, 162, 198.

84   David Martín López and Francisco José Aranda Pérez, "La conformación de la provincia jesuítica de Toledo en torno al generalato de Diego Laínez (1556–1565)," *Hispania sacra* 66, extra 2 (2014): 357–96, here 382. Martín López and Aranda Pérez suggest that further research may reveal why this was the case.

85   Javier Burrieza Sánchez, "Los ministerios de la Compañía," in Egido, Burrieza Sánchez, and Revuelta González, *Jesuitas en España*, 107–50, here 107.

86   Superior General Muzio Vitelleschi to Provincial Pedro Continente, May 30, 1633, Archivo Histórico Nacional, hereafter AHN, Jesuitas, hereafter J, legajo, hereafter leg., 253 documento, hereafter doc., 180. Archival documents are not listed in the bibliography.

     I use the most common English-language spelling of the names of generals of the Society of Jesus in my text; however, in referencing archival correspondence, I use the given names that the correspondence employs. In representing the names of Jesuits referenced in these letters, I will add the necessary accent marks to my text.

87   Bailey, "'Style jésuite n'existe pas,'" 70. See Jeffrey Muller, "Historiography of the Art and Architecture of the Jesuits," ed. Robert Aleksander Maryks, *Jesuit Historiography Online*; https://referenceworks.brillonline.com/entries/jesuit-historiography-online/historio graphy-of-the-art-and-architecture-of-the-jesuits-SIM_192594 (accessed April 28, 2020) for the origins of the term "Jesuit style" as a criticism of the order.

AN OVERVIEW OF THE PRE-SUPPRESSION SOCIETY OF JESUS IN SPAIN 23

understand the Colegio Imperial's collection of portraits of Jesuit saints and martyrs that was begun by Ribadeneyra.[88]

The early Society's economic straits meant that it could not afford to employ the best artists and architects; therefore, Bailey classifies much of the "art and architecture" in sixteenth-century Spanish Jesuit churches as "second rate."[89] Ultimately, however, religious images' value never lay solely in their aesthetic qualities. A statue of the Virgin Mary damaged when English forces attacked the city of Cádiz in 1596 first came to be displayed in the chapel of the Jesuit Colegio de San Albano in 1600, where it remains an important devotional object to this day. The mutilated statue is known as the Virgen Vulnerata (Wounded Virgin).[90]

3.4 *The* Spiritual Exercises

According to D. Scott Hendrickson's research, the *Exercises* came back to Spanish soil when Pierre Favre (1506–46) began to give them in Valladolid in 1541.[91] Particularly in the order's early years, making the Exercises introduced Jesuit spirituality to men who later joined the community. For example, three of the seven men who came to Alcalá to make the Exercises in 1547 became Jesuits. This fact is known because Francisco Antonio (1535–1610) and Alcázar included this information in their histories of the province of Toledo.[92] Since the Exercises, in fact, encapsulated the Jesuits' fundamental approach to spiritual and ministerial matters, it did give potential applicants a working idea of the order's positions.[93]

But potential recruitment was far from the goal of guiding the laity through the Exercises, as Jesuits also gave the Exercises to women, whom the order had

---

88   José Simón Díaz, *Historia del Colegio Imperial de Madrid* (Madrid: Consejo Superior de Investigaciones Científicas, Instituto de Estudios Madrileños, 1952), 1:119.

89   Bailey, "'Style jésuite n'existe pas,'" 72.

90   See the Royal English College of St. Alban/Real Colegio de los Ingleses' website (http://www.sanalbano.org/ [accessed April 29, 2020]). The English-language section "Saints and Martyrs" details the history of the statue.

91   D. Scott Hendrickson, *Jesuit Polymath of Madrid: The Literary Enterprise of Juan Eusebio Nieremberg (1595–1658)* (Leiden: Brill, 2015), 30. House style differentiates between the italicized reference to the book, the *Exercises*, and the unitalicized reference to the process of making the Exercises.

92   Alcázar, *Chrono-historia de la Compañia de Jesvs, en la provincia de Toledo*, 1:88, 1:115–16, 2:65–67, and Francisco Antonio, *Historia de la provincia de Toledo* (1604), 1:15–16, cited in Martín López and Aranda Pérez, "Conformación de la provincia jesuítica de Toledo," 367–68.

93   O'Malley, "Some Distinctive Characteristics," 165–66.

24 MANNING

no interest in recruiting.[94] Men and women from various sectors of Spanish society made the Exercises. Whereas those who made the Exercises in urban areas tended to be well placed in the social, academic, or religious hierarchies, those who made them in less elite settings, like market towns, were of more modest means. Certain Jesuits, like Baltasar Álvarez (1533–80), who is best known today as spiritual director to Teresa de Ávila (1515–82), became known for their skills as spiritual directors, and for giving the Exercises in this context.[95] It was this volume and practices established for its usage that started what is now a standard practice in Catholic spirituality, namely the retreat.[96]

O'Reilly attributes the early circulation of the *Exercises* in manuscript rather than printed form to initial "hesitan[cy]" on the part of Ignatius and later on the part of the Society to circulate the *Exercises* widely.[97] Such reticence is understandable considering that Cano's suspicions about *alumbradismo* extended to the *Exercises*. And Cano encouraged Silíceo to evaluate the *Exercises*. Likely because of these concerns, the *Exercises* were not printed in Spanish until 1615, and the Spanish-language text was printed in Rome rather than in Spain.[98] Combined with the Spanish Inquisition's investigations of Loyola and the increasing suspicions on the part of the Holy Office of works of popular piety in the vernacular, this disinclination seems to have been quite prudent.

Beyond concerns about potential denunciations to the Inquisition, handwritten documents continued to be preferred for particular types of texts as manuscript culture coexisted with print culture after the invention of the printing press. As Fernando Bouza explains, certain genres tended to circulate in handwritten form, including "las meditaciones espirituales" (spiritual meditations) because they "cumplirían funciones de privacidad o de sociabilidad cerrada y detrás de ellas se descubriría una voluntad de expresa incomunicación" (would serve purposes of privacy or of sociability in a closed circle. And behind these purposes, one would discover a wish for an express lack of communication).[99] It is this ethos that underpins the oral delivery style in which the person giving the Exercises reads the text aloud to the person making them, as described in the text. This method benefited the illiterate and those who "could not read Latin" once the Bible in the vernacular was

---

94 O'Malley, *First Jesuits*, 75.

95 Hendrickson, *Jesuit Polymath of Madrid*, 30.

96 O'Malley, "Some Distinctive Characteristics," 166.

97 O'Reilly, "Early Printed," 664.

98 Hendrickson, *Jesuit Polymath of Madrid*, 30–31. See Astrain, *Historia de la Compañía de Jesús*, 1:366–84 for criticisms of the *Exercises*.

99 Fernando Bouza, *Corre manuscrito: Una historia cultural del Siglo de Oro* (Madrid: Marcial Pons Historia, 2001), 21.

AN OVERVIEW OF THE PRE-SUPPRESSION SOCIETY OF JESUS IN SPAIN   25

prohibited in the Spanish Inquisition's 1559 Index of Prohibited Books.[100] The *Exercises*, however, did not emerge entirely unscathed from this Index.

In practical terms, the lack of printed versions of the *Exercises* may have posed some challenges in giving them. In 1589, Superior General Claudio Acquaviva (1543–1615, in office 1581–1615) asked that the province ensure that Jesuits used Ignatius's original text rather than Father Joseph Blando's (dates unknown) commentary on the *Exercises*.[101] This issue likely in part arose due to the scarcity of manuscript copies of the *Exercises* in Spain.

3.5   *Exclusion Redux*

Despite the legal precedents for an all-male religious community, in 1554 they were set aside for a member of the Spanish royal family. When Juana de Austria, who was princess of Portugal, daughter of Charles V, sister of Philip II (and his sometimes regent), wanted to join the order, she was humored. The gender politics involved in this decision merit comment. Not only was the admission of the Spanish princess kept secret, but according to O'Malley only "a few" Jesuits knew about it, and she was given a male codename, Mateo Sánchez.[102] As Wenceslao Soto Artuñedo observes, this coded surname became Montoya after 1556.[103] Juana needed a male guise to conceal her identity in case correspondence about her came to the attention of those who did not know about her presence in the order.

---

100 O'Reilly, "Early Printed," 662–63. Also see 662n132 for the references to this delivery method in the *Exercises*.

101 Superior General Claudio Acquaviva to Provincial Hieronimo Roca, 1589, AHN J leg. 252 doc. 165. I maintain Latinate forms of names, such as Joseph, when I lack sufficient information to decide between the Castilian José or Catalan Josep.

  This essay was completed after the Covid-19 pandemic shuttered libraries and archives, including the Archivum Romanum Societatis Iesu. In several cases, without access to this archival documentation, it has not been possible to differentiate between multiple Jesuits with the same name or to determine the manner in which these documents spelled or Latinized a particular surname. In other cases, it has not been possible to determine as much as one would normally be able to ascertain about Jesuits' life dates. As a result of my more limited access to sources, the biographical information and publication dates for the texts mentioned in this essay may not be as precise as they would have been under other circumstances. Under these conditions, it has been particularly challenging to reconcile sometimes widely differing data about dates of publication for the same work with limited sources. I apologize in advance for any errors or omissions.

102 O'Malley, *First Jesuits*, 75–76.

103 Wenceslao Soto Artuñedo, "Juana de Austria, ¿de la compañía de Jesús?," in *V Reunión científica asociación española de historia moderna*, vol. 1, *Felipe II y su tiempo*, ed. José Luis Pereira Iglesias and Jesús Manuel González Beltrán (Cádiz: Servicio de Publicaciones de la Universidad de Cádiz, Asociación Española de Historia Moderna, 1999), 1:579–88, here 1:582.

At that point in time, the relationship between the early Society of Jesus and the Spanish monarchy was rather strained. King of Spain and Holy Roman Emperor Charles v and then Prince Philip seemed unimpressed with the new religious order.[104] So Juana could have provided a needed connection to the royal family. Despite the papal exemption from having a female branch, the order did not wish to reject the princess and risk offending such a potentially powerful ally. Soto Artuñedo notes that no archival record exists of Juana's vows because of their highly secret nature, but Loyola and the small circle of Jesuits who knew about Juana's request discussed the vows that Mateo Sánchez (i.e., the princess) would take. As Soto Artuñedo specifies, given such detailed planning for such a highly unusual eventuality, it would be very strange indeed if Juana did not take the vows that were designed especially for her. Juana demonstrated such a level of commitment to the Jesuit community that it seems logical that she took the vows that were prepared for her.[105] In terms of this royal's dedication to the order, when Archbishop Hernando de Aragón (1498–1575), a relation of Borja, who, despite this familial tie, nonetheless opposed the Jesuits, impeded the Society's establishment of a house in Zaragoza, Juana facilitated the order's presence by appealing to the viceroy (and ultimately the Inquisition's) authority.[106] Moreover, in addition to putting the Jesuits in charge of the education of her son, Juana played a role in the foundation of a number of Jesuit *colegios*.[107] In 1573, for example, she underwrote a chaired position in theology at the Jesuit house in Madrid, which would later become the Colegio Imperial.[108]

Like the Roser case, this episode disquieted the limited number of Jesuits who knew about it. Some of these concerns might have been justified. Juana's Jesuit vows likely soured the relationship between her brother Philip ii and the order. Rumors about an affair between his sister Juana and Borja greeted Philip ii on his return to Spain after residing in England during his marriage to Mary Tudor (1516–58, r.1553–58).[109] Both Philip ii's sister and Borja were, in fact, keeping a secret, but rather than a romantic liaison, they were concealing the depth of their commitment to the Society of Jesus. Nonetheless, the gossip

---

104   See the already cited portion of Lozano Navarro, *Compañía de Jesús*, 89–91, 93.
105   Soto Artuñedo, "Juana de Austria," 1:582–86.
106   Burrieza Sánchez, "Establecimiento, fundación y oposición," 60.
107   Soto Artuñedo, "Juana de Austria," 1:586–87.
108   Burrieza Sánchez, "Establecimiento, fundación y oposición," 72.
109   O'Malley, *First Jesuits*, 76, 318.

AN OVERVIEW OF THE PRE-SUPPRESSION SOCIETY OF JESUS IN SPAIN   27

about the perceived affair between the princess and Borja became so wide-spread that Laínez suggested that Borja depart from court.[110]

3.6   *Borja and the Order's Expansion in Spain*
Like Ignatius's story, the account of how Borja came to dedicate himself to re-ligious life is striking. In 1539, Borja accompanied the body of Empress Isabella (1503–1539) (wife of Charles V) to the site of her burial in Granada. Before her interment, the identity of the cadaver had to be verified. When the coffin was opened, Borja was stunned by how much her body had decayed. And Borja continued to recollect that moment throughout his life: in the spiritual diary he kept as an older man, he remembered Empress Isabella on the anniversary of her death and continued to gratefully acknowledge the lessons he learned via her death.[111] Visual depictions of Borja, like Juan de Valdés Leal's (1622–90) *San Ignacio y san Francisco de Borja contemplan una alegoría de la Eucaristía* (Saint Ignatius and Saint Francisco de Borja contemplate an allegory of the Eucharist [1671]), often recall this episode, through the skull wearing a crown in Borja's hands.[112]

Borja did not make an immediate change in his life circumstances. But fol-lowing his wife's death, in 1548 Borja secretly joined the order. Once his mem-bership in the Society became public in 1551, Borja's presence boosted the Society to such a degree that the order became more successful in recruiting new members in Spain.[113] Although Borja's entrance raised the profile of the Jesuits, the fact that powerful nobles in Philip II's government supported the order also contributed to its expansion.[114]

In 1554, the year Borja became the order's *comisario* (a commissioner, who in the early Society was designated by the superior general to supervise a prov-ince or several provinces or to assist with a particular issue) in Spain, Spanish Jesuit communities were divided into three provinces: Castile, Andalusia, and

---

110   José Martínez Millán, "Transformación y crisis de la Compañía de Jesús (1578–1594)," in *I religiosi a corte: Teologia, politica e diplomazia in antico regime; Atti del seminario di studi, Georgetown University a Villa Le Balze, Fiesole 20 ottobre 1995*, ed. Flavio Rurale (Rome: Bulzoni, 1998), 101–29, here 103.

111   See Cándido de Dalmases, *Francis Borgia: Grandee of Spain, Jesuit, Saint*, trans. Cornelius Michael Buckley (St. Louis, MO: Institute of Jesuit Sources, 1991), 15–18, and *El padre Francisco de Borja* (Madrid: Biblioteca de Autores Cristianos, 1983), 20–23 for more details about this journey.

112   See Hendrickson, *Jesuit Polymath of Madrid*, 127 for an image of this painting.

113   Doris Moreno, "Los jesuitas, la Inquisición y la frontera espiritual de 1559," *Bulletin of Spanish Studies* 92, no. 5 (2015): 655–75, here 662–63.

114   Martínez Millán, "Transformación y crisis," 102.

Aragon. During Borja's term in that office, the order began building a number of establishments in Spain.[115] This expansion occurred not only in Iberia but also across the order. As O'Malley suggests, there was "no master plan" to govern the expansion of the Society's *colegios*. In addition to sometimes overlooking the financial and practical considerations as to whether *colegios* had sufficient means of support or would attract enough students, the early Society frequently failed to consider whether it had sufficient members available to teach and perform other necessary tasks in new foundations.[116]

Despite the growing acceptance of the order in Spain, its building plans were not welcomed in all locales. Since 1547, the order had worked to establish a house in Zaragoza. Although a donor willed a house to the Jesuits, his heirs sued. Other religious orders opposed the Jesuits' purchase of other properties. The archbishop, believing the Jesuits did not recognize his jurisdictional authority, also opposed their presence. As previously mentioned, it took the intervention of Juana de Austria to bring about a positive resolution for the Society in this situation.[117]

3.7 Protestantism in Spain, the 1559 Index of Prohibited Books, and the Society of Jesus

Events in 1558 and 1559 would negatively affect Borja's reputation and that of the Jesuit order. In 1557–58, several circles of practicing Protestants were uncovered in Seville and Valladolid.[118] According to information Borja provided to Laínez, rumors identified the Jesuits as one of the loci spreading Protestant thought. In Valladolid, Ana Enríquez (b. *c.*1535), an in-law of the Borja family, was arrested for her role in that Protestant group. Borja visited his relative during her detention, and several other Jesuits attended to the spiritual needs of those accused of being Protestants who were imprisoned in Valladolid and Seville.[119] When Enríquez was sentenced to wear a *sanbenito* (a penitential garment worn as part of a sentence from the Inquisition) as punishment for being one of the Valladolid Protestants, according to Kamen's research, Borja

---

115 Burrieza Sánchez, "Establecimiento, fundación y oposición," 71; I. [Ignacio] Echarte, "Comisario" in "Gobierno: Sumario," in *Diccionario histórico de la Compañía de Jesús: Biográfico—temático*, ed. Charles E. O'Neill and Joaquín María Domínguez (Madrid: Universidad Pontificia Comillas, 2001), 2:1749–50, here 2:1749. See the "Gobierno: Sumario" section for definitions of offices in the order (2:1745–62).

116 O'Malley, *First Jesuits*, 232.

117 Astrain, *Historia de la Compañía de Jesús*, 1:438–64.

118 See Kamen, *Spanish Inquisition*, 101–4 for details.

119 Moreno, "Jesuitas, la Inquisición y la frontera espiritual," 665, 668.

AN OVERVIEW OF THE PRE-SUPPRESSION SOCIETY OF JESUS IN SPAIN 29

intervened so that she, and the family's reputation, would not have to suffer this public shame.[120]

Beyond the implication of this member of Borja's extended family, this discovery had serious consequences for spiritual practices in Spain. These, in turn, would affect Borja more directly.

When the Spanish Inquisition published its first Index of Prohibited Books in 1551, in Kamen's assessment it "was no more than a reprint of one compiled by Louvain in 1550, with a special appendix devoted to Spanish books." As such, it had a relatively minor impact on the reading materials of most Spaniards. Following the discovery of practicing Protestants in Valladolid and Seville, the subsequent 1559 Index had a devastating impact on devotional literature written in Spanish, as many popular works of piety in the vernacular were prohibited.[121]

One such work was titled *Obras del Cristiano* (Works of the Christian) and was attributed to Borja. However, as Doris Moreno indicates, the precise work to which the prohibition refers is unclear. According to Moreno's research, Luis Gutiérrez (*fl.* early to mid-sixteenth century), a bookseller in Alcalá de Henares, published a volume titled *Las obras del Cristiano* (The works of the Christian) in Borja's name in 1550, but there are no known exemplars of this text. Also beginning in 1550, another text, *Primera parte de las obras muy devotas y provechosas para cualquier fiel cristiano* (First part of the very devout and useful works for any Christian believer) was attributed to Borja. But Borja was not in fact the author of all the texts attributed to him.[122]

Although Borja attempted to learn the motives for the volume's prohibition, he never succeeded in doing so.[123] Some scholars, like Moreno and O'Malley, suspect that Borja's friendship with the imprisoned archbishop Bartolomé Carranza (c.1503–76) may have influenced the Inquisition's decision, but Cándido de Dalmases (1906–86) does not concur with this opinion. Dalmeses believes that the 1559 Index was hastily compiled and therefore the Inquisition did not take the time to clarify questions of authorship.[124] Ricardo García Cárcel notes Inquisitor General Fernando de Valdés's

---

120 Kamen, *Spanish Inquisition*, 318.

121 Kamen, *Spanish Inquisition*, 124–27.

122 Moreno, "Francisco de Borja," 366–67.

123 Dalmases, *Francis Borgia*, 136; *Padre Francisco de Borja*, 142. Dalmases treats this episode in *Francis Borgia* on 133–47 and in *Padre Francisco de Borja* on 138–54.

124 Moreno, "Francisco de Borja," 368; O'Malley, *First Jesuits*, 318; Cándido de Dalmases, "San Francisco de Borja y la Inquisición española 1559–1561," *Archivum historicum Societatis Iesu* 41 (1972): 48–135, here 126.

(1483–1568) enmity with the Jesuits in general and Borja in particular.[125] In Burrieza Sánchez's estimation, negative feelings about the Jesuits' connections to *alumbradismo* on the part of Bernardo de Fresneda (1509–77), Philip II's Franciscan confessor, and Cano contributed to the Inquisition's attitude toward Borja's work.[126] Regardless of the motive for the prohibition, Borja and other Jesuits obtained testimony from book professionals about the true authorship of the works misattributed to Borja. By the end of 1559, Borja decided to accept an invitation from Cardinal Henrique (1512–80), heir to the Portuguese throne, to visit Portugal. From Portugal, Borja traveled to Rome at the behest of the pope.[127] While no documentation relating to an arrest, or an impending one, of Borja by the Spanish Inquisition has come to light, according to Moreno's research in the Inquisition's files, two brief notations respectively refer to a penitence and a trial for "Francisco de Borja, teatino" (Francisco de Borja, Theatine [Jesuits were often referred to—and often pejoratively—as members of the Congregation of Clerics Regular of the Divine Providence]) and "padre Francisco Duque de Gandía" (Father Francis, duke of Gandía).[128]

A note in the 1583 Index explains that a number of well-respected authors, including Borja, were listed in Indices not because their works contained doctrinal errors but rather for reasons unrelated to religious polemic, including the erroneous attribution of texts to them, printing errors in works that they did author, or because the texts' content was not appropriate for circulation in the vernacular.[129]

The prohibition of works attributed to Borja was not the only blow dealt to the Society of Jesus by the 1559 Index. As a means of limiting access to topics deemed inappropriate for consumption in the vernacular, this Index prohibited devotional works that were disseminated in handwritten versions. Since the *Exercises* had not yet been printed in Spanish, this text necessarily circulated in manuscript form. As Kamen relates, Juan Suárez (1528–99), the rector of the Jesuit *colegio* in Seville, inquired to the Inquisition as to whether the *Exercises* would be included in this ban. Suárez was appalled when the Inquisition informed him that handwritten copies of the *Exercises* were prohibited. After

---

125 Ricardo García Cárcel, "La crisis de la Compañía de Jesús en los últimos años del reinado de Felipe II (1585–1598)," in *La monarquía de Felipe II a debate*, ed. Luis Antonio Ribot García (Madrid: Sociedad Estatal para la Conmemoración de los Centenarios de Felipe II y Carlos V, 2000), 383–404, here 385.

126 Burrieza Sánchez, "Establecimiento, fundación y oposición," 67.

127 Moreno, "Francisco de Borja," 369, 370, 372.

128 AHN Inquisición, hereafter Inq., leg. 2136 expediente, hereafter exp., 7 and AHN Inq. leg. 3190 exp. 179 (August 29, 1571), cited in Moreno, "Francisco de Borja," 375.

129 See Dalmases, "San Francisco de Borja," 127–28 for the passage in its entirety.

AN OVERVIEW OF THE PRE-SUPPRESSION SOCIETY OF JESUS IN SPAIN   31

submitting the *colegio*'s copies to the Inquisition, Suárez wrote to Laínez explaining that the proscription of the handwritten *Exercises* had so affected him that he was confined to his bed.[130]

4   Borja and Mercurian's Generalates

4.1   *Further Expansion*
In 1562, the provincial structure changed and four provinces were created: Castile, Andalusia, Aragon, and Toledo. Among Jesuits in Spain, memories of negative reactions to the first attempts at founding houses no doubt lingered in the group's collective memory. These early attacks had consequences in terms of establishing Jesuit institutions. The Society was perhaps overly inclined to establish houses in places that expressed an interest in having them, without necessarily investigating their viability in the longer term. Inevitably, this strategy meant that some houses were located in small towns.

By 1565, however, the challenges involved in the unchecked creation of *colegios* in the order as a whole were beginning to become evident. In the interest of ensuring the sustainability of Jesuit establishments, the Second General Congregation (1565) requested that the pace of construction be slowed and that already established *colegios* be supported further.[131] As a result, only eight new Jesuit establishments were founded in Spain during the years that Borja was general.[132] The general congregation's decree required endowments for new *colegios*, and generous patrons, including women like Leonor de Mascareñas (1503–84) and Magdalena de Ulloa (1525–98), provided sufficient funding so that the order could carry out its building projects.[133] Such patronage became a standing practice in the order. At the same time, propriety became a point of such urgent concern that it could interfere with the order's relationship to female patrons. When the Society sought to forbid Ulloa from entering the *colegio* at Villagarcía, which she helped to underwrite, because of her gender, her

---

130   Kamen, *Spanish Inquisition*, 127.
131   Burrieza Sánchez, "Establecimiento, fundación y oposición," 71. General Congregation (hereafter GC) 2, decree (hereafter d.) 8, in *For Matters of Greater Moment: The First Thirty Jesuit General Congregations*, ed. John W. Padberg, Martin D. O'Keefe, and John L. McCarthy (St. Louis, MO: Institute of Jesuit Sources, 1994), 113–14.
132   Francisco de Borja Medina, "Everard Mercurian and Spain: Some Burning Issues," trans. Walter P. Krolikowski, in *Mercurian Project*, ed. McCoog, 945–66, here 957. Also see 955–57 for summaries of the state of the Spanish provinces upon Borja's death and the eight foundations.
133   See Burrieza Sánchez, "Establecimiento, fundación y oposición" and "Ministerios de la Compañía," 71, 78–79, 112 for more information about Mascareñas and Ulloa's roles.

brother Domingo de Ulloa (d.1601), a Dominican provincial of Spain, and her other male relatives protested vehemently.[134]

4.2 (Re-)Assessing Borja's Generalate

In the estimation of some scholars, Borja's generalate proved problematic for the order. For example, Flavio Rurale, citing Mario Scaduto's study, asserts: "Francis Borja's extreme pro-Spanish and strict generalate exacerbated real schismatic tendencies, which burst into flame in the 1580s during the administration of Claudio Acquaviva."[135] The documentary basis that justifies such conclusions, however, is far from objective. Italian Jesuits, including Palmio and Antonio Possevino (c.1533–1611), addressed *memoriales* (documents that make requests or ask favors of an authority) to Superior General Everard Mercurian (1514–80, in office 1573–80) that detailed the challenges facing the community, which they attributed to past Spanish superiors general. Yet, in Esther Jiménez Pablo's analysis, the aftereffects of Spain's imperial policy in Italy also influenced this critique of Spanish Jesuit generals. The memory of the Spanish troops' sack of Rome and other misdeeds was fresh enough in the minds of Italian Jesuits to fuel animus toward Spanish superiors who seemed to employ a governance style rooted in the methods of the Spanish Empire.[136] Admittedly, Borja's tendency to appoint Spaniards to important supervisory posts in Italy only exacerbated these negative feelings.[137]

In terms of the order's continuing admission of *converso* members during Borja's generalate, this decision cannot be classified as "pro-Spanish." In point of fact, the general's decision to maintain the status quo greatly displeased the Iberian—both Spanish and Portuguese—sector of the community. As Borja appointed Jesuits with *converso* origins, like Polanco, to positions of note in the order, the general also offered advice in favor of appointing Diego de Avellaneda (1529–98), who had some questionable elements in his lineage, as provincial of Andalusia. At the same time, in this same letter and in another a year later, Borja suggested that the order should consider refusing admission

---

134 Wright, "Jesuits and the Older Religious Orders," 921.

135 Flavio Rurale, "Carlo Borromeo and the Society of Jesus in the 1570s," in *Mercurian Project*, ed. McCoog, 559–605, here 559.

136 Esther Jiménez Pablo, "El final de la hegemonía hispana en la Compañía de Jesús: Los memorialistas italianos (1585–1593)," *Hispania sacra* 69 (2017): 619–37, here 620, 623, 621.

137 See Mario Fois, "Everard Mercurian," in *Mercurian Project*, ed. McCoog, 1–33, here 21–22 for a summary of the Spanish nationals whom Borja appointed to positions of authority in Italy.

AN OVERVIEW OF THE PRE-SUPPRESSION SOCIETY OF JESUS IN SPAIN

to *converso* candidates in areas like Andalusia where negative feelings toward *conversos* could have negative effects on the Jesuits' work.[138]

4.3 *Mercurian's Generalate and Spain*

Partisans of a number of national and extra-national interests urged against the election of another Spanish superior general prior to the Third General Congregation (1573). In addition to the Italians' objections, King Sebastian of Portugal (1554–78, r.1557–78) expressed a preference for a candidate who was not from *converso* stock and opposed *conversos*' admission to the Society. The *converso* origins of a number of the Spanish candidates, including Polanco, proved problematic. But issues surrounding *conversos* were "reformulated" "into a question of nationality" in Rome, and Pope Gregory XIII (1502–85, r.1572–85) requested that no Spaniards be considered for election during this general congregation. The exclusion of Spanish Jesuits from contention for the position had a notable impact: as a result, only twenty of the forty-seven attendees of the general congregation were eligible for election as superior general.[139]

The behavior of the Spanish king undoubtedly created anxieties about a potential fourth Spanish superior general. Beginning in 1560, Philip II began to petition the pope for permission to undertake a series of reforms of religious communities in Spain. Through a number of proposals made to several pontiffs, Philip asserted that orders with heads that resided outside of Spain did not adequately supervise their Spanish members and that these same orders siphoned Spanish funds away from the country. Pope Pius IV (1499–1565, r.1559–65) did concede some changes regarding the administration of a number of religious orders that operated in Spain. For example, after this reform, the Spanish Cistercians' superior was no longer a French abbot but rather a papal representative. After this initial success, the Spanish monarch continued to request that Rome place Spanish members of other religious orders under the supervision of Spanish superiors.[140] Against this backdrop, the pope's

---

138 Alison Weber, "Los jesuitas y las carmelitas descalzas en tiempos de san Francisco de Borja: Amistad, rivalidad y recelos," in *Francisco de Borja y su tiempo: Política, religión y cultura en la edad moderna*, ed. Enrique García Hernán and María del Pilar Ryan (Valencia: Albatros Ediciones, 2011), 103–13, here 106–7.

139 Fois, "Everard Mercurian," 22–25; Medina, "Everard Mercurian and Spain," 946.

140 See José García Oro, "Conventualismo y observancia: La reforma de las órdenes religiosas en los siglos XV y XVI," in *Historia de la iglesia en España*, vol. 3.1, *La iglesia en la España de los siglos XV y XVI*, ed. José Luis González Novalín (Madrid: Biblioteca de Autores Cristianos, 1980), 3.1:211–350, here 3.1:317–23. See 3.1:317–34 for more details of the monarch's plans.

counsel to the Third General Congregation to elect a non-Spanish general was designed to assert his primacy over that of the Spanish monarch and maintain the independence of a religious order headquartered in Rome over Philip II's regalist ambitions. Since Mercurian was a Flemish subject of Philip II, the monarch still had a tie to the Society's leader.[141]

Spanish Jesuit superiors warned that the pope's preference for a non-Spanish general could motivate Philip II to mandate that Spanish Jesuits not follow such a general and therefore break off a "Spanish branch" of the Society with a separate supervisory structure.[142] While this did not happen, Mercurian's election set the stage for new complaints against the Society of Jesus on the part of the Spanish monarchy. Ultimately, these would lead the order to renounce some of its privileges and alter its relationship to the Spanish Inquisition.

This was not the only long-term legacy of Mercurian's election. After assuming the generalate, Mercurian began to remove *converso* Jesuits from leadership positions. As a result, a number of these Jesuits returned to Spain where, as Maryks details, several of them reoriented their careers toward writing. Whereas some, like Polanco and Ribadeneyra, composed historical works, others, like Dionisio Vázquez (1527–89), began to write *memoriales* to various authorities to complain about aspects of the governance of their order.[143]

Leaving aside the *memorialistas* (writers of *memoriales*) for the moment, tensions between Mercurian and Spanish Jesuits arose over certain contemplative practices. Spanish Jesuits Antonio Cordeses (1518–1601) and Álvarez were the most prominent members of a group of fellow Jesuits who used meditative techniques other than those that appear in the *Exercises*. Cordeses and Álvarez did not receive strong "formation[s] in the *Exercises*," as Philip Endean notes. Cordeses was close to Borja and his meditative approach, although Borja criticized Cordeses's techniques in a 1571 visit. Cordeses's method emphasized the importance of divine love as part of an affective prayer style. In 1574, Mercurian requested that Cordeses cease talking about prayer techniques that were not grounded in the *Exercises*.[144] In this context, it is important to note that many Spanish-language texts related to affective spirituality (devotional practices that involve the emotions in prayer life) were banned

---

141 Jiménez Pablo, "Final de la hegemonía hispana," 623.

142 Jiménez Pablo, "Final de la hegemonía hispana," 623.

143 Maryks, *Jesuit Order as a Synagogue of Jews*, 117, 123–28.

144 Philip Endean, "The Strange Style of Prayer: Mercurian, Cordeses, and Álvarez," in *Mercurian Project*, ed. McCoog, 351–97, here 380, 352–54, 356, 358–60, 380; Joseph de Guibert, *The Jesuits: Their Spiritual Doctrine and Practice; A Historical Study*, trans. William J. Young (St. Louis, MO: Institute of Jesuit Sources, 1986), 223.

AN OVERVIEW OF THE PRE-SUPPRESSION SOCIETY OF JESUS IN SPAIN   35

in the Spanish Inquisition's 1559 Index.[145] Álvarez also employed contemplative techniques that were not strictly in keeping with the *Exercises*. Joseph de Guibert (1877–1942) defines Álvarez's technique as infused contemplation, in which the mind becomes totally centered on God after being given this ability from the divine.[146] In 1577, *Visitador* (inspector) Diego de Avellaneda informed Álvarez that he should teach the practices outlined in the *Exercises*.[147] Despite this counsel from the general about their prayer lives and the techniques they taught, both men continued to hold important positions in the Jesuit community in Spain. Cordeses remained in office as provincial of Castile, and Álvarez trained Jesuits in formation at Villagarcía and later became *visitador* in the province of Aragon, among other leadership posts.[148]

In practical terms, regardless of the absence of Spaniards from top leadership positions and despite the controversy over contemplative prayer, the Society of Jesus continued to flourish in Spain under Mercurian. By 1580, as Francisco de Borja Medina observes, despite dispatching over one hundred Jesuits on missions to points in the Spanish Empire, membership in the Spanish provinces totaled "approximately 1,440." According to Medina's calculations, this figure represents a forty-four percent increase during Mercurian's term in office.[149]

No gains were made for the order against the wishes of locals. During Mercurian's generalate, support beyond underwriters, extending to the local community in individual localities, continued to be crucial to the Society in establishing new *colegios*. This was particularly the case in the 1570s, when the Dominicans took legal action to oppose Jesuits' plans in Soria, Salamanca, and Ávila. In 1579–80, Mercurian expressed displeasure with Spanish Jesuits for agreeing to accept support for a *colegio* in Pamplona over the objections of residents of the area and postponed the plan.[150]

Mercurian's decision to ground the Society's approach to prayer in the meditative techniques referenced in the *Exercises* was a significant one that deserves further consideration. In Endean's opinion, issues of nationality, specifically

---

145   Melquiades Andrés Martín, *La teología española en el siglo XVI* (Madrid: Biblioteca de Autores Cristianos, 1976), 1:362, cited in Gillian T. W. Ahlgren, *Teresa of Avila and the Politics of Sanctity* (Ithaca, NY: Cornell University Press, 1996), 19.
146   Guibert, *Jesuits*, 225.
147   Endean, "Strange Style of Prayer," 365–66.
148   Guibert, *Jesuits*, 223; Endean, "Strange Style of Prayer," 371–72.
149   Medina, "Everard Mercurian," 960.
150   Wright, "Jesuits and the Older Religious Orders," 922, 927. See Bernabé Bartolomé Martínez, "Las librerías e imprentas de los jesuitas (1540–1767): Una aportación notable a la cultura española," *Hispania sacra* 40 (1988): 315–88, here 381–82 for a listing of the current location of documents relating to Jesuit *colegios* in Spain and 386–88 for information about the processing of their papers when they were confiscated by the Spanish state.

Spanish Jesuits' feelings regarding the pope's advice to avoid the election of another Spanish superior general, likely underpinned this discussion of contemplative styles. There is no doubt that this decision was—and continues to be—controversial. Again according to Endean, a more accurate representation of Mercurian's attitude toward mystical practices is that Mercurian emphasized the Jesuits' commitment to "ministerial purpose," as opposed to pure contemplation.[151]

But one issue concerning ministry was fundamental to this polemic over prayer, namely serving as spiritual directors to women. Avellaneda's instructions to Álvarez specified that the latter should curtail the amount of time he dedicated to women, particularly Carmelite nuns, and instead spend more time advising men, "where there is less danger and more profit." (As others have signaled, it is important to note this advice was given before future doctor of the church Teresa de Ávila's meditative approach had become mainstream.)[152] This advice also distanced the Society of Jesus from the Discalced Carmelites. Before this point, Jesuits had served as spiritual advisors in eleven of the seventeen convents that Teresa de Ávila established. As Alison Weber notes, no documentary evidence has been found to suggest that this break was motivated by Mercurian's anti-*converso* stance. But in Weber's estimation, it was motivated by the Carmelites' connections with spiritual currents, including *alumbradismo*, that had become suspicious.[153]

Outreach to women was not the only potential problem with Álvarez's contemplative methodology. In 1574, Provincial of Castile Suárez asked Álvarez to compose a treatise offering advice on how to avoid *alumbrado* terminology.[154] Whereas Endean characterizes Álvarez's work as "a balanced, somewhat pedestrian extension" of Ignatius's thinking on the matter, Weber instead finds a "bold defense of laywomen's spirituality" in a work that advocates for an Ignatian "golden mean" that avoids the pitfalls of contemplative prayer while not abandoning it altogether. Álvarez does not restrict interior devotion to the educated clergy. Suárez was not pleased with the text and instructed Álvarez to revise it.[155]

Superiors in the Jesuit community were particularly concerned with distancing themselves from contemplative prayer and women because of several

---

151   Endean, "Strange Style of Prayer," 390, 378.
152   Endean, "Strange Style of Prayer," 365. This translation is Endean's. See Endean, "Strange Style of Prayer," 370n62 for several scholars who make this point.
153   Weber, "Jesuitas y las carmelitas descalzas," 105, 113.
154   Weber signals that this detail appears in Luis de la Puente's biography of Álvarez in "Jesuit Apologias," 333.
155   Endean, "Strange Style of Prayer," 362; Weber, "Jesuit Apologias," 333–34, 337.

AN OVERVIEW OF THE PRE-SUPPRESSION SOCIETY OF JESUS IN SPAIN 37

issues of importance to the Spanish Inquisition: the Inquisition's growing concern with priests' solicitation of female penitents during confession and an *alumbradismo* case in southern Spain. As in the *alumbradismo* cases investigated after 1525, *alumbradismo* also seemed to travel in the company of *conversos*. In Stefania Pastore's interpretation, Mercurian's mandated reform of contemplative practices sought to distance the order from controversies concerning *alumbrados* and *conversos*.[156]

5 Encounters with the Inquisition

5.1 *Renewed Accusations of* Alumbradismo

Beginning in the early 1570s, Dominican Alonso de la Fuente (1533–92) complained that the Jesuits were *alumbrados* to a variety of legal authorities, including both the Spanish and Portuguese Inquisitions, the king of Spain, and the pope. Astrain relates that Fuente played a role in uncovering practitioners of *alumbradismo* in Llerena. His motives for implicating the Jesuits differ according to scholars. In Menéndez Pelayo's analysis, after Jesuit Diego de la Cruz (d.1577) came to the area and addressed Fuente's criticisms of the Society in a sermon, Fuente simply decided to denounce the Jesuits as well.[157] In Wright's assessment, however, the actual source of this Dominican's complaint was different: "The denunciation was truly typical of a more profound objection, common among Spanish regulars, to the supposed conduct and institutional identity of the Society in Spain." In addition, Wright adds that the Jesuits that Fuente implicated in the order's supposed revival of *alumbradismo* were of *converso* origins.[158] So the order's acceptance of men descended from practitioners of Judaism also implicitly related to these grievances.

However, the presence of *conversos* in the order was not the only issue involved in Fuente's denunciations of the Society. In addition to Jesuits from converted Jewish families, Fuente was also concerned with gender, more specifically with interior piety as it was practiced by women in Andalusia and Extremadura. Along with problematic meditative practices on the part of

---

156 Stefania Pastore, "La 'svolta antimistica' di Mercuriano: I retroscena spagnoli," *Dimensioni e problemi della ricerca storica* 1 (2005): 81–93, here 88.

157 Astrain, *Historia de la Compañía de Jesús*, 3:58–59 and Menéndez Pelayo, *Historia de los heterodoxos españoles*, 2:543, cited in Astrain, *Historia de la Compañía de Jesús*, 3:58–59. In formatting the last names of historical personages that involve "de," I use the format that the Real Academia de la Historia employs in the *DB~e*, except when house style overrules this choice.

158 Wright, "Jesuits and the Older Religious Orders," 924.

women, the Dominican preacher found inappropriate sexual relationships between women and their confessors. (This had been a feature of *alumbradismo* earlier in the sixteenth century as well.) According to Fuente's denunciations, he uncovered what Weber terms "demonic sexuality." When Fuente interviewed one of his nieces who had become a *beata* about her practices, she revealed that her mental prayer generated lewd and sacrilegious thoughts. Eventually, Fuente came to assert that Jesuit clerics were using sorcery to attract adherents. He also believed that he discovered satanic influence in these mental prayer practices.[159]

Royal and ecclesiastical authorities, however, did not concur that erotic and demonic elements had mixed with heretical thought as this Dominican believed. When the Inquisition began investigating in Llerena, the body did not incorporate Fuente's ideas about sexual activities tied to demonic forces in the "edicto de fe" (edict of faith, a listing of heterodox behaviors that inquisitors in Spain, or their designates, read aloud to begin a visit to a particular area) that was read at the beginning of the Inquisition's visit in 1574. As these investigations led to arrests and, according to the Inquisition's methods, questioning under torture, defendants were interrogated about sex acts between priests and female disciples without reference to demonic influence. As Weber observes, with one exception, the women involved were given lighter sentences than the clerics with whom they had sexual relations. Thus, in contrast to Fuente's focus on women, the Inquisition's judges determined that the clerics bore greater levels of culpability for this misconduct. More generally, again in Weber's analysis, this incident belies a common assertion in the historiography of the Catholic Church, namely "that the ecclesiastical elites were unremittingly hostile to the varied forms of embodied piety in post-Tridentine Spain." The practitioners of interior piety targeted by Fuente were supported by the bishop of Badajoz, the archbishop of Seville, and other ecclesial authorities.[160]

As the Inquisition's investigations in Llerena continued, Fuente turned to the Portuguese Inquisition to make new accusations against the Society of Jesus. According to Fuente, not only did Jesuits indulge in inappropriate sexual contact with their penitents while in ecstatic states but they also used magic and worshipped the devil. Faced with these wild accusations against the Society, Cardinal Henrique, then the Portuguese inquisitor general, complained to

---

159 Menéndez Pelayo, *Historia de los heterodoxos españoles* (Mexico City: Porrúa, 1982), 4:322, cited in Alison Weber, "Demonizing Ecstasy: Alonso de la Fuente and the *Alumbrados* of Extremadura," in *The Mystical Gesture: Essays on Medieval and Early Modern Spiritual Culture in Honor of Mary E. Giles*, ed. Robert Boenig (Aldershot, UK: Ashgate, 2000), 141–58, here 141, and Weber, "Demonizing Ecstasy," 143, 144–46, 148.

160 Weber, "Demonizing Ecstasy," 147, 150, 151, 155.

AN OVERVIEW OF THE PRE-SUPPRESSION SOCIETY OF JESUS IN SPAIN   39

Philip II. After being found guilty of libel, Fuente was forced to retract his assertions and was subjected to other punishments, including a period of confinement to the monastery of Portaceli in Seville and restrictions on his preaching about his notions of the *alumbrado* heresy.[161]

When the Llerena investigations culminated in a 1579 *auto de fe* (literally, act of faith, an often public ceremony in which the sentences of those tried by the Inquisition were read), no members of the Society were among those punished. In Weber's estimation, however, this case had long-lasting consequences for the order, in that it motivated Mercurian's distancing of the Society from contemplation not included in the *Exercises*.[162]

The Spanish Inquisition had other concerns with the Society. Specifically, the Inquisition objected to the Jesuit order's admission of *conversos*, its seeming lack of interest in taking positions in the Inquisition, and its jurisdictional privileges. Because of papal privileges, a number of religious orders, including the Society, were exempted from certain mandates from the Inquisition. Whereas many other members of the Spanish populace, including clerics, were required to report heretical actions to the Inquisition, members of the Society of Jesus only needed to give an account to their superiors. The order's resolution of the case of a Jesuit who solicited a penitent during confession without reporting the behavior to the Inquisition became a particular point of contention.[163]

5.2   Solicitation in the Confessional

In Weber's assessment, the Inquisition's attention to the Llerena case was motivated by the body's desire to curtail solicitation. The Holy Office began to more seriously consider Fuente's charges once they involved sexuality. The Llerena case was only one manifestation of the Inquisition's desire to control solicitation in the confessional. According to Weber's research, from December 1573 to July 1576, the Suprema sent five *cartas acordadas* (letters from a higher-level court to a lower one, in this case from the Supreme Council of the Inquisition to its tribunals) mandating severe sanctions for those found guilty of soliciting their penitents.[164]

This growing attention to the sexual practices of the clergy formed part of the Spanish Inquisition's pivot to policing sexual practices in earnest, including those of people of the cloth. Before this point, Spanish bishops and

---

161   Weber, "Demonizing Ecstasy," 151–52; Astrain, *Historia de la Compañía de Jesús*, 3:60–62.
162   Weber, "Jesuit Apologias," 333.
163   Kamen, *Spanish Inquisition*, 207; Astrain, *Historia de la Compañía de Jesús*, 3:369.
164   Weber, "Demonizing Ecstasy," 157.

occasionally the Inquisition had dealt with cases of clerics who solicited their penitents during confession. In 1561, Pope Pius IV granted the Spanish Inquisition jurisdiction over solicitation. As Stephen Haliczer explains, this decision emphasized the seriousness with which authorities had come to view this transgression, as sexual solicitation by clerics while administering the sacrament of penance could undermine increased participation in confession, a goal of the reforms of the Council of Trent (1545–63).[165]

Beginning in the mid-1580s, the Society of Jesus clashed with the Inquisition over jurisdiction for Jesuits accused of solicitation and other matters over which the Inquisition believed it held exclusive jurisdiction. In 1584, Jesuit Diego Hernández (*fl.* mid- to late sixteenth century) denounced his own religious community to the Inquisition because he was displeased with the manner in which the case of Sebastián de Briviesca (*fl.* mid- to late sixteenth century) had been handled by the order. Briviesca had been accused of solicitation and was sent to Rome without the Society informing the Inquisition of the charges. (As a result of Hernández's denunciation to the Inquisition and the case of another Jesuit who was sent to Rome for preaching incorrect doctrine, again without the matter being referred to the Inquisition, the provincial and three other Jesuits were detained by the Inquisition between 1586 and 1588.) From the Inquisition's relatively light sanction for Provincial Antonio Marcén (d.1603), who was excluded from the position of superior for two years, and the lack of any sanction for the other three Jesuits, we may conclude that no evidence was found against them.[166] In José Martínez Millán's assessment, these flimsy charges formed part of a campaign to discredit Jesuits allied with the non-Spanish superior general.[167]

Subsequently, both the Jesuits and the Spanish Inquisition appealed to Rome to resolve the matter. In 1591, the Society secured a papal opinion that specified that the papal nuncio, not the Inquisition, was the proper adjudicating authority for matters concerning the Society. The following year, however, the Roman Congregation of the Inquisition decided that superiors of regular religious orders were not invested with the authority to adjudicate cases against their own members. Subsequent papal bulls further defined the Inquisition's authority on this matter. In 1605, a papal bull from Pope Paul V (1550–1621, r.1605–21) removed authority from superiors in any situation over which the Inquisition had jurisdiction. Specifically concerning solicitation, in 1622 another bull endowed the Inquisition with special authority over this

---

165 Stephen Haliczer, *Sexuality in the Confessional: A Sacrament Profaned* (New York: Oxford University Press, 1996), 42.

166 Astrain, *Historia de la Compañía de Jesús*, 3:372–73, 376–79, 400–1.

167 Martínez Millán, "Transformación y crisis," 114.

AN OVERVIEW OF THE PRE-SUPPRESSION SOCIETY OF JESUS IN SPAIN 41

crime, regardless of whether the accused cleric was a regular (member of a religious order) or secular (diocesan) cleric.[168]

This cluster of Inquisition cases that began with charges of solicitation by a Jesuit was unusual for the order in Spain. According to Haliczer's research on the topic, most solicitation complaints involved members of the regular (as opposed to secular) clergy; however, very few Jesuits were denounced for such behavior. Basing his analysis on H. [Henry] Outram Evennett (1901–64), Haliczer attributes this fact to the Society's admission standards, its training of its members as well as "their freedom from the boring and stultifying routines of convent life, and the order's emphasis on avoiding the kinds of activity leading to immorality and scandal."[169] Correspondence between Rome and Jesuit provinces reveals an important element of the order's plan to avoid solicitation: the Society generally sought to limit the contact that younger priests had with female penitents, particularly in the cases of young noblewomen seeking Jesuit confessors. When reports of Jesuits' potentially inappropriate relationships with women reached Rome, generals reminded provincials of this practice. In relating the reports that Father Jerónimo Vilar (*fl.* early to mid-seventeenth century) had visited and exchanged "love letters" with a young woman, Superior General Muzio Vitelleschi (1563–1645, in office 1615–45) chided Provincial Pedro Continente (1587–1651) that, if this accusation proved true, it was the result of allowing a young priest of not entirely firm virtue to hear the confession of a young woman.[170]

Haliczer's research reveals that clerics found guilty of solicitation received official "admonition[s]," formal reproofs that were typically read before their sentences to encourage the newly convicted to behave better in the future. With this goal in mind, these documents evoked the goals of their religious orders. In 1687, the reprimand for a Jesuit offender emphasized the Society's commitment "to preaching and missionary work." Since non-Catholics judged Jesuits "to be their most dangerous opponent[s]," a Jesuit's misbehavior would "inevitably give comfort to the heretics, who would be able to hold the entire order up to ridicule."[171] These comments also tie into concerns among members of the order that any negative behavior by their number would serve as more fuel for criticism of the entire community.

---

168 Haliczer, *Sexuality in the Confessional*, 60.

169 Haliczer, *Sexuality in the Confessional*, 86–87. Haliczer mentions "only three cases" against Jesuits during an era of increasing membership for the Society. And an analysis of records dating from 1723 to 1820 reveals that Jesuits accounted for "3.2 percent" of allegations of solicitation (86–87).

170 Vitelleschi to Continente, May 30, 1634, AHN J leg. 253 doc. 209.

171 Haliczer, *Sexuality in the Confessional*, 43–44. The translations are Haliczer's.

5.3 Policy Changes in the Society to Address Spanish Concerns

While the Holy See did clarify the relative roles of religious orders in judging cases of solicitation, the Jesuits' privilege to read prohibited books and their reluctance to assume positions in the Inquisition remained unresolved. These matters might have been decided more slowly were it not for the complaints made by the *memorialistas*, Spanish Jesuits who complained about the Roman governance of the Society of Jesus to authorities outside the order, including to the Inquisition and royal representatives. In looking ahead to Acquaviva's decision to exclude *conversos* from the Jesuit community, it is not incidental that a number of the *memorialistas* were of Jewish descent.[172]

One such individual was Juan de Mariana (1536–1624), who was a member of a *converso* family. As a *memorialista*, he collaborated with Francisco de Estrada (*c*.1519–84).[173] Mariana's manuscript *Tratado del gobierno de la Compañía* (Treatise on the governance of the Society [composed before 1609]) outlined his grievances. Among other objections, Mariana complained about the "monarchical" style of governance of the Society in which the best candidates for offices were passed over in favor of weaker ones. Moreover, penitences were not imposed on those who deserved them. This text was printed posthumously as *Discurso de los grandes defectos que hay en la forma del gobierno de los jesuitas* (Discourse on the great defects that there are in the form of governance of the Jesuits) in 1625.[174] Astrain believes that the work came to be published after it was taken from Mariana's papers following his arrest by the Spanish Inquisition in 1609.[175] Whatever the means by which it came to the printed format, the volume was soon translated into French. Excerpts were published in French in 1625 and 1631.[176]

A faction at court including royal secretary Mateo Vázquez (*c*.1544–91) made certain that complaints concerning the Society of Jesus reached the monarch.[177] Even before learning of these specific grievances, Philip II already took such a dim view of the supervision of Spanish men of the cloth by non-Spaniards that he sought to have new structures developed in a number of religious orders to prevent this occurrence. Given these circumstances, it is unsurprising that the Spanish monarch began to lobby the pope to abolish the Jesuits' exemption from diocesan supervision and from the purview of the

---

172   Maryks, *Jesuit Order as a Synagogue of Jews*, 143.
173   Maryks, *Jesuit Order as a Synagogue of Jews*, 107, 128, 212. See Astrain, *Historia de la Compañía de Jesús*, 3:557–60 for more details about Mariana's behavior in Spain.
174   García Cárcel, "Crisis de la Compañía de Jesús," 388, 390, 386–87.
175   Astrain, *Historia de la Compañía de Jesús*, 3:560.
176   García Cárcel, "Crisis de la Compañía de Jesús," 386–87.
177   Martínez Millán, "Transformación y crisis," 110–13.

AN OVERVIEW OF THE PRE-SUPPRESSION SOCIETY OF JESUS IN SPAIN   43

Spanish Inquisition. In the king's estimation, the fact that the Jesuits needed to receive permission from their superior in order to work for the Inquisition did not exhibit sufficient commitment to the Holy Office. In an attempt to sway the pope, the king included some of the *memorialistas'* texts. Philip II also advocated for the appointment of an external assessor to evaluate the Society. For its part, the Society of Jesus sent two Jesuits, naturalist José de Acosta (c.1539–1600) and Robert Persons (1546–1610), who played a prominent role in the order's missions to the British Isles, to defend the order's point of view to the king. As Martínez Millán signals, it was not coincidental that both these priests had carried out important work in territories that were significant to the king who was once the spouse of Mary Tudor.[178]

It is important to note that Spanish and Italian Jesuits were not the only ones who employed similar strategies to make complaints to authorities outside of the Society. For example, Cardinal Mariano Pierbenedetti (1538–1611) sent a *memorial* to the Roman Inquisition in 1592 in which he traced what he deemed were the negative aspects of the Society's governance to its Spanish heritage.[179] The Fifth General Congregation's (1593–94) regulations sought to prevent the development of any future *memorialista* movements. To this end, decree 54 addresses Jesuits who are "disturbers of our accustomed peace and authors of sedition." These Jesuits "place their judgment ahead of that of the entire Society and even of its founder" and seek to upend the practices of the Society. Those suspected should be asked to promise to obey the *Constitutions*, the general congregation's decrees, and any relevant bulls. If they refuse to do so or later do not abide by their oaths, such individuals are to be dismissed from the order, "even if they are professed or of advanced years." Moreover, decree 55 specifically addressed the "calumnies and lying accusations" about the Society that were directed at Philip II. The general congregation resolved to inform the Spanish king that these allegations were untrue. Using correspondence and Jesuits traveling home to Spain to communicate with the sovereign, the Society would ensure that Philip II obtained accurate information.[180]

The general congregation specified that the order's privileges that disturbed Philip II had been resolved before the meeting of the congregation. Within the Spanish sphere of influence, the Society agreed to cease reading prohibited books and pardoning heretical behavior without recourse to the Spanish

---

178   Martínez Millán, "Transformación y crisis," 115–17, 121. See 115 for an excerpt of a letter that Philip II wrote to the count-duke of Olivares about these points.

179   Jiménez Pablo, "Final de la hegemonía hispana," 629.

180   GC 5 d. 54–55, in *For Matters of Greater Moment*, ed. Padberg, O'Keefe, and McCarthy, 205–7.

Inquisition. In 1589, the Society also set aside a privilege from Pope Gregory XIII that compelled Jesuits to seek "the expressed consent and mandate of the superior himself" in order to undertake work for anyone "of whatever ecclesiastical or secular dignity or authority" for the entire Jesuit community. Decree 21 of this general congregation affirmed these decisions and acknowledged that these changes were made at the behest of Philip II.[181]

5.4   *The Evolution of Jesuits' Service to the Spanish Inquisition*
In terms of specific service to the Inquisition, the Fifth General Congregation's decree 21 urged Jesuits in Spain's territories to aid the Holy Office in whatever manner possible.[182] However, Jesuits were prohibited from actively seeking positions in the Inquisition for themselves or for others. According to decree 28, if Jesuits were to do so, they would be excommunicated. Furthermore, if the threat of exclusion from the church proved to be an insufficient deterrent, the general congregation authorized the general to impose more serious punishments.[183]

By formally allowing Jesuits to take positions in the Spanish Inquisition, the order answered complaints from Philip II and settled long-standing criticisms on the part of other religious orders in Spain. Some twenty years before, during the Third General Congregation, the order was inclined to continue to refuse certain placements in the Inquisition. One question in the questionnaire to assist voters in that congregation in determining the best candidate for the office of superior general asked whether the candidate would "seriously attempt to free our Society from the many things that are not in agreement with our institute and thus burden us." This specifically included "acting as judges in meetings of the Inquisition and the Signatura of the Penitentiary."[184]

Ignatius preferred that Jesuits decline positions as judges or *calificadores* (assessors who were charged with evaluating the doctrinal soundness of texts or ideas expressed by defendants in the Inquisition) because these offices would take time away from their ministerial work.[185] But early Jesuits did assist the Inquisition in Spain on an *ad hoc* basis. As Astrain details, when Favre and Araoz came to the Spanish court in 1545, they were met with a cordial reception from the Inquisition. Over the ensuing years, clergy from various orders, including Jesuits, tended to the spiritual needs of those imprisoned

---

181   GC 5 d. 21, in *For Matters of Greater Moment*, ed. Padberg, O'Keefe, and McCarthy, 192.

182   GC 5 d. 21, in *For Matters of Greater Moment*, ed. Padberg, O'Keefe, and McCarthy, 193.

183   GC 5 d. 28, in *For Matters of Greater Moment*, ed. Padberg, O'Keefe, and McCarthy, 194.

184   GC 3 d. 5 (prior to election), in *For Matters of Greater Moment*, ed. Padberg, O'Keefe, and McCarthy, 136–37.

185   *FN1*, 728, 732–33.

AN OVERVIEW OF THE PRE-SUPPRESSION SOCIETY OF JESUS IN SPAIN   45

and sentenced to death by the Holy Office. Astrain mentions three Jesuits who also served as *calificadores* for the Inquisition.[186] Luis de Valdivia (1561–1642), in his history of Jesuit *colegios* in Castile, described the role played by his fellow Jesuit Juan de Prádanos (1529–97) in the discovery of the Protestant circle in Valladolid. In this version, Prádanos encouraged one of his penitents to denounce the Valladolid group to the Inquisition.[187] Moreno is more skeptical about Prádanos's part: in her estimation, Jesuits created the version of events that gave their priest a crucial role.[188] In Astrain's analysis, during Acquaviva's generalate, the Inquisition began to complain about the previously mentioned privileges and exemptions enjoyed by the Jesuits.[189] Following the Fifth General Congregation, Jesuits' roles in the Inquisition grew in the seventeenth century.

6   Admission Redux: Excluding *Conversos* from the Society

The 1593–94 general congregation reassessed more than the order's relationship to Spain's Holy Office. As various institutions in Spanish society started to impose statutes to exclude those with non-Christian branches in their family trees, the presence of *converso* Jesuits in Spain began to generate controversy. The first such exclusionary law in Spain was implemented in 1449 in Toledo.[190] (Whereas purity-of-blood laws in Spain applied initially to those of Jewish origin, they eventually were extended to those of Muslim origins as well.) As we have seen, the early Society of Jesus did not require genealogical purity for admission. If the admission of particular Jesuits from *converso* families caused comments in Iberia, the Society typically sent the men to Rome, where the issue of their lineage was not problematic.[191] But those in Iberia who favored excluding people descended from practitioners of Judaism and Islam were powerful, and their point of view gained ground. Archbishop of Toledo Silíceo was a significant proponent of these exclusions. In 1547, Silíceo made purity of blood a requirement for ecclesiastical appointments in his archdiocese. Not only was Silíceo the most powerful cleric in Spain but his archdiocese also

---

186   Astrain, *Historia de la Compañía de Jesús*, 3:368–69.
187   Burrieza Sánchez, "Establecimiento, fundación y oposición," 63.
188   Moreno, "Jesuitas, la Inquisición y la frontera espiritual," 666–67.
189   Astrain, *Historia de la Compañía de Jesús*, 3:369.
190   See J. [John] H. Elliott, *Imperial Spain 1469–1716* (London: Penguin, 2002 [1963]), 220–24, and Maryks, *Jesuit Order as a Synagogue of Jews*, 1–39 for more details about the evolution of these exclusionary laws.
191   Maryks, *Jesuit Order as a Synagogue of Jews*, 83–84.

housed the Society's *colegio* in the university town of Alcalá de Henares. That this institution became, in Maryks's assessment, "a hotbed of Jesuit (*converso*) vocations" must have galled Silíceo. According to Jesuit Diego de Guzmán (*c.*1522–1606), Silíceo actively attempted to influence the Jesuits' thinking on the *converso* question. In a 1593 letter to Acquaviva protesting the recent exclusionary decree, Guzmán related that Silíceo promised Nadal a "great *colegio*" if the order would retract its admission of *conversos*.[192]

Official disagreement with the order's acceptance of *conversos* was not limited to Spain but was a broader Iberian phenomenon. The Portuguese ecclesiastical hierarchy and Inquisition as well as Portuguese royals were in favor of this exclusion. In advance of the Fifth General Congregation, in the last decade of the sixteenth century, Kamen relates that a "whispering campaign initiated by its enemies" against the Society represented it as heavily populated by Jewish men, presumably meaning *conversos*. As a result, fewer men chose to join the Jesuit order.[193]

Iberian concerns compelled the Fifth General Congregation to abolish the admission of *conversos* to the order. According to decree 52, the Society came to this decision because those whose genealogy includes non-Christians "have routinely been in the habit of inflicting a great deal of hindrance and harm on the Society (as has become clear from our daily experience)." This decree mandated that any individual "who is descended of Hebrew and Saracen stock" should not be admitted. In the case of discovery of such lineage after admission, such a Jesuit "should be dismissed as soon as the impediment will have been shown to exist, at whatever time before profession it becomes known." In these cases, superiors were to notify the general and wait for his response. Although decree 52 "does not give the impediment the force of an essential one," no one, including the general himself, "may give dispensation from it."[194] In 1608, the Sixth General Congregation revisited this requirement. Decree 28 limited the genealogical inquiry "to the fifth degree of family lineage inclusive"; however, as Maryks signals, this change was not very meaningful. Many whose ancestors had converted could not meet this bar.[195]

At the ideological level, the Society abandoned an early policy that was significant to the founder in order to conform to the restrictions that other

---

192   Elliott, *Imperial Spain*, 222; Maryks, *Jesuit Order as a Synagogue of Jews*, 82, and ARSI, *Instit. 186e*, fols. 354ᵛ–355, cited in Maryks, *Jesuit Order as a Synagogue of Jews*, 84. The translation is Maryks's.

193   Kamen, *Spanish Inquisition*, 320.

194   GC 5 d. 52, in *For Matters of Greater Moment*, ed. Padberg, O'Keefe, and McCarthy, 204.

195   GC 6 d. 28, in *For Matters of Greater Moment*, ed. Padberg, O'Keefe, and McCarthy, 232; Maryks, *Jesuit Order as a Synagogue of Jews*, xxviii, 159.

AN OVERVIEW OF THE PRE-SUPPRESSION SOCIETY OF JESUS IN SPAIN

Iberian institutions had placed on the *converso* population. In 1590, Acquaviva wrote to Spanish provincials asking that *converso* Jesuits not be given leadership positions in which they would have to interact with royal or inquisitorial officials because so many notable people cautioned the order against its position vis-à-vis *conversos*. At that point, Acquaviva urged for more stringent admission. The general admitted that the opinions of highly placed authorities necessitated this decision in order to preserve the standing of the Jesuit community.[196] But there were motives unrelated to external pressures that affected this decision and the subsequent exclusionary decree of the Fifth General Congregation. In Maryks's analysis, following Acquaviva's election in 1581, highly placed Jesuits, including Paul Hoffaeus (*c.*1530–1608), Lorenzo Maggio (1531–1605), and Manuel Rodrigues (1534–96), stressed *conversos'* involvement in the *memorialista* movement. The 1593 ban on *conversos'* admission was as such "orchestrated as a punishment for the alleged participation of *conversos* in the revolt against the way in which Acquaviva and his assistants general governed the Society."[197]

At the practical level, if the Society instituted purity-of-blood statutes in hopes of boosting recruitment efforts, this endeavor failed. The previously mentioned Diego de Guzmán noted that a number of productive members of the community left because of their *converso* background. Moreover, admissions fell notably in the Spanish and Portuguese spheres of influence.[198]

A *memorial* written by Guzmán suggests other issues that he believed would arise as a result of the exclusion of *conversos*. As Maryks relates, Guzmán asserted that some families chose to avoid Jesuit schools because if their sons subsequently wanted to join the Society, the genealogical investigation would reveal their *converso* origins and end up shaming the family. At the same time, some men looking to prove their genealogical *bona fides* who had no religious vocations would join the order simply to obtain evidence of their non-*converso* lineage. Guzmán's *memorial* is only one example of a larger group

---

196   ARSI *Inst. 184/II*, fols. 347, 366–67, cited in Maryks, *Jesuit Order as a Synagogue of Jews,* 147–48.

197   Maryks, *Jesuit Order as a Synagogue of Jews,* 143, 149.

198   Diego de Guzmán, ARSI *Inst. 186e*, fol. 355ᵛ, and Francisco de Borja Medina, "Precursores de Vieira: Jesuitas andaluces y castellanos en favor de los cristianos nuevos," in *Terceiro centenário da morte do Padre António Vieira: Congresso Internacional; Actas* (Braga: Universidade Católica Portuguesa, Província Portuguesa da Companhia de Jesus, 1999), 491–519, here 501, both cited in Maryks, *Jesuit Order as a Synagogue of Jews,* 151.

of documents that protested the 1593 decree and ultimately led to the 1608 modification of the 1593 decision.[199]

In general terms, opinions differ over the effectiveness of policies to exclude those of *converso* descent from religious orders, ecclesiastical positions, and some *colegios mayores* (colleges) of universities. Kamen maintains that statutes mandating purity of blood were not widespread or strictly enforced. He also argues that those required to demonstrate lineages free of non-Christian antecedents could launder their lineage through money: either by bribery or by purchasing fraudulent documents that would incorrectly affirm a Christian genealogy.[200] Nonetheless, Kamen does concede that in later eras "the rules about blood purity continued in force in several parts of Spain down to the nineteenth century." These later *limpieza* exclusions "affected many individuals to varying and by no means negligible degree, though by then they were in the nature of a tool to exclude competitors for posts rather than a weapon of racialism."[201]

Other scholars believe that these exclusionary laws became consequential much earlier. Albert A. Sicroff (1918–2013), for example, cites the misgivings expressed by Fernando de Vera (1582–1639), the bishop of Cuzco, when he learned in 1636 that his nephew was seeking entrance into the military— religious Orden de San Juan (Order of Saint John). (These institutions were both highly selective and strict in their application of purity-of-blood laws.) In a letter that the bishop cautioned his nephew Jacinto (*fl.* mid-seventeenth century) to read in private, the bishop informed the younger man of some issues with his maternal line. The elder Vera offered his nephew a number of strategies to employ, including bribery. And he sent his younger relative funds for this purpose. The bishop also cautioned the younger man that seeking such an honor could ultimately damage the family's reputation: either the suspension of his nephew's application for additional investigations or his admission with a waiver would have negative repercussions on the family's standing.[202]

In Kamen's estimation, it was the question of honor that ultimately motivated *limpieza* restrictions.[203] As a relative "newcomer" when compared with

---

199   Maryks, *Jesuit Order as a Synagogue of Jews*, 186, xxviii. See 159–217 for more about these *memoriales*.

200   Kamen, *Spanish Inquisition*, 312–13.

201   Henry Kamen, *Imagining Spain: Historical Myth and National Identity* (New Haven: Yale University Press, 2008), 146–47.

202   Albert A. Sicroff, *Los estatutos de limpieza de sangre: Controversias entre los siglos XV y XVII*, trans. Mauro Armiño (Madrid: Taurus, 1985), 309–13.

203   Kamen, *Imagining Spain*, 147.

AN OVERVIEW OF THE PRE-SUPPRESSION SOCIETY OF JESUS IN SPAIN 49

more established religious orders in Spain, the Society of Jesus needed to be concerned with its image, particularly as the order's critics were waiting to exploit any perceived misstep. Kamen rightly signals that a variety of institutions, "most notoriously of all, city councils and cathedrals which had statutes of blood purity systematically ignored them when it suited their purpose."[204] Considering the Jesuits' position, in contrast to those of more established entities, the order had a greater need to prove its members' *limpieza* in order to maintain the order's social standing. While the Society of Jesus likely was not as stringent in applying *limpieza* laws as the notoriously strict Orders of Santiago and Calatrava, surviving records do indicate that the Society investigated the origins of applicants. When the now renowned writer Baltasar Gracián y Morales (1601–58) applied to enter the Society, Gracián's witness Cosme Ferrer (b. *c.*1559) affirmed that Gracián's parents and all four grandparents were free from non-Christian origins. It seems, however, that there were some concerns about the veracity of this information. In Gracián's case, a "special note" that Miquel Batllori (1909–2003) indicated does not figure in other proofs offers additional clarification about Gracián's paternal line. In addition, it seems that further inquiries might have been made because a summary of these investigations appears later in the same book of records. There also is one more "anomaly" in terms of the manner in which Gracián's documentation was archived, which suggests that the order thought it might need access to Gracián's proof in the future. According to Batllori's analysis, the order kept the original documents concerning Gracián rather than the standard practice of simply recording the data in their register of proofs of *limpieza*.[205] Maryks's research on the surname Gracián explains the order's care in maintaining the documentation concerning Gracián's lineage, as questions might have arisen over Gracián's ancestry because his family shared several traits with *conversos*. A number of people with this surname were *conversos* who rendered the Hebrew last name Hen as Gracián. Moreover, the fact that so many of Gracián's siblings joined religious orders follows a pattern often seen in *converso* households.[206] Beyond Gracián himself, cautious families, like that of the aforementioned bishop Vera, might well have urged their sons not to seek

---

204   Kamen, *Imagining Spain*, 146.
205   Miguel Batllori, *Gracián y el barroco* (Rome: Edizioni di Storia e Letteratura, 1958), 13–14. Catalan Miquel Batllori used the Castilian version of his first name in his publications in Spanish. (The linguistic policy of the Franco regime made Spanish the only official language of the country.)
206   Maryks, *Jesuit Order as a Synagogue of Jews*, 153–54.

50 MANNING

admission to the Society because of the potential negative impacts of genealogical research on their reputations.

7 Aiding Catholics under Siege

As the debate over *converso* membership was building in the latter part of the sixteenth century, ministering to the needs of Catholics under the rule of Protestants in the British Isles was an area of particular concern for Spain and for Spanish Jesuits. As the situation for Catholics in the British Isles became more difficult, Catholic powers took various steps to assist them, including establishing seminaries on the Continent to train mostly British, Scottish, and Irish Catholic clergy for service in British domains. Spain hosted a number of these seminaries, among them the Seminario de Ingleses and the Seminario de Escoceses in Madrid, the Colegio Inglés in Seville, and the Colegio de los Ingleses, the Colegio de San Albano, in Valladolid. In the late 1500s, Spain alone provided financial support to the English *colegios*.[207]

One Spanish noblewoman took an active role in assisting English Catholics after an association with the Jesuits in Spain. Luisa de Carvajal y Mendoza (1566–1614) spent years on a Catholic mission in Protestant England. Because Catholic priests' movements were restricted, women working with English Catholics performed more active roles than they did in areas where Catholic clergy could minister more freely. Under these circumstances, traditional gender roles were set aside to combat Protestantism, particularly to serve the needs of Catholics in officially Protestant England.[208]

Carvajal's writings offered differing versions about how her interest in the plight of English Catholics began. On some occasions, Carvajal traced it to her teens, whereas on others, she dated it to her time in Madrid. While in Madrid, however, she did not write about the possibility of going to England herself.[209]

---

207 Thomas M. McCoog, *The Society of Jesus in Ireland, Scotland, and England: "Our way of proceeding?"* (Leiden: Brill, 1996), 264, cited in Anne J. Cruz, "Introduction," in *The Life and Writings of Luisa de Carvajal y Mendoza*, ed. and trans. Anne J. Cruz (Toronto: Iter, Centre for Reformation and Renaissance Studies, 2014), 1–109, here 67.

208 Elizabeth Rhodes, "Luisa de Carvajal's Counter-Reformation Journey to Selfhood (1566–1614)," *Renaissance Quarterly* 51, no. 3 (1998): 887–911, here 906; Alison Weber, "Introduction: Devout Laywomen in the Early Modern World; The Historiographical Challenge," in *Devout Laywomen*, ed. Weber, 1–28, here 10–11. Weber mentions Raymond of Capua's (c.1330–99) defense of Catherine of Siena's (1347–80) "public role" in this context.

209 Cruz, "Introduction," 54–55.

AN OVERVIEW OF THE PRE-SUPPRESSION SOCIETY OF JESUS IN SPAIN   51

When Carvajal arrived in England in 1605, English Catholics initially declined to house her because they feared her presence would attract too much attention and would therefore endanger the entire group. So Carvajal resided with the Spanish ambassador. Despite this initially cool reception, eventually Carvajal helped to import Catholic texts into the country, found sanctuary for priests, visited imprisoned Catholics, taught new converts, and preached. In time, the Spanish noblewoman came to live with other similarly minded women; this group worked to preserve the remains of those executed for the practice of Catholicism. In correspondence with her cousin, Carvajal described how the remains of executed Catholics were disinterred and the manner in which this group of women cleaned and preserved the bodies. Since the archbishop of Canterbury George Abbot (1562–1633) classified Carvajal as a "Jesuitess," Glyn Redworth suggests that Carvajal, rather than Mary Ward (1585–1645), whose female congregation based on the Society was eventually suppressed by Pope Urban VIII (1568–1644, r.1623–44), might deserve the title of "the first Jesuitess in England."[210]

Carvajal was not the only woman with ties to the Society who took on ministerial roles in Protestant England. When future saint Anne Line (c.1565–1601) became widowed, she engaged in similarly public work with London's Catholics. In 1601, Line was executed for these efforts. Henry Garnet (c.1553–1606), the superior of the Jesuit community in England, related that Line voluntarily took vows of chastity, poverty, and obedience, but regarding the latter, "there was no one who would receive it." Members of the Society were not permitted to accept women's vows of obedience.[211]

Both Carvajal's life as a *beata* and her association with the Society began back in Spain. As a young woman living with her uncle in Madrid, she converted the highest floor of his home into a space where she could live an austere life centered on prayer.[212] Following the death of her surviving relatives, Carvajal bought a house in Madrid's calle de Toledo from the Society to establish her own household. When the Spanish court moved to Valladolid, Carvajal followed in order to continue her lawsuit over her inheritance. While there, she

---

210   Glyn Redworth, "A New Way of Living? Luisa de Carvajal and the Limits of Mysticism," in *New Companion to Hispanic Mysticism*, ed. Kallendorf, 273–95, here 276, 277, 282–83; Cruz, "Introduction," 70–75, 85–86. For a selection of Carvajal's writings in translation, see *Life and Writings of Luisa de Carvajal*, ed. and trans. Cruz, and *This Tight Embrace: Luisa de Carvajal y Mendoza (1566–1614)*, ed. and trans. Elizabeth Rhodes (Milwaukee, WI: Marquette University Press, 2000), for English and Spanish texts.

211   Robert E. Scully, "The Lives of Anne Line: Vowed Laywoman, Recusant Martyr, and Elizabethan Saint," in *Devout Laywomen*, ed. Weber, 276–93, here 277, 284, 279.

212   Redworth, "New Way of Living," 275.

came to live beside the Society's Colegio de San Albano, an institution founded to train Jesuits for the priesthood in England, and prayed in the presence of the Virgen Vulnerata in the *colegio*'s chapel. In Valladolid, Carvajal headed a small community of devout women, and their ties to one another endured through her years in England. She continued to correspond with Inés de la Asunción (*fl.* mid- to late sixteenth to early seventeenth century), one of her companions in Valladolid, along with a number of other Spanish women interested in religious matters.[213]

Although Carvajal expressed a willingness to abandon her lawsuit over her inheritance, she wrote that the Society would not allow her to do so.[214] According to Anne J. Cruz's research, "the donation of her [Carvajal's] inheritance to the English Jesuits had facilitated her desired voyage to England," but "her contact with the order's hierarchy was tenuous at best."[215] In Burrieza Sánchez's estimation, it was two of the Walpole brothers, Michael (*c.*1570–1625) and Richard (1564–1607), Jesuit priests who trained at the Colegio de San Albano, who personally, rather than formally on behalf of the English Jesuits, encouraged Carvajal's journey to England.[216] Several Jesuits corresponded with Carvajal while she was in England, including Joseph Creswell (1557–*c.*1623), the rector of San Albano, and John Blackfan (1561–1641).[217] (Carvajal and Blackfan's correspondence will be discussed later in terms of seventeenth-century mortification practices.)

Whatever the degree to which the order officially knew about Carvajal's undertaking, Spanish Jesuit priests memorialized her in posthumous sermons after she died of illness in 1614 following her release from prison in London.[218] Michael Walpole also wrote a *vita* (literally, a life, in this case a life story) to celebrate her virtues. Yet, despite these tributes to Carvajal's life, the Society did not follow her request concerning the disposition of her remains. In leaving her fortune to the Society, Carvajal requested burial in a Jesuit chapel; but the order did not comply. Although some English Catholics hoped to keep

---

213 María J. Pando-Canteli, "Letters, Books, and Relics: Material and Spiritual Networks in the Life of Luisa de Carvajal y Mendoza (1564–1614)," in *Devout Laywomen*, ed. Weber, 294–311, here 307n24; Cruz, "Introduction," 13; Lehfeldt, *Religious Women*, 209.

214 Elizabeth Rhodes, "About Luisa de Carvajal y Mendoza, 1566–1614," in *This Tight Embrace*, ed. and trans. Rhodes, 1–37, here 7.

215 Cruz, "Introduction," 67, 54.

216 Burrieza Sánchez, "Percepción jesuítica," 91.

217 Pando-Canteli, "Letters, Books, and Relics," 294–95 discusses the correspondence with Creswell, and Redworth, "New Way of Living," 291–92 and Glyn Redworth, *The She-Apostle: The Extraordinary Life and Death of Luisa de Carvajal* (Oxford: Oxford University Press, 2008), 156–58, 223 with Blackfan.

218 Burrieza Sánchez, "Percepción jesuítica," 92; Cruz, "Introduction," 1.

AN OVERVIEW OF THE PRE-SUPPRESSION SOCIETY OF JESUS IN SPAIN 53

Carvajal's body in England, King Philip III (1578–1621, r.1598–1621) instructed his ambassador in Spain to send the body to the Convento de la Encarnación in Madrid. When Rodrigo Calderón (1576/78–1621) claimed Carvajal's remains, he absconded with them to Porta Coeli. Eventually, the Spanish monarch forced Calderón to turn the remains over to the bishop. Magdalena de San Jerónimo (*fl.* late sixteenth century to early seventeenth century), a woman of the cloth who founded various reformatories for women and corresponded with Carvajal, complied with the king's wishes to turn the coffin over to the Convento de la Encarnación, where it remains.[219]

Beyond Carvajal and Spanish-trained Jesuits who traveled to England to minister to Catholics, Spanish members of the Society of Jesus undertook other efforts to assist British mariners, whether coreligionists or not. In 1618, Vitelleschi wrote to inform Provincial Juan Sanz (d.1627) that the English monarch had released a number of imprisoned priests, including eleven Jesuits. The general requested that some of these freed Jesuits be accommodated in port cities in the province of Aragon in order to aid Catholic and non-Catholic sailors who worked on English flagged vessels.[220]

When called upon, Jesuits assisted Catholics who had been captured and held for ransom by pirates, corsairs, and other kidnappers.[221] Juan de Torres (1546–99) and Gabriel Bautista del Puerto (1525–78), as well as Puerto's companion Gaspar López (1533–1601), Jesuits stationed in North Africa with financial assistance from Magdalena de Ulloa, worked to pay for captives' release from African-based captors.[222] When necessary, other Jesuits ransomed themselves or other members when they were taken hostage. A party of Spanish Jesuits, including the provincial of Castile Gil González Dávila (1532–96), Martín Gutiérrez (1524–73), Juan Suárez, and their companion Diego de los Ríos (*fl.* mid- to late sixteenth century), were captured by Huguenots in France when traveling to Rome for the Third General Congregation. As John W. Padberg signals, their kidnappers never learned that the men were Catholic religious, but their situation was nonetheless serious. Gutiérrez died while captive. By the time Suárez, who was freed to raise the needed funds, returned with the ransom money, González Dávila was too unwell to be able

---

219   Cruz, "Introduction," 94, 100–101, 98, 101–2.
220   Vitelleschi to Provincial Juan Sanz, August 6, 1618, AHN J leg. 253 doc. 63.
221   See María Antonia Garcés, *Cervantes in Algiers: A Captive's Tale* (Nashville: Vanderbilt University Press, 2002), 15–60 for an introduction to captives' lives in the city of Algiers.
222   Burrieza Sánchez, "Ministerios de la Compañía," 79. See F. B. [Francisco de Borja] Medina, "Puerto, Gabriel Baptista de" and "López, Gaspar" in *Diccionario histórico de la Compañía de Jesús*, ed. O'Neill and Domínguez, 4:3257–58 and 3:2414 for more details. I modernize Baptista to Bautista in my text.

to continue immediately to Rome. Although Suárez did resume his journey to Rome, he arrived too late to cast a vote for the new general.[223] These Jesuits were not the only Spanish members who were waylaid and held for ransom during overland or sea journeys to Rome.

Other members of the order were captured under other circumstances. A 1612 document references the need to repay funds for the ransom of Jesuit Juan Alcover (*fl.* early to mid-seventeenth century).[224] The order also attempted to aid members' captured relatives. In 1638, Vitelleschi expressed his appreciation for the alms that Andalusian Jesuits collected for the ransom for Jesuit Antonio Perlas's (*fl.* seventeenth century) mother, sisters, and other relatives.[225]

8   The Question of Religiously Minded Women

8.1   *Women of the Cloth*

The prohibition of religious texts written in Spanish in the Spanish Inquisition's 1559 Index was a particular blow to women interested in religious topics, because so few women could read Latin. Teresa de Ávila was motivated to begin writing in order to fill this gap.[226] In considering the influence of Teresa's writings, it is important to note that they were circulated in handwritten form beginning in the latter 1560s, which is to say prior to their publication in printed form in 1588.[227] This publication generated a great deal of controversy. Among those who denounced Teresa's writings to the Inquisition, Fuente condemned them as the product of *alumbradismo*.[228]

As previously mentioned, in 1577 Jesuit spiritual director Álvarez was told to spend less time providing spiritual advice to women in general and specifically to Carmelite nuns, like his directee, the future saint. On a fairly frequent basis, advice from superiors general to provinces in Spain reminded Jesuits

---

223   John W. Padberg, "The Third General Congregation April 12–June 16, 1573," in *Mercurian Project*, ed. McCoog, 49–75, here 51; Medina, "Everard Mercurian," 946.

224   Letter to Pedro Planes, procurator of the Colegio de San Pablo (Valencia), 1612, AHN J leg. 259 doc. 132.

225   Vitelleschi to Provincial Luis de Ribas, May 28, 1638, AHN J leg. 253 doc. 326. This may well be Antonio Perlas (d.1682), but without access to ARSI documents, I do not want to present this supposition as fact.

226   Ahlgren, *Teresa of Avila*, 20, 2–3.

227   Redworth, "New Way of Living," 278. Occasionally, when a woman is best known by a given name combined with a place name or other very common qualifier like "de Jesús" (of Jesus), I use her first name to avoid confusion with other individuals who used the same qualifiers.

228   Weber, "Demonizing Ecstasy," 152–53; Ahlgren, *Teresa of Avila*, 115–17.

AN OVERVIEW OF THE PRE-SUPPRESSION SOCIETY OF JESUS IN SPAIN 55

that they should not become regular confessors of nuns. In 1635, for example, Provincial of Aragon Luis de Ribas (1576–1647) was reminded that Jesuits should not be hearing confessions at convents more than three or four times per year.[229] Ironically, the wider circulation of Teresa's texts made possible by their printed format likely motivated more women to seek spiritual guidance from Jesuits. As Maria Laura Giordano notes, Teresa's writings educated her female readers about mystical practices to the point that many wanted to follow them themselves.[230] As Rhodes surmises, since the future saint described the positive role that Jesuits played in her spiritual development, other women naturally looked to the order for similar guidance.[231]

8.2   Laywomen

While Jesuits' interactions with women of the cloth were governed by the *Constitutions*, older Jesuits of established virtue continued to offer regular spiritual advice to laywomen. One group of women would have been particularly interested in such counsel. The pattern that emerges in Carvajal's life in Spain and England, of a woman living a devout life in her home and later a group of devout women living communally, is one that was followed by many *beatas*. In Spain, she, and many such women, lived in close proximity to the religious order whose members provided their spiritual direction, in Carvajal's case two Jesuit establishments in Madrid and Valladolid.

Ángela Atienza López notes that for some women, the lifestyle of a *beata* was a preliminary step toward a formal tie to a particular religious order, and the Tridentine reforms reinforced these existing tendencies.[232] For example, the *beata* Mariana de Jesús (1565–1624) lived in a *casita* (a small house or hut) in the shadow of the Discalced Mercedarian friary of Santa Bárbara in Madrid. Later in her life, after a vision of the Virgin Mary encouraged her to wear the Mercedarian habit, she came to do so. Soon thereafter, she took vows as a tertiary, but the question of whether she did so to the Calced or Discalced Mercedarians is debated. Regardless of the branch to which she made tertiary vows, Mariana never moved behind the convent wall and continued to reside outside of it.[233] As this example demonstrates, even in the early modern era,

---

229   Vitelleschi to Ribas, November 30, 1635, AHN J leg. 253 doc. 254.
230   Maria Laura Giordano, "Historicizing the Beatas: The Figures behind Reformation and Counter-Reformation Conflicts," in *Devout Laywomen*, ed. Weber, 91–111, here 99.
231   Rhodes, "Join the Jesuits," 41.
232   Atienza López, "De beaterios a conventos," 151, 155.
233   Jodi Bilinkoff, "A Saint for a City: Mariana de Jesús and Madrid, 1565–1624," *Archive for Reformation History* 88 (1997): 322–37, here 324, 332.

56   MANNING

people were not easily able to differentiate a devout laywoman from a woman who had taken tertiary vows based on her lifestyle.[234]

The simple vows of a tertiary, in contrast to solemn vows made to a religious organization that were binding, could be set aside. *Beatas* also sometimes took similar vows, which were essentially private, personal promises rather than official ones to a religious order. Such *beatas* likely are the referents for the term *beatas profesas* (professed *beatas*).[235] Despite the Society's lack of a third order, women who received spiritual advice from Jesuits took similar vows.[236]

In order to examine such vows, we will return to the case of Luisa de Carvajal y Mendoza. As evidence of the non-binding nature of such promises, in 1600 Carvajal set aside her previous set of vows.[237] As we have seen in the case of Line, Jesuits could not accept vows of obedience from women, but this did not preclude *beatas* from taking informal vows of obedience. Carvajal's vow of obedience contains a clause that obligated her even if her superior did not accept her promise. As Rhodes signals, this clause relating to non-acceptance was necessary because a member of the Society could not accept such a vow from a woman. Despite promising obedience, Carvajal stated that she retained the power to choose her own superior (i.e., confessor). In Rhodes's characterization, these details in Carvajal's vow of obedience "show a marked influence of Jesuit casuistry and are purposefully ambiguous. Carvajal declares obedience at the same time she pries the door open to remarkable freedom."[238] As this vow demonstrates, *beatas'* vows could be more idiosyncratic than the vows of poverty, chastity, and obedience made in most religious orders. In addition to this vow, the noblewoman also swore to commit herself to continue to strive for perfection.[239] But these were not the most original promises that

---

234   Atienza López, "De beaterios a conventos," 147.

235   See Atienza López, "De beaterios a conventos," 147n9. See Alicia Fraschina, *Mujeres consagradas en el Buenos Aires colonial* (Buenos Aires: Eudeba, 2010) for the fascinating case of María Antonia de San José (1730–99), a Jesuit *beata profesa* from what today is Argentina. After the Society's expulsion from Spain's territories and the subsequent papal suppression, San José continued some Jesuit practices. Fraschina's research found that San José received permission to "organize" the *Exercises* (215). I thank Sarah E. Owens for reminding me of Fraschina's work.

236   See Carlos A. Page, "De beatas y beaterios jesuitas de la provincia del Paraguay, siglos XVII–XVIII," *Región y sociedad* 30, no. 73 (2018): 1–22, here 8 for a more detailed explanation.

237   See the documentation of this fact in *This Tight Embrace*, ed. and trans. Rhodes, 106–7.

238   "Voto de obediencia," in *This Tight Embrace*, ed. and trans. Rhodes, 112–17, 113n11, 117n13.

239   See "Voto de mayor perfección," 116–19. Carvajal's vow of poverty will be discussed in short order.

AN OVERVIEW OF THE PRE-SUPPRESSION SOCIETY OF JESUS IN SPAIN   57

Carvajal took. She also took a truly extraordinary one: in 1598, she took a vow of martyrdom.[240]

Once Carvajal established her community, the Company of the Sovereign Virgin Mary, in England, the women took three vows of chastity, poverty, and obedience. Beyond the obvious influence of the Society in the name of the organization, the women also imitated Jesuits' vows by taking a fourth vow to the pope.[241]

From the point of view of ecclesial and judicial authorities, a significant distinguishing factor among *beatas* was whether they had a close relationship with a clerical spiritual director. According to Jodi Bilinkoff's assessment, without the protection of Mariana de Jesús's confessor, the Mercedarian friar Juan Bautista del Santísimo Sacramento (1554–1616), she might have been punished by the Inquisition and therefore forced to abandon her lifestyle, as other *beatas* were during this era in Madrid.[242] Such a clerical protector became more necessary as time passed. By the seventeenth century, issues concerning women, both lay and of the cloth, and their potentially false sanctity were judged to be a serious threat by the Inquisition and prosecuted accordingly.[243] Between 1609 and 1645, the Inquisition issued penances to twelve *beatas* from Seville and the surrounding areas, so there was potential danger for laywomen without ties to clerics to guide (and potentially defend) them in case of detention by the Inquisition.[244]

Unfortunately, this stratagem could have the opposite effect. *Beatas* with connections to a particular religious order could find that such an affiliation led to negative treatment in legal settings. Even though the Jesuits did not support Isabel Ortiz (*fl.* mid- to late sixteenth century) when the Inquisition tried her following her 1564 arrest on charges of *alumbradismo*, Giordano nonetheless suggests that the resultant censure of Ortiz's writings can be interpreted as a rebuke of the Society's support of laywomen interested in religion. Ortiz was not alone in this regard. In other situations, women could find that their loyalties conflicted with those of the men who evaluated the orthodoxy of defendants' beliefs on behalf of the Inquisition. As Isabel de Briñas (*fl.* mid- to

---

240   See "Voto de martirio," 118–21.

241   Redworth, *She-Apostle*, 149, 150–51, 155.

242   Jodi Bilinkoff, *Related Lives: Confessors and Their Female Penitents, 1450–1750* (Ithaca, NY: Cornell University Press, 2005), 26.

243   Maria Laura Giordano, "Al borde del abismo: 'Falsas santas' e 'ilusas' madrileñas en la vigilia de 1640," trans. Josep Monter, *Historia social* 57 (2007): 75–97, here 77.

244   Mary Elizabeth Perry, *Gender and Disorder in Early Modern Seville* (Princeton: Princeton University Press, 1990), 104, 106, 108–9.

late seventeenth century) experienced in Madrid beginning in 1639, her connection to the Order of Preachers did not endear her to the Jesuit *calificadores* who assessed her case for the Inquisition.[245]

On the part of religious orders and individual clerics, *beatas* could enhance their standing. In the case of a wealthy woman like Carvajal, there could be financial benefits to such an association. In point of fact, Rhodes observes that Esteban de Ojeda (*fl.* mid- to late sixteenth to early seventeenth century), the rector of the Colegio Imperial in Madrid, kept a holographic version of Carvajal's vow of poverty in order to allow the Society to access her funds and cover her expenses.[246]

Beatas provided advantages beyond financial gain. Visionary *beatas* could offer religious orders insight into matters of interest to their communities, including the Society. Testifying before the Inquisition, the Jesuit Juan Muñoz (d.1640) provided a text composed by Luisa Melgarejo de Soto (1578–1651), a devout woman in the circle of future saint Rose of Lima (1586–1617), that revealed that Jesuits asked Melgarejo to discern the fates of deceased members of the order.[247] Jesuit spiritual directors were not the only clergy to receive such favors: Mariana de Jesús, for example, had a vision that demonstrated divine support for Juan Bautista del Santísimo Sacramento's plans to reform the Mercedarian order. Beyond her capabilities as a mystic, Mariana assisted in these plans through her ties to the court. Moreover, her reputation as a woman of great virtue no doubt brought distinction to the Mercedarians and to her spiritual director himself. This was one motive that prompted men of the cloth to circulate the life stories of their penitents, sometimes including *beatas*. (See the section on *vitae* for more details.)[248]

9   Theological Debates

9.1   *The Changing Nature of Opposition to the Jesuit Order*

Eventually, much of the opposition to the Jesuit order did not protest its mere existence but rather contested Jesuits' theological practices and stances on the burning questions of the day. Although the theological debate between the Jesuits and Dominicans was especially vehement, discussion among Catholic

---

245   Giordano, "Historicizing the Beatas," 98; Giordano, "Al borde del abismo," 87–93, 96.

246   *This Tight Embrace*, ed. and trans. Rhodes, 107n2.

247   Stacey Schlau, "Flying in Formation: Subjectivity and Collectivity in Luisa Melgarejo de Soto's Mystical Practices," in *Devout Laywomen*, ed. Weber, 133–51, here 136–37.

248   Bilinkoff, *Related Lives*, 26–27, 19.

AN OVERVIEW OF THE PRE-SUPPRESSION SOCIETY OF JESUS IN SPAIN 59

authorities over evolving doctrine and preferred practices was impassioned. Catholic religious orders attempted to gain support for their own points of view by bringing them to the attention of the reading public. Criticism of opposing religious orders in print was a common tactic. To counteract this behavior, the Spanish Inquisition often prohibited the further circulation of texts and pamphlets on certain matters. But such orders were not always respected. In a particularly heated moment, the *definidor general* (definitor general) of the Carmelites, José de la Encarnación (*fl.* mid- to late seventeenth century), published his displeasure with those who would not follow the Inquisition's decrees mandating silence in "Respeto a los decretos del Consejo Supremo de la fe, contra los que no le guarden" (Regard for the decrees of the Supreme Council of the Faith [the Supreme Council of the Spanish Inquisition] against those who may not follow them [1655]), while summarizing the attacks against the Carmelites by other religious orders and reiterating the Carmelites' position.[249]

Members of the Society of Jesus actively participated in formulating Catholic theology, doctrine, and practices, including some of the most polemical issues of the sixteenth and seventeenth centuries: the immaculate conception, the *de auxiliis* (literally, on help; the debate concerned the roles of grace versus free will) matter, and casuistry.

9.2 Casuistry

The Society of Jesus did not begin the study of cases of conscience, which began in medieval Scholastic thought prior to the order's inception and ultimately traced its origins to classical rhetoric. Nonetheless, casuistry was important to the Society. According to O'Malley's research, the order was offering lectures on cases to "mixed audiences of clergy and laity" in Goa in 1555. In 1556, Jesuits studying at the Collegio Romano attended "daily lectures" on the topic. Interest in the subject matter was not limited to members of the order. By 1564, the second year in which the course was open to those who were not Jesuit scholastics, the venue for the lectures had to be changed—only the church could accommodate the crowd, which included local clerics not affiliated with the order.[250] As Hilaire Kallendorf signals, Spanish Jesuits, such as Nadal, Diego de Ledesma (1524–75), and Juan Azor (1536–1603) were prominent

---

249   José [Josef] de la Encarnación, "Respeto a los decretos del Conseio Svpremo de la fe, contra los qve no le gvarden," see AHN Inq. leg. 4455 exp. 2 for a copy and the context of the larger debate.

250   O'Malley, *First Jesuits*, 145–46.

moral theologians and casuists in Rome.[251] Maryks considers *Theologiae moralis summa* (Compendium of moral theology [1591]), the work of Jesuit Enrique Enríques, or as he is also known Henrique Henríquez (1536–1608), to be the "first Jesuit manual of moral theology." (Enríques was sent to Spain to avoid negative commentary about his lineage in his home country of Portugal.)[252] In James F. Keenan's analysis, it was Mercurian's interest in "institutional systematization" that led to the publication of the earliest Jesuit works on casuistry. In this venue as well, Spanish Jesuits were a significant presence. Francisco de Toledo's (1532–96) *Summa casuum conscientiae* [...] (Compendium of cases of conscience [...] [1598]), published after the author's death, was based on his teaching at the Collegio Romano in the 1560s. Toledo's *Summa* proved so successful that it did not go out of print until 1716. Subsequently, Azor and Tomás Sánchez (1550–1610) also published works of moral theology that explored cases of conscience.[253]

Although the Jesuit order became closely associated with probabilism, it was the Dominican Bartolomé Medina (1527–80) who first articulated the concept. Probabilism, in John Harty's (1867–1946) definition, is "the moral system which holds that, when there is question solely of the lawfulness or unlawfulness of an action, it is permissible to follow a solidly probable opinion in favour of liberty even though the opposing view is more probable."[254] Admittedly, scholarship concurs that the Spanish Jesuit Francisco Suárez (1548–1617) was the "clearest early modern proponent" of this school of thought.[255] Not coincidentally, both casuistry and probabilism led to accusations of laxity against the Jesuit community. As one considered the individual and his or her circumstances and not just the sin committed in the study of cases of conscience, probabilism considered one's intentions and not merely the end result of an action. Whereas Blaise Pascal (1623–62) in particular and Jansenism in general highlighted—and exaggerated—the potential for moral relativism in probabilism, their interpretations strayed quite far from the origins of the concept. Patrick J. O'Banion, echoing Jean Delumeau (1923–2020), points out that probabilism originated in the clerical "need to respond to excessively scrupulous

---

251 Hilaire Kallendorf, *Conscience on Stage: The* Comedia *as Casuistry in Early Modern Spain* (Toronto: University of Toronto Press, 2007), 8–9.

252 Maryks, *Jesuit Order as a Synagogue of Jews*, 65.

253 James F. Keenan, "The Birth of Jesuit Casuistry: *Summa casuum conscientiae, sive de instructione sacerdotum, libri septem* by Francisco de Toledo (1532–1596)," in *Mercurian Project*, ed. McCoog, 461–82, here 467, 468.

254 John Harty, "Probabilism," in *The Catholic Encyclopedia*, vol. 12 (New York: Robert Appleton, 1911); http://www.newadvent.org/cathen/12441a.htm (accessed April 28, 2020).

255 O'Banion, *Sacrament of Penance*, 30.

AN OVERVIEW OF THE PRE-SUPPRESSION SOCIETY OF JESUS IN SPAIN   61

confessants who agonized over the moral implications of every decision."[256] Thus, probabilism sought to alleviate either the early modern moral equivalent of "analysis paralysis" or worse, a cycle of self-castigation over the small decisions one must make on a daily basis.

Not all Jesuits supported probabilism: Spanish missionary preacher Tirso González (1624–1705), for example, was a proponent of probabiliorism, which constrained the degree of choice involved in probabilism. Probabiliorism maintained that one could only follow the "less safe opinion" if it was "more probable." After the Society declined to authorize González's text on probabiliorism, in 1680, the Roman Holy Office issued a decree that allowed him to write his opinions and mandated that the general of the Society of Jesus permit opposition to probabilism.[257] Once he became superior general himself, González (in office 1687–1705) asked the pope to recognize probabiliorism as the solution to this question in moral theology; González did not succeed.[258]

In addition to Latin treatises on casuistry, Jesuits also wrote manuals in vernacular languages to help clergy (and to a lesser degree the laity) prepare for the confessional.[259] And Spanish Jesuits participated in this trend. As O'Banion details, by 1665 Jesuit Antonio de Escobar y Mendoza's (1589–1669) *Examen de confesores y práctica de penitentes* (The examination of confessors and exercises for penitents [1630]) had been printed fifty-three times. Again according to O'Banion's research, women more often read saints' lives than confessional manuals. Jesuit Bernardino de Villegas's (1590–1653) *Esposa de Cristo instruida* (The wife of Christ, instructed [1625]) advised women preparing for confession in the context of the life of Saint Lutgarde (1182–1246).[260] As Elena del Río Parra notes, apart from formulaic references to penitents in titles and front matter, books of cases specifically directed toward the laity were relatively rare, but interested laypeople could pursue their interests in other ways, including reading confessional manuals written for a clerical audience.[261] Those who followed Spanish theater, and play-going was a significant social phenomenon, had a ready venue to study casuistry. Kallendorf's research describes the manner in which cases of conscience played out in Spanish theatrical works.[262]

---

256   O'Banion, *Sacrament of Penance*, 31.
257   Harty, "Probabilism."
258   Burrieza Sánchez, "'Las glorias del segundo siglo' (1622–1700)," in Egido, Burrieza Sánchez, and Revuelta González, *Jesuitas en España*, 151–78, here 177.
259   See Robert Aleksander Maryks, "Census of the Books Written by Jesuits on Sacramental Confession (1554–1650)," *Annali di storia moderna e contemporanea* 10 (2004): [415]–519.
260   O'Banion, *Sacrament of Penance*, 27, 132.
261   Elena del Río Parra, *Cartografías de la conciencia española en la Edad de Oro* (Mexico City: Fondo de Cultura Económica, 2008), 54.
262   See Kallendorf, *Conscience on Stage*, 1–205 for examples.

9.3   *The* De auxiliis *Controversy*

As Astrain asserted in 1908, the traditional starting point for the controversy over the role of grace versus free will was a 1581 debate between the Jesuit Prudencio de Montemayor (1556–99) and the Dominican Domingo Báñez (1528–1604) in Salamanca.[263] A few years later, however, Astrain explained that he found information in an Inquisition case brought against Luis de León (1527–91) concerning his comments on the matter of grace versus free will surrounding the debate. These Inquisition documents stated that the Montemayor—Báñez debate took place on January 20, 1582. References to 1581 might have used a different manner of calculating the beginning of the year.[264] To summarize the main point of contention between the two orders: whereas the Dominicans believed that the influence of grace was more significant than free will, the Jesuits maintained that free will was the more important element. For both communities, the temporal relationship between divine grace and human action was significant. The Dominicans maintained that God exerted his influence first and then humans acted. For the Jesuits, divine influence and human action occurred simultaneously. From the Jesuits' point of view, if God acted prior to humans, God would seem to be responsible for any poor choices that humans might make subsequently. In the Jesuits' system, human beings' free will made sufficient grace efficacious. In 1588, Spanish Jesuit Luis de Molina (1535–1600) posited in *Concordia liberi arbitrii cum gratiae donis* [...] (Harmony of free will with gifts of grace [...] [1588]) that divine *scientia media* (middle knowledge) expected humans to accept grace.[265]

Some Jesuits, such as Mariana and Enríques, disagreed with Molina's position.[266] While Leuven and Rome also were significant foci in this debate, this section focuses on the debate as it relates to Spain.[267]

---

263   Antonio Astrain, "Congregatio de Auxiliis," in *The Catholic Encyclopedia*, vol. 4 (New York: Robert Appleton Company, 1908); http://www.newadvent.org/cathen/04238a.htm (accessed April 28, 2020).

264   Astrain, *Historia de la Compañía de Jesús*, 4:130.

265   Astrain, *Historia de la Compañía de Jesús*, 4:118–20, and Joseph Pohle, "Controversies on Grace," in *The Catholic Encyclopedia*, vol. 6 (New York: Robert Appleton Company, 1909); http://www.newadvent.org/cathen/06710a.htm (accessed April 28, 2020).

266   Joseph Pohle, "Luis de Molina," in *The Catholic Encyclopedia*, vol. 10 (New York: Robert Appleton Company, 1911); http://www.newadvent.org/cathen/10436a.htm (accessed April 28, 2020). See Pohle, "Controversies on Grace," for a more detailed explanation of the question of grace versus free will.

267   Astrain, "Congregatio de Auxiliis."

AN OVERVIEW OF THE PRE-SUPPRESSION SOCIETY OF JESUS IN SPAIN 63

For reasons of space, I only highlight some of the most notable moments in this controversy.[268] As Dominicans and Jesuits publicly defended their own positions on the relative roles of grace and free will, each order periodically denounced the other to the Spanish Inquisition. This ongoing discussion was not an exclusively theological one taking place behind the closed doors of ecclesial institutions or in the confines of university buildings. All of Valladolid was eagerly following the debate: Jesuits' complaints to the papal nuncio and the Inquisition mentioned that nuns and even laywomen were discussing the question of free will.[269] For a variety of Catholic authorities, the public nature of this increasingly acrimonious debate became problematic. Therefore, in 1594, Pope Clement VIII (1536–1605, r.1592–1605) took jurisdiction over the question and imposed silence on the parties involved. In 1597, three years after Clement VIII called for silence on the matter, three inquisitors in the Spanish city of Toledo signed a document that reminded the Jesuit and Dominican orders that they had agreed not to engage in any debate regarding "la gracia suficiente y eficaz" (sufficient and efficacious grace), either in public or private. Sermons and lessons on the matter were also proscribed.[270]

In 1598, the pope convened the Congregatio de Auxiliis (Congregation on grace) to examine the question. Spanish Jesuit Pedro de Arrúbal (c.1560–1608) played an important part in contesting the Dominicans' point of view in this debate, particularly in oral arguments before Pope Clement VIII.[271] In 1607, the papal Congregatio de Auxiliis decided that both the Dominican and Jesuit orders could maintain their own opinions, but that they could not criticize the other point of view. In 1611, however, the Roman Inquisition prohibited further publication on efficacious grace; this prohibition stayed in place for much of the seventeenth century.[272]

When in 1655 Matías Borrull (1615–89) was allowed to submit a treatise on the *scientia media* to textual reviewers within the Society of Jesus for permission to publish from the Society, Superior General Goswin Nickel (1584–1664, in office 1652–64) reminded Provincial Diego de Alastuey (d.1674) that reviewers would not authorize any text concerning the *de auxiliis* matter. Material on this topic was not to be circulated in print. But the general's response strongly suggested that he anticipated the text's approval, as he also stated that he looked forward to receiving his copy of the printed work. In 1656, after the

---

268   See Astrain, *Historia de la Compañía de Jesús*, 4:115–385 for a detailed treatment of the topic.

269   Astrain, *Historia de la Compañía de Jesús*, 4:132–33, 183, 197.

270   AHN Inq., July 21, 1597, leg. 4437 exp. 2.

271   Pohle, "Controversies on Grace."

272   Astrain, "Congregatio de Auxiliis."

Society's reviewers decided that Borrull's text did not stray into prohibited topics concerning free will, Nickel authorized the publication.[273] Despite this care on the part of the Society, the Inquisition embargoed the volume to determine whether it could circulate freely. In 1658, Nickel was pleased to relate to the province that the embargo was to be lifted. Although this correspondence simply referenced Borrull's work on the *scientia media*, the timing suggests that the text under discussion was Borrull's *Divina scientia futurorum* [...] (Divine knowledge of future things [...] [1656]).[274] Borrull's subsequent *Tractatus de voluntate dei* (Treatise on God's will), which was published in 1661, raises an important point.[275] As theological thinking developed, the degree to which the earlier decisions regarding the *de auxiliis* matter needed to be respected became a matter for discussion in the latter part of the century.

A new edition of Suárez's texts brought this issue to the fore. In 1660, Jesuit Ignacio Arias de Arbieto (d.1676) wrote to the Inquisition about a passage in a recent imprint of Suárez's works, which in Arbieto's estimation was prohibited in a bull by Pope Clement VIII.[276] After reading Arbieto's opinion, Doctor Diego de Vergara (*fl.* mid-seventeenth century) recommended that the Inquisition assess the text and consult with the pope to resolve the issue.[277]

When two *calificadores* from the Society of Jesus were asked by the Inquisition how such material came to be included in a new imprint, and was publicly defended, the Jesuits readily admitted that it had been prohibited in the past, but that thinking surrounding matters of grace and free will had changed: "Respondieron era verdad que antiguamente se prohibio la proposicion refexida; pero oy la trahian los authores modernos por probable: y que siendo un Author tan graue no era justo poner este impedimento" (They responded that it was true that long ago the referenced proposition was prohibited, but today modern authors treat it as probable. And being such a serious author, it was not just to put this impediment [on him]).[278]

Cristóbal de Castilla y Zamora (d.1683) and Álvaro de Ibarra (1619–75) requested additional opinions "como esta materia es de la grauedad que se reconoce por tocar a un author tan docto, y a una religion tan ilustre" (as this

---

273 Superior General Goswin Nickel to Provincial Diego de Alastuey, September 24, 1655, AHN J leg. 254 doc. 134 and to Provincial Jacinto Piquer, August 30, 1656, AHN J leg. 254 doc. 156.

274 Nickel to Piquer, March 2, 1658, AHN J leg. 254 doc. 184.

275 Carlos Sommervogel, *Bibliothèque de la Compagnie de Jésus* (Brussels: Oscar Schepens, 1899), 1:col. 1823.

276 Ignacio Arias de Arbieto to the Inquisition, October 17, 1660, AHN Inq. leg. 4467 exp. 3. Most of the Inquisition's papers are not foliated. I use dates when they are helpful in locating a particular document in a file.

277 Diego de Vergara, Parecer, December 13, 1660, AHN Inq. leg. 4467 exp. 3.

278 Document signed by Cristóbal de Castilla y Zamora and Álvaro de Ibarra, October 11, 1662, AHN Inq. leg. 4467 exp. 3.

AN OVERVIEW OF THE PRE-SUPPRESSION SOCIETY OF JESUS IN SPAIN   65

material is of a seriousness that is recognized since it touches on such a learned author, and such an illustrious religious order). In order to obtain an additional opinion from Vergara, who was a *calificador* for the Inquisition, they remitted the documents. Unfortunately, there is no extant record of a final decision regarding this passage on the part of the Inquisition in this file. An appended letter dated 1664 does, however, offer the assessment that Suárez's text contains "false doctrine," but that it does not violate Clement VIII's decree.[279]

Around 1650, an anonymous text titled *Relación de la variedad que ha habido en la comunicación de disputas con los padres de la Compañía en la provincia de España de la Orden de Predicadores* (Account of the range that there has been in the communication of disputes with the fathers of the Society [of Jesus] in the province of Spain of the Order of Preachers), which offered a summary of disputes between the Jesuits and the Dominicans on the question of grace versus free will, came to the attention of the Inquisition. In 1650, this *relación* (account) was prohibited by the Inquisition in Spain. It lacked the requisite elements: licenses, *censuras* (literally censorships, one of the terms used for official approvals of printed texts), and *aprobaciones* (literally, approbations, another of the terms used for official approvals of printed texts), to certify that it had been licensed by the Council of Castile.[280] Despite the text being printed without the requisite approvals, it apparently circulated widely. Pedro M. Guibovich Pérez finds reference to its prohibition by the Inquisition in Lima.[281] When the next Index of Prohibited Books was printed in 1707, this *relación* is listed as prohibited.[282]

This brief text serves as a case study for the manner in which theological controversy was used to criticize the Jesuits in a text for circulation to a broader, non-ecclesiastical public. This two-folio, not quite four-page-long text, offers a summary of the status of public debates about grace and free will between the Jesuits and Dominicans from 1594 until Philip IV's (1605–65, r.1621–65) reign. According to this text, following the 1594 debate in Valladolid between the Jesuit Antonio de Padilla (1557–1611) and the Dominican Diego Nuño (d.1614), Philip II invited the provincials of the two communities to court to discuss

---

279   AHN Inq. leg. 4467 exp. 3.
280   August 9, 1650, AHN Inq. leg. 4438 exp. 13.
281   Pedro M. Guibovich Pérez, *Censura, libros e inquisición en el Perú colonial, 1570–1754* (Seville: Consejo Superior de Investigaciones Científicas, Escuela de Estudios Hispano-Americanos, Universidad de Sevilla, Diputación de Sevilla, 2003), 352.
282   In the 1707 Index, the title is slightly different: "Relacion de la variedad, que ha avido en la comunicacion de disputas, con los padres de la Compañía de las provincias de España, y de la Orden de Predicadores," *Novissimus librorum prohibitorum et expurgandorum Index pro Catholicis Hispaniarum regnis Philippi V* (Madrid: Ex Typographia Musicae, 1707), 2:195; https://books.google.com/books?id=f9lQAAAAcAAJ&printsec=frontcover&source=gbs_ge_summary_r&cad=0#v=onepage&q&f=false (accessed May 19, 2020).

66 MANNING

the matter in hopes of bringing about an amicable conclusion. Among other points, the two religious communities agreed not to characterize the opinions of the opposing side as "heretical" or "erroneous." Also, the two religious orders agreed to burn any "papers" (presumably handwritten comments) concerning the "customs" of other religious orders. The handwritten comments at the beginning of the text express skepticism that Philip II directly intervened in this question or that he would have asked his confessor to play a role. Despite the skepticism on the part of this reader/commentator, Astrain cites documentation that Spanish Jesuits prepared for this meeting and details the agreement that royal confessor Diego de Yepes (1529–1613) brokered between the two orders.[283]

During Philip III's era, public debates were revived. But during Philip IV's reign, they were prohibited except in university towns. Although two types of debates were allowed, one in public and the other within convents or *colegios*, the anonymous author of this imprint asserted that the second type should be banned and promised to explain his reasoning in another publication.[284]

Although this *relación* purports to offer an update on the status of the debate over the relative roles of grace and free will until "este año de 1636" (this year of 1636), it does not offer a neutral assessment of both religious orders. Rather, the narrative repeatedly characterizes the Jesuits in a negative fashion. For example, the Jesuits employ "gran artificio y astucia" (great artifice and cunning) to win acclaim in debates. Moreover, according to this *relación*, the Society of Jesus was not content with the status quo (i.e., no debates between the two religious orders). Instead, the Jesuits aggressively lobbied both Philip II and Philip III to once again allow public debates on the matter. For this reason, the handwritten comments at the beginning of the text characterize the *relación* as "en desafecto a la Compañia" (in opposition to the Society) and "infame" (despicable).[285]

Presumably, the Inquisition followed its usual practice and prohibited this work by decree in 1650 prior to its inclusion in the next Index, in this case in

---

283 Astrain, *Historia de la Compañía de Jesús*, 4:206–10; *Relacion*, fol. 1^{r-v} and handwritten comments on fol. 1^r. The comments appear in the BNE manuscript, hereafter MS, 18174. (Although house style abbreviates manuscript as MS, for readers interested in searching for these manuscripts in the BNE's electronic catalog, it is important to note that it abbreviates manuscript as mss.) This text forms part of a volume titled *Papeles de Gil González Dávila*, which is available in electronic form in the BNE's BDH. See http://bdh-rd.bne.es/viewer.vm?id=0000135516&page=1 (accessed May 19, 2020). The *relación* begins on pane 132 of the electronic version.

284 *Relacion*, fol. 2^{r-v}.

285 *Relacion*, fols. 2^v, 1^r, and marginal handwritten comments at the beginning of the *relacion* on fol. 1^r.

AN OVERVIEW OF THE PRE-SUPPRESSION SOCIETY OF JESUS IN SPAIN 67

1707. Whether or not this decree was issued, the handwritten annotations at the end of the *relación* suggest that it was in circulation close to the turn of the century. These comments fretted that the November 8, 1697 royal decree issued by King Charles II (1661–1700, r.1665–1700) concerning the need to demonstrate knowledge of Thomism in order to obtain *cátedras* (chaired teaching positions at universities) would come to be used against the Society of Jesus. The enmity of King Charles II's confessor, the Dominican father Pedro de Matilla (d.1698), against the Society fueled this commentator's worry.[286]

9.4   *The Immaculate Conception, Part 1*

Following the conflict over the matter of grace, another skirmish broke out between the Dominicans and Jesuits, this time concerning the immaculate conception. The debate over the question of the immaculate conception (whether Mary, the mother of Jesus, was without original sin from the moment of her conception) was a lengthy one that involved a number of religious orders in many countries. Frederick Holweck (1856–1927) situates the first instances of debate about this point to twelfth-century Europe. Most religious orders came to defend this concept; however, the Dominicans concluded that Thomas Aquinas's (1224/25–74) writings did not support the immaculate conception. And the Order of Preachers followed this opinion. Aquinas maintained that Mary only was freed from original sin after she was conceived.[287]

As the question of Mary's conception was hotly debated throughout the Catholic world, scholars concede that the immaculist position was quite popular among the populace in Iberia and that the Spanish monarchy's support of it was a significant factor in its eventual elevation to dogma. Suzanne L. Stratton traces Iberian royal interest in the immaculate conception to the thirteenth century and details the artistic representation that this support helped to create.[288] In most scholars' estimation, circumstances forced Emperor Charles V and King Philip II to be discreet in their devotion, as they did not

---

286   Handwritten comments at the end of the *relacion* on fol. 2ᵛ. Since these comments reference 1697 as "este año" (this year), it is reasonable to assume that they were composed in 1697.

287   Frederick Holweck, "Immaculate Conception," in *The Catholic Encyclopedia*, vol. 7 (New York: Robert Appleton Company, 1910); http://www.newadvent.org/cathen/07674d.htm (accessed April 28, 2020); Suzanne L. Stratton, *The Immaculate Conception in Spanish Art* (Cambridge: Cambridge University Press, 1994), 3. See Holweck's section titled "The Controversy" for a summary of the debates.

288   Stratton, *Immaculate Conception*, 4–5; Adriano Prosperi, "L'immaculée conception à Séville et la fondation sacrée de la monarchie espagnole," *Revue d'histoire et de philosophie religieuses* 87, no. 4 (2007): 435–67, here 435, 445. See Stratton, *Immaculate Conception*, 1–146 for the history of the Spanish monarchy's support.

68 MANNING

want to further ideological rifts within the Catholic community.[289] After the loss of Spain's inaptly named Invincible Armada in 1588, the political and religious situation led to further interest in the promulgation of the immaculate conception in Spain.[290]

Public opinion in Spain firmly sided with the point of view of the Society and other religious orders against the Dominicans' point of view. (The Franciscans were such strong supporters of the immaculate conception that attendees at a 1621 general chapter meeting in Seville swore an oath indicating that they would be willing to die in defense of Mary's conception without sin.)[291] A large number of short publications about the immaculate conception were printed because of interest in the topic among the laity.

Printed, painted, or sculpted images served an important function in the promulgation of the immaculate conception; as Stratton indicates, when papal bulls prohibited the public dissemination of either maculist or immaculist ideas in written texts and oral sermons, art was not included.[292] Surviving material products confirm the strength of this devotion among the populace. In 1644, a printer in Zaragoza produced twelve *autos sacramentales* (short, generally allegorical, plays with religious thematics) by the playwright Lope Félix de Vega Carpio, most often referred to as Lope de Vega (1562–1635), which contained a number of statements in favor of the immaculate conception.[293] Moreover, household inventories demonstrate that the immaculate conception became an extremely popular object of devotion. In Madrid, paintings and statues depicting Nuestra Señora de la Concepción (Our Lady of the Immaculate Conception) often figure in household inventories at a variety of price points over a lengthy period of time. For example, a master tailor and vendor of second-hand clothing of French origin possessed a "hechura y Quadro de nuestra señora de la Concepcion" (statue and painting of Our Lady of the Immaculate Conception) valued at ten *reales* (a monetary unit) in 1666.[294] Early in the eighteenth century, Josefa María de Suazo (d. *c.*1709),

---

289 See, for example, Pierre Civil, "Iconografía y relaciones en pliegos: La exaltación de la Inmaculada en la Sevilla de principios del siglo XVII," in *Las relaciones de sucesos en España (1500–1750): Actas del primer coloquio internacional (Alcalá de Henares, 8, 9 y 10 de junio de 1995)*, ed. María Cruz García de Enterría et al. (Paris: Publicaciones de la Sorbonne, 1996), 65–77, here 67n10.

290 Prosperi, "L'immaculée conception à Séville," 447–49.

291 Stratton, *Immaculate Conception*, 87.

292 Stratton, *Immaculate Conception*, 71.

293 Lope de Vega, *Fiestas del Santissimo Sacramento, repartidos en doze avtos sacramentales, con sus loas, y entremeses* (Zaragoza: Pedro Verges, 1644). BNE.

294 Archivo Histórico de Protocolos Madrid, hereafter AHPM, protocolo 5439, May 6, 1666, fol. 43ᵛ.

AN OVERVIEW OF THE PRE-SUPPRESSION SOCIETY OF JESUS IN SPAIN   69

widow of Manuel de Olivares (*fl.* late seventeenth or early eighteenth century), and a woman of some means, left a painting of Nuestra Señora de la Concepción that was valued at one hundred *reales.*[295]

A series of printed and handwritten texts compiled in a manuscript in Spain's Biblioteca Nacional describes the tactics the Dominicans used to defend their point of view in the first decades of the seventeenth century. Considering that this compilation begins with a series of printed texts in favor of the immaculate conception, the person who collected the texts may have been a partisan of this point of view. Even if some of the texts may have exaggerated events, as a whole they do seem to present a pattern of negative behavior on the part of Dominicans when confronted with celebrations of the immaculate conception. One text relates the "grauissimo escandalo" (very grave scandal) that the Dominicans in Seville caused on February 7, 1615 when they planned to publicly defend the point of view that Mary was conceived in original sin. While this in and of itself provoked a negative reaction, the outcry became louder when the Dominicans apparently hit children in the street who were singing about the immaculate conception.[296] Although the violence involved in this protest appears to have been relatively anomalous, the Dominicans did not countenance processions in celebration of Mary's conception without original sin. Another document in the same compilation copies a letter that Diego de Acuña (*fl.* early seventeenth century), governor and captain general of Cartagena de Indias (today Cartagena, Colombia), wrote to Philip III in 1616. Acuña related that Dominicans, "offended" by processions, made "demostraciones escandalosas" (scandalous demonstrations). Siding with the Dominicans, Bishop Pedro de la Vega (1560–1616) "insulted" a procession celebrating the immaculate conception. Acuña related that sermons against the immaculate conception "scandalize[d]" those who heard them, including a number of listeners who were recent converts to Catholicism.[297] As demonstrated by several letters in Italian, such episodes were related to people outside of Spain.[298]

Given their long-standing theological disputes, the Society of Jesus was a particular object of the Dominicans' ire in this acrimonious dispute about the immaculate conception. One of the other texts in this collection relates

---

295   AHPM protocolo 11571, January 3, 1710, fol. 63ʳ. Given the early January date for this valuation document, it seems likely that Suazo died in 1709.

296   "Memorial sumario de los veynte y quatro informaciones que el Arçobispo de Seuilla mandò hazer [...]," BNE MS 9956, fols. 43ʳ and 44ʳ. I thank Felipe Pereda for bringing this manuscript to my attention in his talk at CORPI in June of 2015.

297   Copy of the letter from Diego de Acuña to Philip III, August 22, 1616, BNE, MS 9956, fol. 100ʳ⁻ᵛ.

298   See, for example, BNE MS 9956, fols. 93ʳ, 94ʳ.

three sonnets containing "libelos infamatorios" (defamatory libels) against the Jesuits, even directly naming one individual for preaching favorably about the immaculate conception.[299] Beyond the insults hurled at defenders of the doctrine who are "unos bellacos, Iudios, borrachos" (rogues, Jews, [and] drunks), Jesuits are "Iudios" (Jews) and "perros judios" (Jewish dogs). Jesuit preachers are dismissed as "unos moçuelos atreuidillos, desuergonçados" (somewhat audacious [and] shameless young men). Meanwhile, as the text signals, Dominicans had a different pedigree: they founded the Inquisition.[300] It is extremely unlikely that such texts would have been licensed to circulate in printed form. In this context, it is important to consider handwritten texts in order to understand the vehemence of polemic around contested points of theology in Spain. While this manuscript concerns the immaculate conception, Astrain remarks on the large body of handwritten texts that relate to the *de auxiliis* controversy, particularly once printing on the topic was prohibited.[301]

To expand on a point mentioned in the context of handwritten copies of the *Exercises*, manuscript culture developed specific functions after the invention of print. As Bouza demonstrates, texts circulated in handwritten forms for a variety of reasons, but the one that concerns us here is "la transmisión de contenidos comprometidos" (the transmission of delicate content). While this strategy allowed for the circulation of texts that would not have been able to obtain printing licenses from the Council of Castile, the handwritten format did not provide *carte blanche* for the free circulation of whatever content one wanted. As Bouza signals, from time to time manuscripts did come to the attention of the Inquisition and were prohibited in Indices of Prohibited Books. Despite this possibility, again according to Bouza, manuscripts passed between individuals who knew one another, and therefore these texts circulated "in a closed circle."[302] This type of circulation included an implicit vetting process that would keep the group of readers (and the texts they consumed) safer from denunciation to the Inquisition. In such a situation, negative texts about either the Jesuit or Dominican communities would presumably be kept away from certain passionate supporters of each order, who would be more likely to denounce such works to the Inquisition.

To return to the uproar created by the processions in Seville, the papal nuncio in Madrid, Antonio Gaetano, or Caetani in the version of his last name more common outside of Spain (1566–1624), expressed his displeasure to the

---

299   BNE MS 9956, fol. 49^r.

300   BNE MS 9956, fols. 51^{r-v}, 53^r.

301   Astrain, *Historia de la Compañía de Jesús*, 4:x.

302   Bouza, *Corre manuscrito*, 63, 67, 21.

AN OVERVIEW OF THE PRE-SUPPRESSION SOCIETY OF JESUS IN SPAIN 71

Spanish king. Gaetano felt that the spectacle in Seville humiliated the church. Clergy in Seville were also discussing the possibility of a municipal vow to support the immaculate conception. In 1616, Pope Paul V issued a new bull, which reiterated previous prohibitions of the public discussion of the matter of Mary's conception.[303]

King Philip III ensured that the royal bureaucracy actively participated in the immaculist cause. Beginning in 1616, the king convened the first of several *juntas* (temporary royal councils) to promote the cause of the immaculate conception. In the estimation of some scholars, the presence of Philip III's confessor, the Dominican Luis de Aliaga Martínez (1565–1626), on these *juntas* virtually guaranteed that unanimous decisions would be difficult to achieve. Aliaga was so faithful to his order's maculist point of view that he was known to draw up long lists of objections to his fellow committee members' work.[304] Despite the internal politics of the committee, in 1617, Pope Paul V issued a brief that forbade the public circulation of the idea that Mary was conceived in original sin. In Stratton's assessment of the 1618 session of the *junta*, the two Dominican members were "pressure[d]" to acquiesce to the monarch's opinion.[305]

Because distinguished men of the cloth, such as the archbishop of Zaragoza Pedro González de Mendoza (1571–1639), continued to object to the negative effects of the Dominicans' position, the king felt obligated to attempt to address these concerns. To this end, Philip III attempted to pressure the Dominicans to alter their position. At a 1618 meeting of some members of the Order of Preachers in Spain, which was held at the monarch's request, the Dominicans present were divided about favoring the immaculist cause; but Aliaga surprisingly advocated for doing so.[306]

After Philip III's death and Aliaga's exile from court, Philip IV took action on the immaculate conception early in his reign. As a new monarch, he lobbied the pope to issue a new bull on the matter, but the ultimate result was not definitive enough to please the king. In 1622, Pope Gregory XV (1554–1623, r.1621–23) ordered that critics of the immaculate conception not preach, write about, or discuss the question (even in private) until the pope resolved the issue.[307]

While the Dominicans were forced into silence on the maculist point of view, the opposing immaculist viewpoint gained ground in Spain, as demonstrated

---

303 Stratton, *Immaculate Conception*, 74–75; Holweck, "Immaculate Conception."
304 See Emilio Callado Estela, "El confesor regio fray Luis Aliaga y la controversia inmaculista," *Hispania sacra* 68 (2016): 317–26, here 320–24 for the strategies employed by Aliaga.
305 Holweck, "Immaculate Conception"; Stratton, *Immaculate Conception*, 81–82.
306 Callado Estela, "El confesor regio," 322–23.
307 Holweck, "Immaculate Conception."

by Pedro de Valpuesta's (*c*.1614–68) painting, *Felipe IV jurando defender la doctrina de la inmaculada concepción* (Philip IV pledging to defend the doctrine of the immaculate conception [*c*.1634–66]).[308] In seeking to advance Mary's cause, the monarch also sought to return to an era in which the Spanish king could influence the pope. The king's devotion to Mary became part of his public persona. In a two-day festival in 1643, Philip IV's court sought aid from the Virgin Mary in defeating heretics. In 1645, the immaculate conception became a feast day in Spain.[309]

There were, however, setbacks. In 1644, the Roman Congregation prohibited the use of the adjective "immaculate" to describe Mary's conception.[310]

The immaculate conception was also incorporated into religious occasions at court. A printed text issued upon the death of Luis Crespí de Borja (1607–63), Philip IV's extraordinary ambassador for the immaculate conception to Pope Alexander VII (1599–67, r.1655–67), includes the funerary sermons delivered by Jesuit Pedro Francisco Esquex (1610–76). The imprint begins with an image celebrating the immaculate conception.[311] When Philip IV passed away, the immaculate conception also figured in sermons preached about the deceased monarch. In a funeral panegyric for the monarch at the Colegio Imperial that was published in 1666, the year following Philip IV's death, Jesuit Jacinto González (1600–*c.* 1670) affirmed that the grateful Virgin Mary eased the monarch's death.[312]

9.5 *Immaculatism and Jurisdictional Tensions in the Case of Juan Bautista Poza*

Although public criticism of the immaculate conception was constrained after 1622, the conflict continued to play out via proxies. And one of these was the Jesuit Juan Bautista Poza (1588–1659). In the first decades of the 1600s, Poza taught philosophy, theology, and sacred scriptures in Alcalá, Murcia, and Madrid. In assessing Poza's temporary assignment to Cuenca, José Martínez Millán and Teresa Sánchez Rivilla propose that this sentence was less related to Poza's compositions than to an increasing rivalry between the Jesuit and

---

308   This painting is on display at the Museo de Historia de Madrid.

309   Stratton, *Immaculate Conception*, 100–101.

310   Stratton, *Immaculate Conception*, 101.

311   Pedro Francisco Esquex, *Sermon en las exeqvias, qve se celebraron el colegio Imperial de la Compañia de Iesvs, al Excelentissimo señor D. Luis Crespi de Borja, del Consejo de su magestad, y su embaxador extraordinario a nuestro muy santo Padre Alexandro Septimo, por el santo negocio de la concepcion* (Madrid: Ioseph Fernandez de Buendia, 1663). BNE.

312   Jacinto González [Iacinto Gonzalez], *Panegyrico fvneral en las honras de D. Felipe IIII el grande, nvestro rey, y señor* (Madrid: Ioseph Fernandez de Buendia, 1666), [28]. BNE.

AN OVERVIEW OF THE PRE-SUPPRESSION SOCIETY OF JESUS IN SPAIN   73

Dominican orders over which order held more influence in the Inquisition and with the monarchy. Fearing that they would lose their positions to Jesuits, the Dominicans vented their ire on Poza.[313]

Unfortunately for Poza, this was not the only external conflict that affected his case. In Moreno and Manuel Peña Díaz's analysis, the decision of the Sacred Congregation of the Index in Rome to censure Poza's *Elucidarium Deiparae* (Encyclopedia of the Mother of God [1626]) involved disputes between the Spanish and Roman Inquisitions and the Society of Jesus as well as the monarchy. (Poza's *Elucidarium* is a work of Marian theology that defends the immaculate conception.) When the Sacred Congregation of the Index in Rome censured Poza's *Elucidarium* in 1628, this decision was not promulgated in Spain because of jurisdictional disputes between Philip IV and Pope Urban VIII.[314]

This was not the only occasion on which the Spanish Inquisition decided not to promulgate a book prohibition from Rome. A similar jurisdictional dispute prevented the prohibition of Galileo Galilei's (1564–1642) *Dialogo sopra i due massimi sistemi del mondo* (Dialogue concerning the two chief world systems [1632]) in Spain. As José Pardo Tomás relates, when the decree was received by Cardinal Cesare Monti (1594–1650), the papal nuncio in Spain, he sent the document to Spanish bishops without consulting the Spanish Inquisition. In Cuenca, the prohibition of Galileo's work was promulgated without the Inquisition's involvement. Offended at the slight made to its jurisdictional rights by its exclusion from this process, the Spanish Inquisition lodged a formal protest with the king. Galileo's *Dialogo* was not prohibited in the Spanish Inquisition's 1640 Index. Pardo Tomás hypothesizes that the Inquisition in Spain did not want to prohibit another text in the same 1634 decree from Rome, *Notitiae Sicilensium ecclesiarum* (Notices of the Sicilian churches [1630]), which defended the Spanish king's right to intervene in ecclesiastical disputes in Sicily. Whereas the pontiff wanted to enforce his opposing point of view by prohibiting the text, the Spanish Inquisition, in order to allow an opinion favorable to the Spanish monarch to circulate, simply ignored Rome's decree.[315]

To return to Poza's case, according to Astrain, Vitelleschi arranged with the pope that Poza would correct his text in order to make it acceptable, but rather

---

313   José Martínez Millán and Teresa Sánchez Rivilla. "El Consejo de Inquisición (1483–1700)," *Hispania sacra* 36 (1984): 71–193, here 101–2.

314   Doris Moreno Martínez and Manuel Peña Díaz, "El jesuita Juan Bautista Poza y la censura," in *Per Adriano Prosperi*, vol. 3, *Riti di passaggio, storie di giustizia*, ed. Vincenzo Lavenia and Giovanna Paolin (Pisa: Edizioni della Normale, 2011), 3:159–70, here 3:159, 3:164.

315   José Pardo Tomás, *Ciencia y censura: La Inquisición española y los libros científicos en los siglos XVI y XVII* (Madrid: Consejo Superior de Investigaciones Científicas, 1991), 186–89.

than do so, Poza began defending his ideas in public, including in a *memorial* to Urban VIII. When the Spanish Inquisition opened its own investigation, Vitelleschi wanted Poza to leave Spain for Naples, but Philip IV intervened to prevent the Jesuit's departure. Displeased with Poza's behavior, the Roman Index banned all of Poza's works in 1632, rather than just the *Elucidarium*. This decision was not promulgated immediately in Spain for several reasons, among them the fact that the Spanish Inquisition wanted the Sacred Congregation to follow the Spanish Inquisition's notification procedures. Once the papal nuncio presented a new decree from the Congregation of Cardinals for the Index of Prohibited Books, Poza's works were banned by the Spanish Inquisition until they could be expurgated.[316] In the 1640 Index, the Spanish Inquisition issued expurgations for the *Elucidarium* and prohibited Poza's *Primeras lecciones que por la cátedra* de placitis philosophorum (Inaugural address that he made on the occasion [of the appointment to] the academic chair concerning the opinions of the philosophers [1629])—*Opinions* was a text by the Pseudo-Plutarch—and three *memoriales* related to Poza's case pending their expurgation.[317]

Moreno, Peña Díaz, and José Martínez de la Escalera (1921–2020) concede that Poza's tendency to write *memoriales* to those involved in his case and his attempts to clarify his positions contributed to his fate. On several occasions, Poza was confined to Jesuit houses under the supervision of the Holy Office. In addition to strongly defending his point of view, Poza criticized the inquisitorial system. In particular, Poza took issue with the uneven training of *calificadores* along with their sometimes self-serving motives. He also objected to the failure of the Indices to distinguish between heretical authors and Catholic authors whose works required corrections for matters such as printing errors. In the same vein, Poza wanted authors to have the opportunity to defend their works to their censors and to change condemned ideas before their works were placed on the Indices.[318] Poza's *memoriales* inevitably gave rise to competing *memoriales* from others holding the opposite point of view. Former Jesuit and former Carmelite Juan de Espino (b.1587) made notable contributions,

---

316   Astrain, *Historia de la Compañía de Jesús*, 5:212–13; Moreno Martínez and Peña Díaz, "Jesuita Juan Bautista Poza," 3:164; J. [José Martínez de la] Escalera, "Poza, Juan Bautista," in *Diccionario histórico de la Compañía de Jesús*, ed. O'Neill and Domínguez, 4:3029.

317   *Novissimus librorum prohibitorum et expvrgandorvm Index pro Catholicis Hispaniarum regnis Philippi IIII* [1640 Index] (n.p.: n.p., 1640), no visible pagination; https://books .google.com/books?id=M1UrC4DVZd4C&printsec=frontcover&source=gbs_ge_summary _r&cad=0#v=onepage&q=Poza&f=false (accessed May 19, 2020).

318   Moreno Martínez and Peña Díaz, "Jesuita Juan Bautista Poza," 3:160, 3:165–67.

AN OVERVIEW OF THE PRE-SUPPRESSION SOCIETY OF JESUS IN SPAIN 75

criticizing Poza and the Jesuits in *memoriales* to the point that the Inquisition forced both sides into silence on the matter.[319]

10 Jesuits' Roles in the Inquisition in the Seventeenth Century

As the dynamics underlying Poza's case suggest (and to the chagrin of the Dominicans), the Jesuits began to participate more in the Inquisition in the seventeenth century. As we have seen, the Fifth General Congregation threatened excommunication for Jesuits who actively sought positions in the Inquisition, either for themselves or for others. From time to time, generals and provincials commented upon whether particular Jesuits had violated this policy. For example, in 1633, Vitelleschi inquired of Continente whether the rector of Barcelona had requested a license from the province of Aragon to take a post in the Inquisition. If any notion of "ambition" or "pretension" was making its way into the Society, Vitelleschi lamented this development and ordered that all possible care be taken to curtail it.[320]

A 1616 *memorial* to the provincial of the province of Toledo clarified that Jesuits were forbidden to "procure" positions as *consultores* (consultants) or *calificadores*, either for themselves or for other members of the order. If the provincial should wish to allow a member of the order to take up such a position, the provincial could allow it, but only after receiving a license from the superior general.[321] In 1620, Vitelleschi asked Provincial Pedro Gil (1551–1622) to make sure that all superiors in the Society understood that it was their duty "acudir a lo que se offrece del seruicio de la Santa Inquisicion en todas ocasiones" (on all occasions to come to the aid of the Holy Inquisition with whatever is sought).[322] As is evident in the requirement for a license from the general, the order did not want just any member to work for the Inquisition. In 1636, the province of Aragon proposed that an unnamed Jesuit become a *calificador* in the Inquisition in Mallorca, but that individual was not judged acceptable by Rome. Therefore, the general requested that another man be put forward because the unnamed individual was not "appropriate."[323] A subsequent letter re-

---

319 Astrain, *Historia de la Compañía de Jesús*, 5:214; Escalera, "Poza, Juan Bautista," 4:3029. Martínez de la Escalera calls the same individual Juan del Espino.

320 Vitelleschi to Continente, July 28, 1633, AHN J leg. 253 doc. 186.

321 Responses to the *memorial* from Father Luis de la Palma to the provincial of the province of Toledo, March 1, 1616, AHN J leg. 253 doc. 3. The notation Aragon below the date suggests that a copy was also sent to this province.

322 Vitelleschi to Provincial Pedro Gil, December 7, 1620, AHN J leg. 253 doc. 119.

323 Vitelleschi to Ribas, July 18, 1636, AHN J leg. 253 doc. 271.

veals that the impetus for this request came from the Jesuit *colegio* in Mallorca, which asked that some Jesuits become *calificadores* because the order had no presence in that tribunal of the Inquisition.[324] The general responded that he found this plan "muy justo" (quite just) and asked the provincial to propose two or three individuals to become *calificadores*, excluding the aforementioned man.[325] Close to a year after this response, discussions were still ongoing about which Jesuits would be appropriate for these positions; deliberations would be required to decide whether Miguel Socies (1593–1669) could take up one of these positions.[326] However, when the inquisitor in Mallorca "insist[ed]" that Socies do so, Vitelleschi relented: "VR le de gusto, pues parece que ya no se puede resistir mas a su voluntad" (Your Reverence is to give him [the inquisitor] his way, as it seems that one cannot resist his determination any more).[327]

As late as 1640, one Jesuit still failed to follow the order's procedures for accepting affiliations with the Inquisition. In that year, Rome informed the province of Aragon that Jacinto Pibernad (d.1648?) had simply taken such a post in the Inquisition without informing his superior. And his superiors found him unacceptable to be a *calificador*. In the same letter, Vitelleschi specified: "Quando los oficios de calificadores de la Inquisicion en los de la Compañia son para credito, util, y servicio suyo, y del Tribunal, parece es raçon tratar de que algunos lo sean" (When the offices of *calificadores* for the Inquisition for those from the Society are for its credit, use, and service [of the Society], and of that of the Tribunal [of the Inquisition], it seems that it is reasonable to negotiate so that some are to become them). Vitelleschi expressed appreciation for the province's careful handling of this matter and requested that Pibernad be encouraged to decline the position. Although this correspondence did not detail the order's concerns with this priest's service to the Inquisition, a marginal comment noted that the improper manner in which Pibernad accepted the position might signal ambition.[328] After Vitelleschi's death, other superiors

---

324 Memorial from Father Martín Pérez, procurator of the province of Aragon, to Vitelleschi, January 4, 1637, AHN J leg. 253 doc. 286.

325 Response from Vitelleschi to a *memorial* that Pérez presented, March 12, 1637, AHN J leg. 253 doc. 287.

326 Vitelleschi to Ribas, January 15, 1638, AHN J leg. 253 unnumbered letter between 317b and 318. Sommervogel, *Bibliothèque*, 7:col. 1344 represents his last name as Socias.

327 Vitelleschi to Ribas, March 12, 1638, AHN J leg. 253 doc. 322.

328 Vitelleschi to Provincial Pedro Fons, February 10, 1640, AHN J leg. 253 doc. 372. Joseph [Josephus] Fejér, *Defuncti secundi saeculi Societatis Jesu 1641–1740* (Rome: Curia Generalitia S.J., Institutum Historicum S.J., 1989), 4:313; http://www.sjweb.info/arsi/documents/Defuncti_1640-1740_vol_IIII_N_R.pdf (accessed July 16, 2020) notes a passing reference to the 1648 death of a Jesuit with this name but lists the year and place of death as uncertain.

AN OVERVIEW OF THE PRE-SUPPRESSION SOCIETY OF JESUS IN SPAIN   77

general continued to authorize Jesuits' work with the Spanish Inquisition—in 1667, for example, Superior General Giovanni Paolo Oliva (1600–81, in office 1661–81) permitted two Jesuits to become *calificadores*.[329]

In the context of internal, and often legalistic, correspondence that frequently deals with staffing and personnel matters, these references to the "credit, usefulness, and service" of the Society are commonplace. However, if the Inquisition were to have learned of this assessment criteria, in which the order prioritized the community's needs over those of the Inquisition, it is likely that some would have judged these priorities to be misplaced because they did not foreground the needs of the Holy Office.

Despite the order's willingness to help staff the Inquisition, the Society's assistance had limits. Because the Inquisition in Spain was a royal institution under the ultimate control of the monarchs, it was used to serve other royal goals from time to time. As Joseph Pérez (1931–2020) observed, the monarch and the count-duke of Olivares Gaspar de Guzmán y Pimentel (1587–1645) found that if tax collectors also held positions with the Inquisition, they became more efficient in procuring revenues for the crown.[330] And religious communities, including the Society of Jesus, were not exempt from these tactics. In 1635, Inquisitor General Antonio de Sotomayor (1557–1648) wrote to an unspecified provincial of the Society of Jesus about a new financial assessment imposed by the king. From the content of the letter, it seems that this provincial had previously declined to donate because of other demands on his funds. However, the inquisitor general wrote on this occasion to ask again for the requested contribution, citing both the needs of the king and the necessity to defend the Catholic faith.[331] In 1641, the inquisitor general again wrote to an unspecified Jesuit provincial to ask for another subsidy that had been assessed by the king.[332]

11   Jesuit *Aprobación* Writers

In addition to working for the Inquisition, Jesuits also served as textual assessors for the pre-publication censorship process of the Council of Castile. Beginning in 1502, a royal pragmatic mandated licenses for the printing of books

---

329   Superior General Juan Paulo Oliva to Piquer, August 26, 1667, AHN J leg. 255 doc. 184, positive microfilm 1360.

330   Joseph Pérez, *The Spanish Inquisition: A History*, trans. Janet Lloyd (New Haven: Yale University Press, 2005), 116.

331   Inquisitor general to Jesuit provincial, August 31, 1635, AHN J leg. 257 doc. 203.

332   Inquisitor general to Jesuit provincial, [month blank in document] 5, 1641, AHN J leg. 257 doc. 234.

in Castile. At that point, the presidents of two *chancillerías* (high courts) and clerics in five towns were allowed to issue licenses. Over time, and particularly following a 1558 law, the process evolved into a system in which the Council of Castile drew textual approvers from a more broad swath of society.[333] As part of the licensing process, the Council of Castile sent manuscripts to reviewers who wrote *aprobaciones* or *censuras* that affirmed that the text did not offend Catholicism, the bounds of propriety, or good practices. Additionally, the text would need to be licensed by a local bishop and the author's religious order if he or she belonged to one; however, as José Simón Díaz (1920–2012) details, all these official approvals could be composed by the same reviewer.[334] If the Council of Castile received positive *aprobaciones* about a work, the text then received its official licenses from civil and religious authorities.[335]

According to Simón Díaz's calculations, "more than one hundred thousand *aprobaciones*" were composed in early modern Spain, with most texts containing more than one. Simón Díaz observes that some members of religious orders, especially those living in Madrid, came to specialize in writing them. In terms of the Society of Jesus, Jesuit Agustín de Castro (1589–1671) composed some seventy-five *aprobaciones* between 1630 and 1666.[336] Many other members of the Society of Jesus wrote smaller numbers of *aprobaciones*. To mention only one example, in penning one of the approvals for the visionary nun María de Jesús de Ágreda's (1602–65) *Mística ciudad de Dios* (Mystical city of God [1670]), Andrés Mendo (1608–84), also a *calificador* for the Inquisition, informed readers that they should not be "surprised" that a woman wrote such a text and situated Ágreda's work in a tradition of female mystical writers.[337] While Mendo proved adept at endorsing the orthodoxy of Ágreda's text, he was less savvy when undertaking the printing of fellow Jesuit António Vieira's (1608–97) works.

Even long after the 1469 marriage of Ferdinand II of Aragon (1542–1516, r.1474–1504 in Castile; r.1479–1516 in Aragon) and Isabella I of Castile (1451–1504,

---

333   See Kamen, *Spanish Inquisition*, 118–23 for a summary in English, and María Marsá, *La imprenta en los siglos de oro (1520–1700)* (Madrid: Ediciones del Laberinto, 2001), 23–30 for more details.

334   José Simón Díaz, *El libro español antiguo: Análisis de su estructura* (Kassel: Edition Reichenberger, 1983), 25–27.

335   Marsá, *Imprenta*, 51–52.

336   José Simón Díaz, *La bibliografía: Conceptos y aplicaciones* (Barcelona: Planeta, 1971), 155, 144.

337   Andrés Mendo, "Censvra de el Reverendissimo Padre Maestro Andrès Mendo," in María de Jesús de Ágreda [Maria de Jesus], *Mystica ciudad de Dios, milagro de sv omnipotencia, y abismo de la gracia* (Madrid: Manvel Rviz de Mvrga, 1701), 1:no pagination. Spencer Research Library.

AN OVERVIEW OF THE PRE-SUPPRESSION SOCIETY OF JESUS IN SPAIN   79

r.1474–1504 as queen of Castile) joined their kingdoms, the two crowns maintained separate legal systems.[338] This system was only in place in the crown of Castile. In the crown of Aragon, the judicial court granted licenses. In contrast to the Castilian system, imprints published in this region did not print the licenses and other approvals in their entirety in the volumes. Instead, Aragonese imprints included the names of the individuals who issued the licenses. When the Bourbons came to power in Spain, Aragon adopted Castile's textual approval system. In the crown of Navarre, this did not occur until 1783.[339]

12   Pedagogy

For the political elite who routinely dealt with the Inquisition and the Council of Castile, for consumers of printed materials, for those unfortunate enough to appear before the Inquisition, and for those who attended its *autos de fe*, the roles that members of the Society of Jesus played in these bodies would have been quite clear. For many in Spain, however, the order was most known for its members' preaching and teaching.

In terms of the teaching mission of the order as a whole, Spanish members played an important part in the development of the *Ratio studiorum*, which governed the administration and curriculum of Jesuit *colegios*. Spanish Jesuits already mentioned for their scholarly prowess, including Ledesma, Acosta, Mariana, and Toledo, as well as Jéronimo de Torres (1530–1611) and Juan de Maldonado (c.1533–83), worked on the commission that formulated the document, circulated a draft version, and eventually produced the final version of the *Ratio* in 1599.[340]

Among other specifications, the *Ratio* allowed for theatrical performances, and Jesuit theater flourished in Spain. Although some students wrote plays, they were more frequently composed by Jesuit faculty members. For example, the first professor of rhetoric at the Colegio Imperial, Pedro Pablo de Acevedo (1521/22–73), wrote plays, as did a number of his fellow members of the order, including Acosta.[341]

In Spain, a significant amount of teaching undertaken by Jesuits took place in *escuelas de latinidad* (Latin schools), also known as *escuelas* (or *estudios*) *de gramática* (Latin grammar schools) as they were termed in Spain, which

---

338   Elliott, *Imperial Spain*, 15, 24, 29–30.
339   Marsá, *Imprenta*, 27.
340   Astrain, *Historia de la Compañía de Jesús*, 4:2–4; Kallendorf, *Conscience on Stage*, 7.
341   Simón Díaz, *Historia*, 1:30; Kallendorf, *Conscience on Stage*, 11–15.

taught classical languages to nine- to fourteen-year-old students in preparation for university enrollment. Since these programs were generally governed by contractual relationships between the Jesuit order and a university or a municipality,[342] the details varied from contract to contract. As Bernabé Bartolomé Martínez notes, the financial underwriting of universities differed substantially between the kingdoms of Aragon and Castile. As a result, fewer Jesuit Latin grammar schools were contractually linked to universities in Castile than in Aragon.[343]

Legal disputes were not uncommon during the process of formulating such educational agreements. In one specific case, tensions arose over the Jesuits' choice for the language of instruction in the grammar school affiliated with the University of Lleida. Whereas Lleida had a lengthy tradition of using Catalan to teach Latin, the Jesuits preferred Castilian in this context. The correspondence from the resulting legal case between the Society and this university includes Vitelleschi's reiteration of previously expressed advice on the importance of "appointing teachers who know the language of the land [...], which without doubt is very important for the benefit of the students."[344]

While this particular conflict over language usage in the classroom was unique to Catalonia, disputes also arose over other details about the teaching of Latin to children and adolescents. For example, in correspondence between Rome and the province of Aragon in 1618, Vitelleschi was content with the resolution reached between the city of Zaragoza and the Jesuit *colegio* there. Vitelleschi cautioned Sanz that the order should not heed requests to expand its offerings to include Greek and rhetoric.[345] Ultimately, the Jesuits ended their agreement with the University of Zaragoza in 1618; but they began another one in 1628. This was not the first instance in which the Society decided to refuse a contract it found onerous. In 1565, then superior general Borja declined a contract for the Jesuits to teach grammar in conjunction with the University of Valencia.[346]

---

342   B. [Bernabé] Bartolomé Martínez, "Las cátedras de gramática de los jesuitas en las universidades de Aragón," *Hispania sacra* 34 (1982): 389–448, here 391.

343   B. [Bernabé] Bartolomé Martínez, "Las cátedras de gramática de los jesuitas en las universidades de su provincia de Castilla," *Hispania sacra* 35 (1983): 449–97, here 468.

344   Bartolomé Martínez, "Cátedras [...] Aragón," 397, 445, and Vitelleschi to Jaime Cornes, June 2, 1626, ARSI *Arag.* 8 fol. 38ᵛ, cited in Bartolomé Martínez, "Cátedras [...] Aragón," 446. This article references the University of Lérida, the Castilian name for the city of Lleida.

345   Vitelleschi to Sanz, December 21, 1618, AHN J leg. 253 doc. 75.

346   Bartolomé Martínez, "Cátedras [...] Aragón," 403, 405.

AN OVERVIEW OF THE PRE-SUPPRESSION SOCIETY OF JESUS IN SPAIN   81

When setting up these Latin programs, Jesuits attempted to exclude others from teaching this subject matter. As Bernabé Bartolomé Martínez notes, the order was more successful in obtaining the exclusive rights to teach Latin in Aragonese universities than in Castilian institutions. At times, the Jesuits' attempts to assert their exclusive rights to teach Latin led to criticism of the order for its seeming opportunism. In 1623, Philip IV issued a royal pragmatic regulating the teaching of Latin. After that point, it became more difficult for Jesuits to receive contracts that designated them as the only official teachers of Latin in urban areas because the royal pragmatic permitted other institutions, such as cathedrals, to do so.[347] Despite possible competition after 1623, the Jesuits nonetheless continued to be a significant force in this sector of education in Spain. Using documents prepared in the wake of the expulsion, Bernabé Bartolomé Martínez counts 118 Jesuit establishments in Spain, most of which served some pedagogical function.[348] In point of fact, the order exerted such dominance over the teaching of the rudiments of Latin that Astrain characterized it as "a type of monopoly for the Jesuits."[349] In the 1740s and 1750s, the Society vigorously defended its domain in the teaching of Latin. The Jesuits won court cases to forbid the Piarists from expanding their schools in Zaragoza and Valencia to include Latin instruction.[350]

Mariana's criticism of his order's methods in teaching Latin is well known; he was especially concerned with the fact that many Jesuits doing this pedagogical work did not have enough knowledge about the subject. However, as John H. Elliott suggests, "Mariana was so passionate a critic of his own Order that his judgements are generally too partisan to be taken purely on trust." Moreover, as Elliott observes, even Mariana conceded that advanced-level coursework functioned more efficiently.[351] But as Enlightenment ideas began to take hold in Spain, the Jesuits' pedagogical methods were perceived to be outdated, particularly by the Portuguese cleric Luís António Verney (1713–92). Although the Jesuit José Francisco de Isla (1703–81) authored a defense of the order's methods, at least at the University of Cervera, there was general agreement with Verney's critique.[352]

Many of the Jesuit *colegios* that taught Latin to adolescents also taught younger children their *primeras letras* (first letters). This early instruction

---

347   Bartolomé Martínez, "Cátedras [...] Castilla," 474–75.
348   Bartolomé Martínez, "Cátedras [...] Aragón," 389.
349   Astrain, *Historia de la Compañía de Jesús*, 3:197.
350   See Bartolomé Martínez, "Cátedras [...] Aragón," 423–24 for details about these cases.
351   Elliott, *Imperial Spain*, 368.
352   See Bartolomé Martínez, "Cátedras [...] Aragón," 442 for a transcribed comment to this effect.

involved reading, arithmetical calculations, catechism, and prayers. Writing generally was taught as a separate skill.[353]

When setting up *colegios*, the order sought out endowments in order to provide *primeras letras* and Latin instruction without charge.[354] And documentary evidence suggests that boys from various social classes attended. The documents that regulated the *colegio* in Mallorca's relationship with that municipality specified that the order would teach both "poor" and "rich" students. Others, including Lleida, Valencia, and Zaragoza, promised equal treatment to those of differing economic backgrounds. When questioned about the attention paid to wealthy students, staff in Zaragoza admitted that those from more privileged backgrounds often needed more help in applying themselves to their work.[355] In terms of the student body that received instruction in Jesuit institutions, Astrain's claim that all the "mother[s]" in a given town sent their sons to the Jesuit *colegio* "at least" to learn "catechism and first letters" is likely to be at least slightly exaggerated.[356] Even in the case of educational opportunities for which one did not have to pay, families had to make an economic calculation: as María del Pilar Ryan signals, a family that chose to send a son to school had to have the economic wherewithal to survive without the income that he would have contributed had he gone to work.[357]

In offering education at no cost to students, the order opened itself up to the accusation that its schools only served as tools for the recruitment of new members. To counter these concerns, several contracts, like those with Girona and Lleida, specified that young students could not join the Society of Jesus without the permission of their relatives.[358]

The potential for the recruitment of young boys was only one issue that arose regarding teaching. In one case, a jurisdictional disagreement that began in Puebla, Mexico, had a negative impact on the Jesuits' ability to collect the portion of wheat that was their payment for their Latin teaching in the Burgo

---

353 Richard L. Kagan, *Students and Society in Early Modern Spain* (Baltimore: Johns Hopkins University Press, 1974), 9, 14.

354 See Bartolomé Martínez, "Cátedras [...] Castilla," 466 for a chart that specifies the amounts of funding obtained by most of the thirty-three *escuelas de gramática* in the province of Castile and the levels of instruction that each offered.

355 Biblioteca de la Real Academia de la Historia, hereafter BRAH, sección, hereafter sec., Jesuitas, hereafter Jes., leg. 9/7295 "Ex variis," cited in Bartolomé Martínez, "Cátedras [...] Aragón," 413 and Bartolomé Martínez, "Cátedras [...] Aragón," 432.

356 Astrain, *Historia de la Compañía de Jesús*, 3:198.

357 Ryan, *Jesuita secreto*, 64.

358 BRAH sec. Jes. leg. 9/7232 *Capítulos propuestos* and *Concordia de Lérida*, cited in Bartolomé Martínez, "Cátedras [...] Aragón," 433.

AN OVERVIEW OF THE PRE-SUPPRESSION SOCIETY OF JESUS IN SPAIN   83

de Osma in the Soria region of Spain. In 1654, Juan de Palafox y Mendoza (1600–59), then bishop of Osma, simply refused to pay.[359]

This denial was rooted in an old dispute between Palafox and the order that traced back to his earlier bishopric in Puebla. In Mexico in 1642, Bishop Palafox decided that religious orders should tithe on the agricultural products grown on their lands; however, local Jesuits did not concur with this assessment. In the ensuing years, the disagreement between the Society of Jesus and Palafox escalated, and Palafox corresponded with the pope about it. Both sides of the disagreement printed publications to support their own point of view and criticize the opposing one. Eventually, the bishop had to give up his see in Mexico for the less prominent one in Osma, Spain. This was not the last time this disagreement would reappear. Palafox's critiques about the Society of Jesus, including of its wealth, were republished in eighteenth-century Spain.[360]

As Gregorio Bartolomé Martínez signals, Palafox's decision to deny payment was not without consequences for the bishop. At least one Jesuit stationed in the area, José Antonio Butrón y Múxica (1657–1734), composed unflattering satirical texts about Palafox in response to his decision not to remunerate the order. Butrón also began to satirize several Carmelites because of their support of Palafox.[361] This event was not the only one to provoke a satirical response from Butrón: he also composed a burlesque sermon about a certain Augustinian named Espinilla who had delivered a sermon against the Jesuits.[362]

Although the Jesuits' work with children was the most visible aspect of the order's pedagogy for a broad spectrum of residents of Spain, the order was also an important presence in teaching at the university level. When Philip IV expressed a desire to establish a program of university-level courses— Estudios Generales (general studies), eventually named Reales Estudios (royal studies)—at the order's Colegio Imperial in Madrid, Spanish universities opposed this plan. And the universities published a number of *memoriales* to support their positions.[363] Beyond this one institution, Jesuits taught at the Jesuit University of Gandía and at other universities in Spain and abroad.

---

359   Archivo Provincial de Toledo de la Compañía de Toledo sec. Palafox, cited in Bartolomé Martínez, "Cátedras [...] Castilla," 465.

360   D. A. [David Anthony] Brading, *The First America: The Spanish Monarchy, Creole Patriots, and the Liberal State, 1492–1867* (Cambridge: Cambridge University Press, 1991), 242–46, 250–51.

361   See Gregorio Bartolomé Martínez, *Jaque mate al obispo virrey: Siglo y medio de sátiras y libelos contra don Juan de Palafox y Mendoza* (Mexico: Fondo de Cultura Económica, 1991), 158–83.

362   Sommervogel, *Bibliothèque*, 2:col. 473.

363   See Simón Díaz, *Historia*, 1:73–81 for a summary of one such *memorial* from the Universities of Alcalá and Salamanca.

84 MANNING

Many Jesuit teachers and professors led peripatetic lives, holding a variety of positions in various places. For example, Juan de Pineda (1557–1637), whose career as a *calificador* for the Inquisition will be the subject of later analysis, began his pedagogical career in Granada, then moved to Seville, Córdoba, and Madrid. He began his time in the classroom as an instructor of the humanities and later taught theology and eventually Scripture.[364] Cuencan-born Molina taught theology in Portugal at the Universities of Coimbra and Évora before teaching in Madrid.[365]

As part of their pedagogical and catechetical missions, Jesuits prepared texts for classroom use. Although Cecilio Gómez Rodeles (1842–1913) found references to Jesuit print shops, including one in Toledo in 1591 and elsewhere, the degree to which these were the "property" of the order remains unclear. Bernabé Bartolomé Martínez believes this to be a more realistic possibility in the eighteenth century.[366] At the beginning of the seventeenth century, Acquaviva advised Provincial Melchor de Valpedrosa (1549–1606) about a matter that had reached his attention concerning the manner in which Jesuit authors were selling their books in Jesuit houses in Valencia. Acquaviva cautioned that Jesuit establishments should not be turned into "bookstores." Instead, as the general previously advised, the books should be sold to booksellers at a price that assured that the bookseller would be able to make a profit. Jesuit authors should only keep a few copies to hand out in the way they saw fit.[367] Three years later, Acquaviva reminded Vice Provincial Pedro Juste (d.1622) that books should not be sold from Jesuit houses.[368] However, texts for classroom usage were regularly sold from the *porterías* (the lobby area of a Jesuit house that is open to the public) of Jesuit institutions, as inventories demonstrate.[369] The sale of books was likely one of the factors that led the anonymous author of an anti-Jesuit poem to remark that (s)he did not know whether a Jesuit establishment should be called a "*colegio*" or a "house of trade."[370]

---

364 Ángel Alcalá, "Góngora y Juan de Pineda: Escaramuzas entre el poeta y el inquisidor," in *Homenaje a Pedro Sáinz Rodríguez* (Madrid: Fundación Universitaria Española, 1986), 3:1–19, here 3:1.

365 Pohle, "Luis de Molina."

366 Cecilio Gómez Rodeles, "Las imprentas de los jesuitas," *Razón y fe* 25 (1910): here 352ff., cited in Bartolomé Martínez, "Librerías e imprentas de los jesuitas," 330–31.

367 Acquaviva to Provincial Melchor de Valpedrosa, December 22, 1601, AHN J leg. 252 doc. 210.

368 Acquaviva to Vice Provincial Pedro Juste, January 12, 1604, AHN J leg. 252 doc. 249.

369 Bartolomé Martínez, "Librerías e imprentas de los jesuitas," 376.

370 "Llave maestra de los entresijos de la sotana y antorcha luciente, que descubre las quatro cumbres del bonete," BNE MS 12880, fol. 94ᵛ, cited in Laura Lara Martínez, "Enfermedades y remedios de la Compañía: El diagnóstico del padre Mariana y otros pensadores jesuitas," in *La actualidad del padre Juan de Mariana: Congreso internacional 22, 23 y 24 de marzo*

13 Preaching

In William V. Bangert's (1911–85) estimation of the order as a whole, "popular preaching was a ministry enthusiastically adopted by the Jesuits."[371] This certainly was the case in Spain. In contrast to many other men of the cloth, Jesuits did not accept monetary remuneration for preaching. The Jesuits' decision represented a notable difference from the practices of other religious orders. As Burrieza Sánchez observes, preaching proved to be a significant income stream, and sermons were "generally well remunerated."[372] But Jesuit superiors in Rome were intent on maintaining non-compensated preaching, as Vitelleschi reminded Sanz in 1618.[373] Despite such warnings, especially as more Jesuit houses in Spain began to experience financial difficulties, some Jesuits apparently accepted funds for preaching. By 1657, Nickel advised Provincial Jacinto Piquer (d.1671?) that he had received information from reliable sources that Jesuit preachers were taking money or other donations in exchange for their services. Nickel reiterated that this practice was forbidden and that all preachers and superiors in the province should be reminded of this point. In addition, any Jesuit who accepted payment was to be punished and his name forwarded to the general "para que yo considere si sera conueniente privarle de voz activa y pasiva" (so that I may consider whether it will be convenient to deprive him of passive and active voice).[374]

For the laity, in addition to regular attendance at Mass, Jesuits advocated for frequent Communion and confession.[375] But taking the sacraments and listening to sermons were not the only roles for laypeople at Jesuit churches. The Society of Jesus frequently established Marian sodalities. According to Fermín Marín Barriguete's research on the sodality of the Nativity of Our Lady at the Casa Profesa in Madrid, members took the sacraments and selected a particular saint to venerate each month on his or her feast day. Lay members

---

de 2017, *Talavera de la Reina*, ed. Jacinto Rivera de Rosales and Francisco Javier Gómez Díez (Pozuelo de Alarcón: Editorial UFV, Universidad Francisco de Vitoria, 2018), 87–95, here 93.

371 William V. Bangert, *A History of the Society of Jesus*, 2nd ed. (St. Louis, MO: Institute of Jesuit Sources, 1986), 113.

372 Burrieza Sánchez, "Ministerios de la Compañía," 114.

373 Vitelleschi to Sanz, September 21, 1618, AHN J leg. 253 doc. 65.

374 Nickel to Piquer, July 14, 1657, AHN J leg. 254 doc. 171. Fejér, *Defuncti secundi*, 4:313 notes that this date corresponds to a Jesuit whose last name is written as Pisquer, so this death date could correspond to a different individual.

375 O'Malley, *First Jesuits*, 136.

of the group helped catechize, visited prisons and hospitals, and performed other charitable work.[376]

Outside these formal groups, others continued to connect themselves to Jesuit communities in more personal ways. Despite their inability to affiliate themselves officially with the Society, *beatas* nonetheless formed informal relationships with particular Jesuit establishments. In the town of Marchena, as Julián J. Lozano Navarro details, a number of *beatas* lived in a house beside the Jesuit church. Although Jesuits served as spiritual directors for these women, and sometimes inherited their possessions upon their deaths, the order oftentimes was ambivalent toward them. Members of the larger community, however, labeled them as "beatas honestas de la Compañía de Jesús" (virtuous *beatas* of the Society of Jesus).[377] Without referring to the Jesuit *colegio* in Marchena, Burrieza Sánchez proposes that the Jesuits distanced themselves from *beatas* in order to protect the Jesuit community if inquisitorial or ecclesiastical authorities inquired about visionary *beatas'* practices.[378] And Jesuits followed this practice vis-à-vis the *beatas* who associated with the order in Marchena. Once the renown of Damiana de las Llagas (1585–1670) began to spread, she enjoyed a closer relationship to the Society. After the deaths of well-known *beatas*, on occasion the order became more interested in their potential sanctity. Lozano Navarro found this was the case with Damiana de las Llagas: after her death in 1670, the Jesuits in Marchena sought to verify her sanctity by checking to see whether her cadaver remained free from decay. The Marchena Jesuits pursued a similar strategy after the death of another *beata*, María de Jesús de los Ríos (d.1735).[379]

13.1 *Mission Preaching in Spain*

It is important to note that the Jesuits did not limit their evangelical efforts to their own churches and schools. In 1633, Vitelleschi requested that Continente focus on "el ministerio de enseñar a los niños la Doctrina Christiana, por las plaças, y calles, y el de visitar las carceles, y hospitales" (the ministry of

---

376 Fermín Marín Barriguete, "Los jesuitas y el culto mariano: La Congregación de la Natividad en la Casa Profesa de Madrid," *Tiempos modernos* 9 (2003–4): 1–20, here 9–10, 4–5. See Bangert, *History of the Society of Jesus*, 106–7 for a short overview of these sodalities in the 1580s.

377 Julián J. Lozano Navarro, "Entre jesuitas y beatas: La percepción de la santidad en el colegio de la Compañía de Jesús en Marchena (siglos XVII y XVIII)," in *Subir a los altares: Modelos de santidad en la Monarquía Hispánica (siglos XVI–XVIII)*, ed. Inmaculada Arias de Saavedra et al. (Granada: Universidad de Granada, 2018), 51–77, here 59–61.

378 Burrieza Sánchez, "Percepción jesuítica," 107.

379 Lozano Navarro, "Entre jesuitas y beatas," 61–67, 69–73.

AN OVERVIEW OF THE PRE-SUPPRESSION SOCIETY OF JESUS IN SPAIN　　87

teaching children Christian doctrine, in plazas, and streets, and that of visiting prisons and hospitals). While Vitelleschi first referenced the importance of these outreach efforts for divine service, he also openly acknowledged their value for the "reputation" and "great credit" of the Society, before reminding the provincial that only those in whom the order had complete confidence should be allowed to carry out these ministries.[380] For some, such thought for the reputation of the community might seem unseemly for men of the cloth. It does speak to the fact that the order was conscious of its image and the need to cultivate good will. Such concern, however, could become a vicious circle. As criticism of the order grew, members became more careful about their reputations, at which point these concerns fed accusations that the community was overly preoccupied with this issue.

Even after the Council of Trent's request for better education of the faithful, Iberian Catholics did not know a great deal about the religion they professed. When men of the cloth reflected on the level of doctrinal knowledge among Catholics on the Iberian peninsula, they often referenced "the Indies" in Spain. This analogy also hoped to foment the same level of enthusiasm for instructing Catholics on the peninsula as for evangelizing in the vast Spanish and Portuguese empires.[381] Religious missions, especially to rural areas of Iberia, attempted to remediate the populace's low level of religious knowledge.

According to Kamen's research, the Society of Jesus began missions in Iberia by 1557 and in the "mountainous areas" of Catalonia in 1566.[382] (I use the term missions in the sense that the Society did, namely to describe visits by Jesuit priests to locales in which there was not a permanent Jesuit presence.) In the 1560s, after the Inquisition in Seville had convicted a number of preachers of Protestantism, Jesuits made missions in the area to ensure that the laity was exposed to proper Catholic doctrine.[383] By the mid-1560s, Jesuits in the province of Toledo were making mission trips to areas south of the town of Toledo. In order to do so, they researched the towns and measured the distance

---

380　Vitelleschi to Continente, February 24, 1633, AHN J leg. 253 doc. 176.
381　See, for example, Federico Palomo, "La doctrine mise en scène: Catéchèse et missions intérieures dans la Péninsule Ibérique à l'époque moderne," *Archivum historicum Societatis Iesu* 74 (2005): 23–55, here 25; Francisco Luis Rico Callado, "Las misiones interiores en la España postridentina," *Hispania sacra* 55 (2003): 109–29, here 111. I use the term Iberian peninsula because, as Palomo details, Catholics in Portugal had similar doctrinal deficits. In addition to Palomo's cited articles, also see his *Fazer dos campos escolas excelentes: Os jesuítas de Évora e as missões do interior em Portugal (1551–1630)* (Lisbon: FCG-FCT/MCES, 2003).
382　Henry Kamen, *The Phoenix and the Flame: Catalonia and the Counter-Reformation* (New Haven: Yale University Press, 1993), 381.
383　Moreno, "Jesuitas, la Inquisición y la frontera espiritual," 671.

between them in order to plan a route, as the document in the ARSI cited by David Martín López and Francisco José Aranda Pérez reveals.[384] In the Spanish provinces, there were several Jesuits who were tasked with preaching on an itinerant basis throughout the year. In 1652, Rome informed the province of Aragon that since Jerónimo López (1589–1658) did not have a fixed *colegio* (he was a full-time itinerant preacher), the province should provide him with clothing and other necessities.[385] In Gómez Rodeles's opinion, López was an innovator in the conduct of missions, having popularized a type of penitential procession known as an "Act of Contrition." In the seventeenth century, Jesuits' missions moved beyond rural zones and began to include urban areas. Between 1665 and 1674, future superior general González and his companion Juan Gabriel Guillén (1627–75) made urban missions in a number of populous Spanish cities, including Seville, Granada, and Madrid.[386] Another itinerant preacher, Gregorio López (d.1673), traveled extensively—a passing reference to him mentioned his mission work in the province of Aragon and in other provinces.[387] Particularly during religiously significant moments in the year, like Lent, Jesuits who held other positions traveled to nearby rural areas to preach and hear confessions.

In the 1550s, preachers in most European nations faced communication challenges because of multiple languages or dialects, but the situation in Spain was especially complicated.[388] The mountainous region in the Pyrenees near the border with France was an area of particular focus because the difficult terrain meant that its residents tended to live isolated lives, in some places without regular access to clergy. Beyond the geographical challenges, ministry in this area was linguistically complex as Basque, Aragonese, and Catalan are spoken there. In point of fact, the Society's province of Aragon, which encompassed a portion of this region, is notable for its number of autochthonous languages. This province was composed of Aragon, Catalonia, Valencia, and Mallorca, each of which was once an independent kingdom with its own language. Repeated requests that Aragonese, Catalan, Valencian, and Mallorcan Jesuits serve outside their home regions did not yield results because the need

---

384   ARSI *Hisp.* 103, fols. 380ʳ–381ᵛ, cited in Martín López and Aranda Pérez, "Conformación de la provincia jesuítica de Toledo," 377–78.

385   Nickel to Piquer, May 24, 1652, AHN J leg. 254 doc. 57.

386   Cecilio Gómez Rodeles, *Vida del célebre misionero Pedro Calatayud de la Compañía de Jesús y relación de sus apostólicas empresas en los reinos de España y Portugal (1689–1773)* (Madrid: Sucesores de Ribadeneyra, 1882), cited in Burrieza Sánchez, "'Glorias del segundo siglo,'" 165–66 and Burrieza Sánchez "'Glorias del segundo siglo,'" 164, 166.

387   Nickel to Alastuey, October 13, 1654, AHN J leg. 254 doc. 112.

388   Kamen, *Phoenix and the Flame*, 362. Kamen mentions the challenge that Cornish posed to English Protestant preachers.

AN OVERVIEW OF THE PRE-SUPPRESSION SOCIETY OF JESUS IN SPAIN   89

to know the autochthonous language of an area made it difficult for Jesuits to work outside their native territory. Therefore, in the 1630s, Roman Jesuit policy requested that members in the province of Aragon learn at least one autochthonous language in addition to their native one so that they could work in more places in the province.[389]

This is not to say that members of the order always preached in the autochthonous language. As Kamen observes, in some urban areas of Catalonia, particularly in Barcelona, Castilian was the preferred language for sermons.[390] This choice appealed to viceroys and other highly placed royal officials who generally spoke Castilian. Indeed, Peña Díaz believes that the Jesuit order played a significant role in the "Castilianization" of Catalonia.[391]

Those attending missions did not merely listen passively to sermons. As Federico Palomo relates, missions often involved kinesthetic activities, like processions with stops to hear doctrinal dialogues around town. Since a number of manuals about preaching in this context include the texts of poems and songs to use, these likely formed part of the overall experience.[392]

Several Jesuits wrote about the order's mission preaching in Spain. In 1678, Martín de la Naja (1606–96) published an account of the life of Jesuit mission preacher Jerónimo López. In 1670, however, one such missionary, Manuel Ortigas (1609–78), was to receive a penance for contravening a decree of the Eleventh General Congregation (1661) that prohibited the publication of texts without the permission of the order. Ortigas had printed several works, including one concerning missions, without obtaining the requisite permissions from the order.[393]

In José Malaxechevarría's (1873–1953) estimation, the Jesuit Pedro de Calatayud (1689–1773) was one of the most well-known missionary preachers in Spain—in the three decades prior to the expulsion, Calatayud preached on mission trips throughout much of the country.[394] In order to facilitate this

---

389 Vitelleschi to Continente, March 25, 1634, AHN J leg. 253 doc. 202. As Kamen details, the Jesuits' position on the use of Catalan has been "misrepresented" based on the order's preference for the use of Castilian in the teaching of Latin and a general preference for instruction in Castilian in university teaching. The Jesuits were well known for preaching in Catalan (*Phoenix and the Flame*, 371–72).

390 Kamen, *Phoenix and the Flame*, 364.

391 Manuel Peña Díaz, "El castellano en la Cataluña de los siglos XVI y XVII," *Manuscrits* 15 (1997): 149–55, here 152.

392 Federico Palomo, "Limosnas impresas: Escritos e imágenes en las prácticas misioneras de interior en la península Ibérica (siglos XVI–XVIII)," *Manuscrits* 25 (2007): 239–65, here 251, 247–48, 254–57.

393 Oliva to Provincial Antonio Perlas, July 19, 1670, AHN J leg. 255 doc. 262.

394 José Malaxechevarría, *La Compañía de Jesús por la instrucción del pueblo vasco en los siglos XVII y XVIII: Ensayo histórico* (San Sebastián: Imprenta y librería san Ignacio, 1926),

work, Calatayud wrote a number of brief texts for the laity to use, including *Incendios del amor sagrado* (Fires of sacred love [1734]). He also produced *Catecismo práctico y muy útil para la instrucción y enseñanza fácil de los fieles* (Practical and very useful catechism for the instruction and easy teaching of the faithful [1747]) and *Doctrinas prácticas que suele explicar en sus misiones el padre Pedro de Calatayud* (Practical doctrine that Father Pedro de Calatayud usually explains on his missions [2 vols., 1737 and 1739]) to help clerics assist the laity in examining their consciences. In the estimation of the Society, leading missions required a specific skillset,[395] and therefore written guides from Jesuits with extensive experience in this field would have been valuable resources for the formation of less experienced mission preachers.

Beyond the work in pulpits and confessionals that one would expect of an eighteenth-century itinerant Jesuit preacher, Calatayud also was instrumental in establishing education for girls. As Malaxechevarría relates, during a 1732 mission in Bilbao, Calatayud arranged for the area's only school to create a separate section for girls. When Calatayud's birthplace of Tafalla wanted to honor him, the preacher requested that the town set up a school for girls. Although the community of Vergara already had a school in place for female education, Calatayud urged for its improvement during his 1750 mission.[396]

14   Publications by Jesuits

14.1   *Works of Popular Piety*

Given the order's interest in preaching and missionary work, it is not surprising that members such as Gaspar Astete (1537–1601) authored catechisms. Among such works, Jerónimo de Ripalda's (1535–1618) *Doctrina cristiana con una exposición breve* (Christian doctrine with a brief exposition [1591]) became the predominant catechism of the era. Although Palomo wonders whether those preaching on missions gave out catechisms during their trips, he indicates that he has not found evidence to clarify this point.[397] Whereas

---

141; http://www.liburuklik.euskadi.eus/handle/10771/25046 (accessed April 28, 2020). See Palomo, "Limosnas impresas," 248 for more details about Calatayud's publications.

395   Trevor Johnson, "Blood, Tears, and Xavier-Water: Jesuit Missionaries and Popular Religion in the Eighteenth-Century Upper Palatinate," in *Popular Religion in Germany and Central Europe, 1400–1800*, ed. Bob Scribner and Trevor Johnson (New York: St. Martin's Press, 1996), 183–202, here 186.

396   Malaxechevarría, *Compañía de Jesús*, 141, 142–45.

397   Palomo, "Limosnas impresas," 250.

AN OVERVIEW OF THE PRE-SUPPRESSION SOCIETY OF JESUS IN SPAIN 91

catechisms like Ripalda's were written to teach the laity about Catholicism, others were directed toward clerics. The *Práctica del catecismo romano y doctrina cristiana* (Exercises for the catechism and Christian doctrine [1640]), published in Juan Eusebio Nieremberg y Ottin's (1595–1658) name, was intended to assist clerics.[398]

In addition to pedagogical texts about the faith, Jesuits also composed other types of religiously oriented works. Nieremberg's *Varones ilustres de la Compañía de Jesús* (Illustrious men of the Society of Jesus [4 vols., 1643–47]) recounted the life experiences of distinguished Jesuits. The continuation of Nieremberg's text by Alonso de Andrade (*c.*1590–1672), and José Cassani's (1673–1750) subsequent additions in the eighteenth century in *Glorias del segundo siglo de la Compañía de Jesús* (Glories of the second century of the Society of Jesus [3 vols., 1734–36]), demonstrate the importance of this work for the order. But Jesuits also wrote about the exemplary lives of those beyond the Society. Texts like Ribadeneyra's *Flos sanctorum* (literally *Flower of saints*, but most commonly translated as *Lives of Saints* [1599]) offer hagiographies.

Despite Poza's difficulties with the Roman and Spanish Inquisitions, his *Práctica de ayudar a bien morir* (Guide to dying well [1619]) remained popular, as demonstrated by the number of times it was reprinted.[399] At the beginning of this guide, Poza explains that it is unlikely that one's confessor will be able to provide continual attention during one's illness; therefore, this work offers guidance for the moments when the ill person finds him or herself alone. In addition to aids for making a good confession and prayers, the volume offers practical guidance on wills and assessments from clerics about visions of "Satan" frequently experienced near death.[400]

Around 1657, Madrid bookseller Gabriel de León's (d. *c.*1690) dedication to the edition of the *Práctica* that he financed attempted to insulate the volume against any damage caused by Poza's earlier difficulties with the Spanish and Roman Inquisitions. (It was common practice for a bookseller who financed a new edition of a work to replace the original dedication with one of his or her own.) First, León seeks a notable level of protection for his imprint through the choice of his dedicatee. His selection is a legal expert affiliated with the

---

398 Hendrickson, *Jesuit Polymath of Madrid*, 54. The question of the authorship of this text is complex. Nieremberg played a significant role in its writing, but his fellow Jesuit Jerónimo López began the project. See 51n1 for more details.

399 Moreno and Peña Díaz count "up to twelve editions and translations" of Poza's *Práctica* ("Jesuita Juan Bautista Poza," 3:169n7).

400 Juan Bautista Poza [Ivan Bavtista Poça], *Practica de ayvdar a bien morir* (Madrid: Domingo Garcia y Morràs, 1648), fols. 1ᵛ, 51ʳ, 59ᵛ, 86ʳ. There is no date on the volume's initial page, but the license is dated 1657. BNE.

royal court system and the Inquisition: Antonio Farfán de los Godos (*fl.* seventeenth century), a judge and royal official in Cartagena de Indias and a *familiar* (a lay official who worked for the Spanish Inquisition) of the Inquisition. Since many book buyers in Madrid would have seen the *memoriales* concerning the Poza case, even if they had not read them, this dedication assures a potentially worried book buyer that this work did not treat Poza's more controversial opinions. Second, in his dedication, León asserts that there are two potential motives for which one dedicates a book to a particular individual: either as an acknowledgment of a benefit provided or to protect the volume from criticism. León claims the second motive: "Porque defendiendole con su afabilidad, ninguno aurà que calumnie a su Autor" (Because defending it with his affability, there will be no one to slander its author).[401] Given Poza's checkered history, it is possible that the literary commonplace of references to the dedicatee's protection of the volume could become an actual necessity. Finally, under these circumstances, rather than make recourse to another common trope in which dedications do not recount the dedicatee's virtues out of respect for his (or her) modesty, León uses a different tactic. To reassure readers and authorities, León recounts various elements of the Farfán de los Godos family's illustrious history.

Although devotional works written in the vernacular are often considered products for the laity (who were significant consumers of these texts), they also formed part of the libraries of religious communities, including those belonging to the Jesuits. As did other readers, Poza's fellow members of the Society of Jesus in Spain continued to read his *Práctica*. A notation in a 1648 imprint of the *Práctica* explains that the library at the Jesuit novitiate in Madrid owned two copies of this work and that for this reason one was removed.[402]

However, Jesuit institutions did not limit their collections of works of popular piety to authors in the community. A handwritten inscription marks a 1640 imprint of a popular collection of poetry, and several prayers, designed to prepare the reader for death entitled *Avisos para la muerte: Escritos por algunos ingenios de España* (Advice for dying: Written by some of the ingenious writers of Spain [1634]) as belonging to the "[l]ibreria de la Casa Profesa de la Compa[ñía] [...] de Madrid" (library of the Casa Profesa of the Society [illegible

---

401   Gabriel de León [Gabriel de Leon], "A Antonio Farfan de los Godos, tesorero, iuez, y oficial por su magestad de la ciudad de Cartagena de las Indias, y su prouincia, y familiar del Santo Oficio de la Inquisicion &," in Poza, *Practica de ayvdar a bien morir*, no pagination. BNE.

402   Handwritten notations on the *portada* of a 1648 imprint of Poza, *Practica de ayvdar a bien morir*; https://books.google.com/books?id=J2ab_sXcGTEC&printsec=frontcover& source=gbs_ge_summary_r&cad=0#v=onepage&q&f=false (accessed May 19, 2020).

AN OVERVIEW OF THE PRE-SUPPRESSION SOCIETY OF JESUS IN SPAIN   93

due to the ink dissolving the paper] in Madrid).[403] Despite the missing word "Jesús" (Jesus), the legible portion of the inscription leaves no doubt as to the Jesuits' ownership of the volume.

14.2   *Exequial Imprints and Necrologies for Jesuits*
When Jesuits died, their fellow members preached at their funerals. Sometimes, these sermons were subsequently printed to commemorate the individual's passing and for private devotional use. Such texts offered readers or hearers the opportunity to contemplate death in order to prepare themselves for it. In 1658, Manuel de Nájera (1604–80) preached a sermon at the funeral of fellow Jesuit Nieremberg. (According to the *portada* [frontispiece] of the printed sermon, the order did not plan an elaborate funeral for Nieremberg; rather, Cristóbal Crespí de Valldaura y Brizuela [1599–1671], a member of the royal council for Aragon, sponsored it.) In his sermon, Nájera portrayed Nieremberg as a warrior against appetites who savored his pain. But illness forced him to cede some ground in his fasting regime. Before his infirmity, Nieremberg "carr[ied] the cross"; however, in his illness Nieremberg suffered with Christ on the cross. The concessions in his normal mortification regime that he was forced to make because of his weakened state were "very hard and very penetrative nails." In death, Nieremberg was equally exemplary. He died in "great peace" proclaiming "what a sweet thing is death!"[404]

In addition to producing printed versions of funerary sermons, Jesuits memorialized their deceased colleagues by recounting the exemplary deaths of members in both printed and manuscript forms. These necrologies were not necessarily composed by noted writers: a number of the Jesuits listed in Carlos Sommervogel's (1834–1902) *Bibliothèque de la Compagnie de Jésus* (Library of the Society of Jesus [1890–1932]) only composed a single necrology or other record of a death. For those who did go on to write other works in the course of their religious lives, their first publication was often a necrology. Such was the case for Gracián.[405]

---

403   Handwritten notation on the *portada* of *Avisos para la mverte: Escritos por algunos Ingenios de España* (Zaragoza: Iuan de Larrumbe, 1640), BNE Raros, hereafter R, 31911.

404   Manuel de Nájera [Manvel de Naxera], "Sermon qve predico el padre Manvel de Naxera predicador de sv magestad en las piadosas exeqvias, que consagrò a la memoria del P. Ivan Evsebio Nieremberg el Ilvstrissimo señor Don Christoval Crespi de Baldavra, vicecanciller del Svpremo y Real Consejo de Aragon" (Madrid: Andres Garcia de la Iglesia, 1658), fols. 15ʳ–16ʳ. BNE.

405   See, for example, the entries for Francisco—listed as François—Franco, and Pedro—listed as Pierre—Fons in Sommervogel, *Bibliothèque*, 3:col. 937, 3:col. 832. See Batllori, *Gracián y el barroco*, 178–80 for Gracián's necrology for García de Alabiano.

94   MANNING

Other, generally longer, texts recounted the lives of notable Jesuits. As the collections of such texts among the documents that once belonged to the order testify, they circulated within the community to provide positive examples for brethren to imitate.[406] Sometimes, these texts were printed to facilitate wide circulation within the community. Printed necrologies, lives, and letters concerning the virtues of deceased members of the order could also bring virtuous Jesuits to the attention of a public beyond the order itself, especially if printed copies were sold to the public as well as sent to Jesuit institutions.

14.3   *Ascetic Practices and Writings about Them*

The level of physical mortification practiced by Nieremberg, and lauded in his exequies, differed from Loyola's advice. As O'Malley explains, "The *Exercises* provided the basic framework for Jesuit piety [...]. They assume that some bodily penance is appropriate during most of the *Exercises* and for the life one will lead afterward, but the counsel is mild."[407] As a number of scholars signal, Ignatius's advice was based on his own experience: his rigorous ascetic practices damaged his health. Therefore, he sought to ensure that his fellow Jesuits avoided this pitfall. After all, Jesuits needed to protect their physical selves for the travel that the order—and the pope—could require of them.[408] But the spiritual climate of the seventeenth century differed from Loyola's era: physical penitential practices had taken on greater importance. In Hendrickson's estimation, "but more than anywhere else, in Spain the Jesuits increasingly began to promote ascetical practices as a model of spiritual perfection, and they moved toward embracing a more eremitical style of living." Nieremberg's own disciplinary practices model this approach as his *Varones ilustres* textually embodies it.[409]

In recounting the lives of the early Jesuits who would have employed more moderate physical devotions in accordance with Ignatian dictates, Nieremberg cleverly manages to introduce the more rigorous practices familiar to his own contemporaries. For example, in recounting the life of Francisco de Villanueva (1509–57), Nieremberg mentions that upon returning from Portugal to the *colegio* in Alcalá, Villanueva found that the presence of one brother who practiced

---

406   AHN J leg. 5 exps. 35–53 collect such documents.

407   O'Malley, *First Jesuits*, 266.

408   A. Lynn Martin, *Plague? Jesuit Accounts of Epidemic Disease in the Sixteenth Century* (Kirksville, MO: Sixteenth Century Journal Publishers, 1996), 59–60; Meissner, *Ignatius of Loyola*, 223; Redworth, *She-Apostle*, 24–25. See J. A. [José Antonio] de Laburu, *La salud corporal y san Ignacio de Loyola* (Montevideo: Editorial Mosca Hermanos, 1938) for a detailed exposition of the manner in which Loyola sought to protect the health of Jesuits.

409   Hendrickson, *Jesuit Polymath of Madrid*, 35.

AN OVERVIEW OF THE PRE-SUPPRESSION SOCIETY OF JESUS IN SPAIN   95

a rigorous regime of physical discipline had motivated the entire community to employ mortifications so excessive that they were ruining their health and neglecting mental forms of penitence. Rather than simply relate this anecdote, Nieremberg then proceeds to detail the excessive physical disciplines that this unnamed brother practiced. At no point does Nieremberg suggest that this anonymous brother's disciplines, including "cilicios extraordinarios" (extraordinary cilices) and multiple whippings per day that drew blood, were not in keeping with Ignatian guidance. Instead, Nieremberg observes that such rigor was not appropriate for everyone.[410]

In Andrade's recounting of the lives of noteworthy Jesuits, no such stratagems were required. His chronologically later subjects were more rigorous in their ascetic routines. To mention only one of numerous possible examples, the missionary life of French-born Estéban Fabro (d.1657) was inspired by a grisly object. On a visit to Avignon, Sebastián de Viera (the version of the name of Sebastián Vieira [c.1573–1634] that Andrade employs), the procurator of Japan, displayed a katana that had been used to behead martyrs. Fabro was "so moved" by this sword that he decided to dedicate himself to missionary work. Fabro went on to serve twenty-seven years in China, all the while severely disciplining himself. This priest restricted his food intake and dressed in such inadequate clothing that he had to endure cold that made his hands swell and bleed in winter. In addition to employing cilices and whips, he fabricated a set of iron pincers that cut into his flesh when he walked.[411]

Such mortifications were not reserved for religious, as laypeople close to the Society also engaged in severe corporal devotional practices. Carvajal's uncle, Francisco Hurtado de Mendoza (c.1532–91), was very devoted to the Society. Hurtado de Mendoza's daughter recollected that her father flagellated himself so diligently that his back was always marked.[412] In her autobiographical writings, Carvajal related the pain she suffered as an adolescent when, at the behest of the aforementioned uncle, servants flagellated her naked upper body. As scholars signal, this practice was doubly inappropriate: first, because

---

410   Juan Eusebio Nieremberg, "P. Francisco de Villanueva," in *Varones ilustres de la Compañía de Jesús*, 2nd ed. (Bilbao: Administración del Mensajero del Corazón de Dios, 1891), 8:5–69, here 8:53–54; https://archive.org/details/varonesilustreso1niergoog/page/n81/mode/2up (accessed April 28, 2020).

411   Alonso de Andrade, "P. Estéban Fabro," in Juan Eusebio Nieremberg, *Varones ilustres de la Compañía de Jesús*, 2nd ed. (Bilbao: Administración del Mensajero del Corazón de Dios, 1889), 2:105–27, here 2:107, 2:124–25; https://archive.org/details/varonesilustresooniergoog/page/n133/mode/2up (accessed April 28, 2020). Sommervogel, *Bibliothèque*, 8:col. 686 renders his last name as Vieira.

412   Redworth, *She-Apostle*, 24, 29.

Carvajal was so young, and second because her uncle did not hold any religious position. He therefore lacked the religious authority to impose such a practice on his niece. Carvajal also chose to mortify her own body.[413] And she continued to discipline her body, as did the devout women who lived with Carvajal in England. Carvajal's "London Rule," the document that governed life in her female community in England, suggested physical discipline three times a week and virtually nightly during Lent. In corresponding with Carvajal, Jesuit Blackfan described the whips he made and sent to three women in Carvajal's community.[414]

The ideals for men and women perceived as holy differed, with ascetic practices that affected one's health becoming *de rigueur* for women. When *beatas* came to the attention of the Inquisition, their mortification practices could be crucial evidence in assessing their religious orthodoxy. Returning to Melgarejo, the devout woman in Lima in the circle of Rose of Lima who was referenced earlier for her connection to the Society, Stacey Schlau notes that Melgarejo's hale and hearty appearance troubled the inquisitors who examined her following her arrest in 1623. Along with five other female associates of Rose of Lima, Melgarejo was accused of being an *ilusa* (delusional) and *alumbrada* (a female follower of *alumbradismo*) by the Inquisition. Admittedly, in the imperial context of Spain's colonies in the Americas, ascetic expectations for devout women were especially high, with devout women's ascetic practices being expected to redeem entire communities. Whereas Rose of Lima's mortification practices were so rigorous that they negatively—and visibly—affected her health and appearance, this was not the case for Melgarejo. After observing that Melgarejo appeared well nourished and took care to put herself together well, the inquisitors concluded that she had not engaged in sufficient castigation of her body. Although the charges against Melgarejo were eventually dismissed, without the intervention of the Society of Jesus, the results could have been more serious. Jesuits removed potentially incriminating materials from the notebooks in which she recorded her visions before the Holy Office

---

413   Anne J. Cruz, "Willing Desire: Luisa de Carvajal y Mendoza and Female Subjectivity," in *Power and Gender in Renaissance Spain: Eight Women of the Mendoza Family, 1450–1650,* ed. Helen Nader (Urbana: University of Illinois Press, 2004), 177–93, here 180–81 and "Introduction," 27–32; Rhodes, "About Luisa de Carvajal y Mendoza," 3–4; Redworth, *She-Apostle,* 19–20, 25–29. See the mentioned pages in Cruz and Rhodes ("Luisa de Carvajal's Counter-Reformation Journey," 892–93) for the relevant passages from Carvajal's autobiographical writings. Both Rhodes ("Luisa de Carvajal's Counter-Reformation Journey," 893) and Redworth (*She-Apostle,* 29) raise the possibility that Hurtado de Mendoza might have observed his household staff mortifying his young niece's body. Cruz ("Introduction," 29) does not concur.

414   Redworth, "New Way of Living," 291; *She-Apostle,* 156–57.

AN OVERVIEW OF THE PRE-SUPPRESSION SOCIETY OF JESUS IN SPAIN   97

confiscated these documents. Not all Jesuits supported Melgarejo so uncondi-
tionally: one member of the Society, Muñoz, turned her in to the Inquisition.
He later withdrew the accusation.[415]

14.4   *Writing* Vitae

Members of the Society wrote about facets of devout life, like ascetic practices and exemplary deaths, in order to share beneficial examples with others.
Jesuits also composed longer works that considered the life stories of notable
devout people, mainly members of the Society and Jesuits' spiritual directees.
Given the emphasis that the Society placed on spiritual direction, it is natural
that it celebrated the exemplary lives of its spiritual directees. There are multiple reasons why large numbers of *vitae* of exemplary individuals circulated in
the early modern Catholic world. As they had done in the medieval era, clerics
wanted to share the details of exemplary lives so that others could take inspiration from positive models. After the Protestant Reformation, the circulation of
the *vitae* of devout Catholics and saints implicitly emphasized Catholicism's
devotion to saints and reinforced doctrine.[416]

Several distinguished Jesuit writers and theologians wrote *vitae*, including
Ribadeneyra.[417] Like Ribadeneyra, a number of Jesuits wrote the life stories of
multiple individuals. Luis de la Puente (1554–1624) was one such Jesuit. In writing the *vita* of fellow Jesuit Álvarez, de la Puente lauded his colleague's abilities
as a spiritual director.[418] De la Puente depicted Álvarez's attitude toward the
Society's directive that he abandon his style of prayer as an example of his
"heroica humildad y paciencia" (heroic humility and patience). Admittedly, as
Camilo María Abad (1878–1969) observes, in the nearly four decades between
that directive and de la Puente's *vita*, thinking had evolved to become more
favorable to Álvarez's approach.[419]

Not only did de la Puente's life of Álvarez provide a pious example for others
to imitate, but in printing it, de la Puente also promoted both men's religious
order. In Bilinkoff's analysis, some writers of *vitae* chose to promote other

---

415   Schlau, "Flying in Formation," 134, 133, 136–38.
416   Bilinkoff, *Related Lives*, 20, 35, 27, 32. I follow the scholarly trend of describing this life
       writing in terms other than hagiography. See Bilinkoff, *Related Lives*, 3.
417   See Jodi Bilinkoff, "The Many 'Lives' of Pedro de Ribadeneyra," *Renaissance Quarterly* 52,
       no. 1 (1999): 180–96 for Ribadeneyra's writing of exemplary life stories.
418   Bilinkoff, *Related Lives*, 20. House style prefers to represent Luis de la Puente's surname as
       de la Puente rather than La Puente, the form used in Spanish sources.
419   Luis de la Puente, *Vida del P. Baltasar Álvarez* [no edition specified], cited in Camilo
       María Abad, *Vida y escritos del V. P. Luis de la Puente de la Compañía de Jesús (1554–1624)*
       (Santander: Universidad Pontificia Comillas, 1957), 391, and Abad, *Vida y escritos*, 390.

elements that were meaningful to them, such as exemplary individuals from their native towns or people who were important to their own lives. Jesuit Marcos Torres (1606–78), for instance, wrote the life story of his mother, María de Pol (d.1659), at the behest of the bishop of Málaga.[420]

Some *vitae* were composed for specific audiences. Ribadeneyra's life of Estefanía Manrique de Castilla (d.1606), a devout laywoman from a noble family, circulated in handwritten form among Jesuit communities. Its purpose, therefore, was not to enlighten many members of the laity, but rather to offer fellow members of the Society what Bilinkoff terms "a guidebook" on how to serve as spiritual directors for well-born women like Manrique de Castilla. To this end, Ribadeneyra included information about how he conferred with Manrique de Castilla's prior confessors. At the same time, in Bilinkoff's analysis, Ribadeneyra stated in the text that he also hoped to provide upper-class women in Toledo with a positive religious example from their own sphere of experience; perhaps the informed clergy would recount her example to women who could benefit from the story.[421]

The seventeenth century marked the high point for the distribution of the lives of devout women composed by male clerics.[422] (It is not incidental that this mid-seventeenth-century boom in the circulation of life stories of devout women coincided with a period that was relatively free from major "scandal[s]" surrounding feigned piety on the part of people in Spain.)[423] As did the secular clergy and members of other religious orders, members of the Society of Jesus wrote the life stories of their confessional daughters, or compiled or edited such women's autobiographies. They also delivered or published sermons about exemplary women. In so doing, these clerics also demonstrated their skills in one of the crucial tasks for clergy of the era, distinguishing true female mystics from those with creative imaginations or those looking to deceive.[424]

Beyond demonstrating their abilities to determine true mystics from false ones, the circulation of the life stories of particular individuals known to the

---

420   Bilinkoff, *Related Lives*, 35–38. Sommervogel, *Bibliothèque*, 8:col. 131 renders his surname as "de Torres."
421   Bilinkoff, "Many 'Lives,'" 188–89; *Related Lives*, 34.
422   J. Michelle Molina and Ulrike Strasser, "Missionary Men and the Global Currency of Female Sanctity," in *Women, Religion, and the Atlantic World (1600–1800)*, ed. Daniella Kostroun and Lisa Vollendorf (Toronto: University of Toronto Press, UCLA Center for Seventeenth- and Eighteenth-Century Studies, and the William Andrews Clark Memorial Library, 2009), 156–79, here 157.
423   Weber, "Jesuit Apologias," 342–43.
424   Bilinkoff, *Related Lives*, 19.

AN OVERVIEW OF THE PRE-SUPPRESSION SOCIETY OF JESUS IN SPAIN   99

Society of Jesus also highlighted the worldwide missionary reach of the order. For this reason, Catarina de San Juan (*c*.1607–88), a devout freed slave in Puebla de los Ángeles, Mexico, who was born in India, kidnapped by pirates who sold her as a slave in the Philippines, and brought to New Spain, was an attractive subject to two Jesuits: her Spanish spiritual director Alonso Ramos (1645–1714) and the German Adam Kaller (d.1702).[425]

Considering the lingering suspicions about interior piety and women's abilities in this realm, the publication of laudatory works about spiritual women was not without controversy. Ramos's life of San Juan was prohibited by the Spanish Inquisition after this body was disturbed by the narration of her visions.[426]

In Spain, before San Juan captured the attention of the Mexican populace, Marina de Escobar (1554–1633) and her parents confessed to the Society's priests in the city of Valladolid. De la Puente would serve as her spiritual director for some two decades. After de la Puente's death, Miguel de Oreña (1576–1656), rector of the Jesuit Colegio de San Ambrosio in Valladolid, took over this role. But Escobar did not rely exclusively on guidance from members of the Society. She also confessed to Andrés de la Puente (b.1560), Luis's brother and a Dominican, for thirty-two years.[427]

Prior to 1603, Escobar lived a devout life in her family's home. Subsequently, she moved into a property owned by her relatives where she came to be joined by a number of other women who shared her interests. The group made clothing for distribution in the area. And Escobar also tutored young women to prepare them for entrance into religious communities. In some cases, she paid the required dowries to enable some to enter convents. Escobar was also a visionary. However, in the final decades of her life, she was so unwell that she was largely confined to her bed.[428] Following a 1615 vision in which St. Bridget of Sweden (also known as Birgitta) (*c*.1303–73) requested that Escobar establish a Brigittine convent in Spain, Escobar worked to lay the groundwork for this foundation. But she died before it could be realized. Following Escobar's

---

425   Molina and Strasser, "Missionary Men," 160, 157.
426   Molina and Strasser, "Missionary Men," 164–65.
427   Isabelle Poutrin, "Una lección de teología moderna: La vida maravillosa de doña Marina de Escobar (1665)," *Historia social* 57 (2007): 127–43, here 128–29.
428   Lehfeldt, *Religious Women*, 202–4; Camilo María Abad, "Escobar (Marine de)," in *Dictionnaire de spiritualité: Ascétique et mystique, doctrine et histoire*, ed. Marcel Viller, Charles Baumgartner, and André Rayez (Paris: G. Beauchesne et ses fils, 1960), 4.1:cols. 1083–86, here 4.1:col. 1083.

death in 1633, the Augustinian nun Mariana de San José (1568–1638) carried out Escobar's plans.[429]

As was the case with many visionaries, particularly women, Escobar wrote down her visions so that her spiritual director could review them. Two Jesuits, de la Puente and Andrés Pinto Ramírez (1595–1654), organized the visions that Escobar largely dictated to one of the de la Puente brothers or to a secretary into two volumes. (Escobar's poor health made it difficult for her to write them herself.) De la Puente's introduction to the first volume complemented his more theoretical writings on mental prayer.[430] In Abad's estimation, de la Puente merely chose and arranged Escobar's writing; he did not contribute much of his own writing to this volume.[431]

Escobar's writings, however, proved problematic. Despite a number of reviews before its publication, the text was denounced to the Spanish Inquisition.[432] (There were concerns that Escobar's meditative methods were not orthodox, namely that her practices bordered on *alumbradismo* or involved another passive form of meditation known as Quietism.)[433] Several examiners for the Roman Inquisition did not believe that Escobar's visions were divinely inspired, and it seemed that the volume would be placed on the Roman Index in 1691.[434] The controversy became so intense that it stalled de la Puente's beatification process for decades. Another Jesuit in Prague, Jean Tanner (1623–94), published two defenses in Latin of Escobar's life.[435] In Abad's estimation, Tanner's work was influential in allowing de la Puente to receive status as venerable.[436]

Once Escobar's orthodoxy was affirmed and her first biographer became venerable, this status became a marketing strategy for new editions of her life story, the *Vida maravillosa de la venerable virgen doña Marina de Escobar, natural de Valladolid* (Marvelous life of the venerable virgin Marina de Escobar, native of Valladolid [1665; later continuation by Pinto Ramírez]). The *portada* of Joaquín Ibarra's 1766 edition noted de la Puente's venerable status.[437]

---

429 Tore Nyberg, "The Prophetic Call of St. Birgitta and of Her Order," *Hispania sacra* 52 (2000): 367–76, here 367, 369, 372–73; Lehfeldt, *Religious Women*, 207–9.

430 Poutrin, "Lección de teología moderna," 131, 135.

431 Abad, *Vida y escritos*, 431.

432 AHN Inq. leg. 4440 exp. 25.

433 See Jacques Le Brun, "Quiétisme," in *Dictionnaire de spiritualité*, 12:cols. 2756–842 for more information about this movement.

434 Abad, *Vida y escritos*, 441, 447.

435 Poutrin, "Lección de teología moderna," 132.

436 Abad, *Vida y escritos*, 450.

437 See Luis de la Puente, *Vida maravillosa de la venerable virgen doña Marina de Escobar, natural de Valladolid* (Madrid: Joachin Ibarra, 1766); https://archive.org/details/bub_gb

AN OVERVIEW OF THE PRE-SUPPRESSION SOCIETY OF JESUS IN SPAIN 101

De la Puente's work was not the first such text to experience problems concerning the veracity or orthodoxy of the female subject's experiences. For example, in 1588, the Portuguese visionary nun María de la Visitación (b.1551), about whom Luis de Granada (1504–88) had written a biography lauding her virtues, was accused of having falsified her visions.[438]

14.5 *Non-Religious Scholarship by Jesuits*

Members of the Society of Jesus wrote widely about topics unrelated to religion. A number ventured into political philosophy in order to counter Niccolò Machiavelli's (1469–1527) ideas on leadership, as did Ribadeneyra in *Tratado de la religión y virtudes que debe tener el príncipe cristiano* (Treatise on the religion and virtues that the Christian prince should have [1595]). Others offered advice for the formation of the sovereign. Mariana's *De rege et regis institutione* (On the king and the instruction of the king [1599]) became infamous for its mention of the possibility of regicide, but it sought to instruct Philip III. As scholars often mention, the question of the justifiability of the murder of a tyrant resonated differently after the 1610 assassination of King Henry IV of France (1553–1610, r.1589–1610).[439] Mendo's emblem book *Príncipe perfecto y ministros ajustados, documentos políticos, y morales* (The perfect prince and upright ministers, political and moral documents [1657; there may have been a 1642 edition but no exemplars exist]) proffered guidance to the future sovereign on a wide range of topics, including the selection of good advisors and matters of social justice for the prince to consider vis-à-vis his subjects.

Other Jesuits offered more concrete policy advice to the sovereign. Mariana warned about the dangers of the king's inflationary monetary policy, most notably in "De monetae mutatione" (On the alteration of money [1609]), but his counsel was ignored. But this was the least of the indignities Mariana would suffer for his ideas about the dire consequences of inflation. He was imprisoned and put on trial by the Inquisition but was eventually let go, without any resolution to the legal case against him. As Gabriel Calzada relates, Philip III requested that his officials destroy all the copies of Mariana's "De monetae." They carried out the monarch's wishes so efficiently that Calzada asserts "that today it is nearly impossible to find a first edition copy of *Septem tractatus* [Seven treatises]" (the work in which this treatise appears).[440] When

---

_Fjk5hAOyg4EC/page/n6/mode/2up (accessed May 12, 2020).

438 Alison Weber, "Spiritual Administration: Gender and Discernment in the Carmelite Reform," *Sixteenth Century Journal* 31, no. 1 (Spring 2000): 123–46, here 142.

439 Astrain, *Historia de la Compañía de Jesús*, 4:99.

440 Gabriel Calzada, "Facing Inflation Alone: Juan de Mariana and His Struggle against Monetary Chaos," trans. Eric Clifford Graf, *Quarterly Journal of Austrian Economics* 21,

Nieremberg proposed a solution to the nation's ills in *Causa y remedio de los males públicos* (Cause and remedy for public ills [1642]), it was religious in nature: he suggested penitence. This suggestion was not a vague, general piece of advice. In point of fact, Nieremberg urged for the creation of a "special commission," a designated group of government officials who would perform mortifications in public in order to inspire the populace to improve their behavior.[441] When Nieremberg advocated for officials to perform public penitential ceremonies to inspire better comportment on the part of the citizenry, he did so as a member of a religious order that conducted rituals in which participants disciplined themselves in public. The missionary preacher Calatayud's guide to preaching on missions, *Misiones y sermones: Arte y método con que las establece* [...] (Missions and sermons: Art and method with which one establishes them [1754]), described such disciplinary ceremonies. One involved participants flagellating themselves in order to share in Christ's pain.[442]

Besides analyzing the issues of the day for the monarch, Jesuits also documented historical events. From the vantage point of their ministry to the *moriscos*, Jesuit chroniclers described unrest in the Alpujarras following the more strict enforcement of laws intended to suppress this group's cultural practices, including distinctive dress, bathing rituals, and language.[443] (After the second rebellion between 1568 and 1571, also known as the Second War of the Alpujarras, the *morisco* population was dispersed.)

Several historical works about Spain by Jesuits—Mariana's *Historia general de España* (General history of Spain [1601]) and Isla's *Compendio de la historia de España* (Compendium of the history of Spain [1754])—were so popular that they continued to be read widely after the expulsion. While these and a number of other historiographical works analyzed matters beyond the Society of Jesus, others focused on the history of their own religious order. Ribadeneyra's multi-volume *Historia de la Compañía de Jesús de las provincias de España y parte de las del Perú y Nueva España y Filipinas* (History of the Society of Jesus in the provinces of Spain and part of those in Peru and New Spain and the Philippines [manuscript]) took a broader approach than many of his colleagues. Some texts, like Alcázar's previously mentioned *Chrono-historia de la Compañía de Jesús en la provincia de Toledo y elogios de sus varones illustres* [...],

---

no. 2 (Summer 2018): 110–36, here 134. See 129–34 for a summary of Mariana's trial.

441   Hendrickson, *Jesuit Polymath of Madrid*, 183–84. See 163–96 for more on Nieremberg's *Causa y remedio* and the broader context of political advice.

442   Palomo, "Limosnas impresas," 245.

443   Stefania Pastore, *Il vangelo e la spada: L'inquisizione di Castiglia e i suoi critici (1460–1598)* (Rome: Edizioni di Storia e Letteratura, 2003), 285n74 references histories from the era, including Jesuit sources.

AN OVERVIEW OF THE PRE-SUPPRESSION SOCIETY OF JESUS IN SPAIN   103

which provides a year-by-year account of the province of Toledo from 1540 to 1580, are better known in the twenty-first century because they were printed. Other historical works circulated in manuscript form, as did Martín de Roa's (1561–1637) and Juan de Santibáñez's (1582–1650) accounts of the province of Andalusia.[444] Members of the order also wrote histories of individual Jesuit institutions, such as Jerónimo Román de la Higuera's (1538–1611) *Historia del colegio de Plasencia de la Compañía de Jesús* (History of the Society of Jesus's *colegio* in Plasencia [1600]), which still survive in manuscript form in archives.[445] Such texts demonstrate that scholarly (and particularly historiographical) work was not only undertaken by well-known Jesuits at the most renowned *colegios* but was also carried out in a systematic manner throughout the order.

At the same time, some of these texts serve a purpose beyond documenting the circumstances of a particular institution. María Amparo López Arandia observes that manuscript histories from Jesuit houses in the province of Andalusia generally relate successful mission trips to underserved populations. She posits that their thematic similarities explain their function: these works provided inspirational examples for other Jesuits.[446]

Scientific inquiry was not outside the scholarly purview of Spanish Jesuits. As Hendrickson explains, works of natural philosophy like Nieremberg's texts describe natural phenomena in order to motivate readers to contemplate them and, in so doing, to praise their creator.[447] After the program of Reales Estudios began at the Colegio Imperial in Madrid, Jesuits produced significant works on mathematics and on cosmography.[448]

14.6   *Pseudonymous Texts*

When Jesuits printed works, they did not always use their own names. In the twenty-first century, one of the best-known Jesuit writers of pre-suppression Spain is undoubtedly Baltasar Gracián. During his own era, however, most of his works were published pseudonymously, usually under the name Lorenzo

---

444   Pastore, *Vangelo e la spada*, 269n40 locates both manuscripts in the Biblioteca Universitaria Granada.

445   Martín López and Aranda Pérez, "Conformación de la provincia jesuítica de Toledo," 384. According to Martín López and Aranda Pérez's research, this manuscript is located in the Archivo Histórico Provincial de Castilla de la Compañía de Jesús.

446   María Amparo López Arandia, "La forja de la leyenda blanca: La imagen de la Compañía de Jesús a través de sus crónicas," *Historia social* 65 (2009): 125–46, here 135–36, 129.

447   Hendrickson, *Jesuit Polymath of Madrid*, 88.

448   See Víctor Navarro Brotóns, "Los jesuitas y la renovación científica en la España del siglo XVII," *Studia historica: Historia moderna* 14 (1996): 15–44 for an overview.

Gracián. (For the first part of *El criticón* [The master critic] [1651], however, he used García de Marlones.)

Since the 1630s, Gracián followed an unauthorized but popular practice in the Society of Jesus: he published his works without submitting them to the order for pre-publication approval. In Batllori's estimation, the skirting of this regulation was so normalized that even Jesuit superiors disregarded this mandate and circulated works without permission of the order.[449] In 1652, Nickel asked that the province investigate whether Baltasar authored the texts published in Lorenzo Gracián's name. In late 1657 or early 1658, after disobeying explicit orders to cease printing texts without the permission of his Jesuit superiors, Gracián underwent penitences, including removal from his chaired position in Scripture in Zaragoza, transfer to the Jesuit house in Graus, and restriction to a diet of bread and water.[450]

Within Jesuit circles, Gracián's authorship of his pseudonymous texts became well known. In 1643 in the *Bibliotheca scriptorum Societatis Jesu* (Library of writers of the Society of Jesus), Jesuit Philippe Alegambe (1592–1652) attributed *Arte de ingenio* (Art of ingenuity [1642]) to Gracián.[451] Although Alegambe made no mention of the other works by the same author, readers more familiar with the Spanish literary scene would assume that Baltasar Gracián also authored Lorenzo Gracián's other texts.

Beyond the Jesuit community, some did learn the pseudonymous author's identity. Cristóbal de Salazar Mardones (d.1670) wrote to Juan Francisco Andrés de Uztarroz (1606–53), royal chronicler and friend of Gracián, about *Arte de ingenio* and asked that he forward the letter to the Jesuit.[452] Another missive from Jerónimo de Ataide (d.1669) to Andrés de Uztarroz included a letter from Ataide to Gracián and a request to Andrés de Uzatarroz to forward it.[453]

At least to some degree, this knowledge did spread beyond the Aragonese circles in which these friends traveled. By 1664, six years after Gracián died,

---

449 Batllori, *Gracián y el barroco*, 91–92; Miguel Batllori and Ceferino Peralta, "La época de *El Criticón* y *El Comulgatorio*," in Miguel Batllori and Ceferino Peralta, *Baltasar Gracián en su vida y en sus obras* (Zaragoza: Institución Fernando el Católico, Diputación Provincial de Zaragoza, 1969), 157–69, here 168–69.

450 Nickel to Piquer, April 13, 1652, AHN J leg. 254 doc. 49, and March 16, 1658, AHN J leg. 254 doc. 190.

451 Philippe [Philippo] Alegambe, *Bibliotheca scriptorvm Societatis Iesv* (Antwerp: Ioannem Mevrsivm, 1643), 549 of the appendix; https://books.google.com/books?id=3YVLAAAAcA AJ&printsec=frontcover&source=gbs_ge_summary_r&cad=0#v=onepage&q&f=false (accessed May 12, 2020).

452 Cristóbal de Salazar Mardones to Juan Francisco Andrés de Uztarroz, June 28, 1642, BNE MS 8391, fol. 426.

453 Jerónimo de Ataide to Andrés de Uztarroz, April 20, 1646, BNE MS 8391, fol. 272.

AN OVERVIEW OF THE PRE-SUPPRESSION SOCIETY OF JESUS IN SPAIN 105

Madrid bookseller Santiago Martín Redondo (d.1709) published an edition of *Obras de Lorenzo Gracián* (Works of Lorenzo Gracián). One exemplar includes a partial dedication to Antonio Manrique de Guzmán (*c*.1630–79) in addition to the one promised on the frontispiece of the volume to García de Velasco (*fl*. mid-seventeenth century). In this fragmentary dedication to Manrique de Guzmán, Martín Redondo expresses uncertainty about the authorship of these texts: "Han sido tan aplaudidas las obras de Gracian (sea Lorenço su Autor, ò sea Baltasar su hermano)" (Gracián's works, [whether Lorenzo is their author or whether his brother Baltasar is], have been so applauded).[454] Lest there be any question as to whether Lorenzo might have been a convenient authorial invention, Belén Boloqui's archival research has demonstrated conclusively that Lorenzo was a flesh and blood sibling, as various religious and legal records testify to his existence.[455] Clearly, Martín Redondo heard about the possibility of the attribution to the correct Gracián brother, but he was not willing to commit to this point.

By continuing to label these texts as Lorenzo's, booksellers were not merely attempting to exploit name recognition or giving in to inertia. The Council of Castile and the Spanish Inquisition's expectations regarding authorial information likely explain this hesitation to publicly attribute the volume to Baltasar Gracián. In licensing reprints, the council checked that the new version followed the previous one and probably would have looked askance at a change in authorship. Martín Redondo conformed so that the imprint he financed would receive its official licenses and so that he could recoup his investment in the printing costs of the volumes. Once the volume was printed, if anyone complained to the Inquisition about what they considered to be an incorrect authorial attribution of Lorenzo Gracián's works, the texts could be withdrawn from circulation. This businessman did what he needed to do in order to safeguard his profit margin, but he also indicated his awareness of the complex nature of the text's authorship in his dedication.

It is less clear how well known the identities of other pseudonymous Jesuit authors became among the public at large. Gracián's fellow Jesuit Sebastián de

---

454 [Santiago Martín Redondo], "Al Ilvstrissimo señor don Antonio Manrique de Guzman, patriarca de las Indias [...]," partial dedication to Antonio Manrique de Guzmán between the folios of the dedication to García de Velasco in *Obras de Lorenzo Gracian: Tomo primero qve contiene* El criticon, primera, segunda y tercera parte; El oraculo; *Y* El heroe (Madrid: Pablo de Val, 1664), BNE R 17585. The included portion does not contain the name of the author of the dedication, but the complete version labels Martín Redondo as the author.

455 Belén Boloqui, "Niñez y adolescencia de Baltasar Gracián," in *Baltasar Gracián: Selección de estudios, investigación actual y documentación*, ed. Jorge M. Ayala (Barcelona: Anthropos, 1993), 5–62, here 20, 40, 49, 55, 58–61.

Matienzo (1588–1644) published several texts under different pseudonyms, as Martínez de la Escalera relates. Using the pseudonym Sebastián de Alvarado y Alvear, in 1628 Matienzo published *Heroida ovidiana: Dido a Eneas con paráfrasis española y morales reparos ilustrada* (An Ovidian heroine: Dido to Aeneas with an illustrated Spanish paraphrase and moral admonitions), a lengthy analysis and commentary on the portion of Ovid's work that concerns Dido and Aeneas. Martínez de la Escalera wonders whether famed playwright Lope de Vega had learned that Matienzo was the author when Lope expressed admiration for the *Heroida* in his *Laurel de Apolo* (Laurel of Apollo [1630]). Again according to Martínez de la Escalera's research, Lope and Matienzo came into contact in 1622 when Matienzo submitted Latin poetry about Xavier to Lope as the secretary of a poetic competition.[456] So perhaps Lope suspected Matienzo's authorship, but we do not know definitively.

In this environment, the actual authorship of pseudonymously published *memoriales* or other short polemical works was grist for the gossip mill. Such texts were often published with pseudonyms to comply with the letter of the Inquisition's rules that banned anonymous publications. At the same time, this strategy circumvented the spirit of that prohibition because the Inquisition had to investigate more in order to determine the actual author of any inappropriate content. This strategy was often employed by writers of *memoriales*, particularly those concerning pending legal matters. One would not want to use one's own name to overtly support one's own legal case or directly attack one's legal opponent in print. Given Poza's prolific use of *memoriales*, it should come as no surprise that he is suspected of resorting to this tactic. As Moreno and Peña Díaz relate, Poza himself admitted to the use of a number of pseudonyms; and fellow Jesuit José Eugenio Uriarte (1842–1909) attributed even more to him.[457]

Some works, either defending the Society or going on the offensive to attack those who did not favor the order, were likely assumed to be composed by members of the Society who concealed their identities with pseudonyms. But the misattribution of controversial works to Jesuits could have more serious consequences. In 1630, for example a *memorial* urging for the reform of the manner in which the Roman Inquisition prohibited books by Catholic authors in Spain was denounced to the Spanish Inquisition as a text composed by Poza, rather than the author to whom it was attributed in the work, Francisco Murcia de la Llana (*fl.* mid-seventeenth century). As Moreno and Peña Díaz specify,

---

456   José Martínez de la Escalera, "Baltasar Gracián desde Pamplona (1640)," *Archivum historicum Societatis Iesu* 55 (1986): 145–53, here 145–46.

457   Moreno Martínez and Peña Díaz, "Jesuita Juan Bautista Poza," 3:159, 3:168n1.

AN OVERVIEW OF THE PRE-SUPPRESSION SOCIETY OF JESUS IN SPAIN 107

Poza and Murcia de la Llana knew one another and shared intellectual connections to the point that Murcia de la Llana even edited one of Poza's publications. So, the question of the authorship of this text is a thorny one. The individual who denounced this imprint to the Inquisition was not alone: Uriarte also attributed this composition to Poza based on a marginal notation in one copy that specified that Poza did not "dare" to circulate it in his own name.[458] At an individual level, this issue could have further damaged Poza's relationship with an institution that was evaluating his work. Moreover, as wagging tongues associated the Jesuit community with this text, some individuals likely lost respect for the order.

As criticism of the order grew, in part because of (mis)attribution of pseudonymous publications to Jesuits, the order came to look far less favorably on publications under *noms de plume*, as Gracián's punishment indicates. By 1661, authors who published without the permission of the order (whether in their own names, under pseudonyms, or anonymously) were to "be chastised with the severe and definite penalties prescribed for them." The specific penalties mentioned include removal from one's position and "corporal punishment."[459] This decree officially ended a long-standing practice of pseudonymous publication without permission of the Society.

14.7   *Prohibitions of Jesuits' Books by the Spanish Inquisition*

Even in the 1630s, when pseudonymous texts by Jesuits were still commonplace, the order sought to exercise more control over members' publications. To prevent future prohibitions of works authored by Jesuits and the ensuing embarrassment to and criticism of the order, Vitelleschi further emphasized the importance of following the order's pre-publication review process in 1632. In letters to the provincials of Aragon and Toledo, Vitelleschi clarified various aspects of the procedure, including the selection of reviewers. The general also urged reviewers to read all the works that they were given to assess and asked provincials to provide reviewers with copies of the order's rules for publications.[460]

In evaluating the Inquisition's censorship procedures, scholars, including Ricardo García Cárcel and Javier Burgos Rincón, are puzzled by the Spanish Inquisition's "presumed incoherence" in carrying out its censorship tasks,

---

458   Moreno Martínez and Peña Díaz, "Jesuita Juan Bautista Poza," 3:167.

459   GC 11 d. 18, in *For Matters of Greater Moment*, ed. Padberg, O'Keefe, and McCarthy, 325.

460   Vitelleschi to Continente, January 17, 1632, AHN J leg. 253 doc. 155; Vitelleschi to Aguado, September 16, 1632, ARSI *Tolet.* 9 *Epp. NN.* copies of letters 1632–34, fol. 6ʳ, cited in Vincenzo Lavenia, "La scienza dell'Immacolata: Invenzione teologica, politica e censura romana nella vicenda di Juan Bautista Poza," *Roma moderna e contemporanea* 18, nos. 1–2 (2010): 179–211, here 194n59.

including the fact that prominent men of the cloth who worked with the Inquisition in censoring books also had their own texts prohibited or expurgated by the same body. While there is no doubt that the Inquisition's approach to censorship was unsystematic, Ángel Alcalá (1928–2017) suggested another motive for the subsequent prohibition of works written by those who worked for the Inquisition's censorship apparatus: payback for their decisions against others' works. Alcalá analyzed this motive in the fate of texts by Mariana.[461] Before turning to this analysis, we first need to consider Mariana's role in the Spanish Inquisition.

As Jesús Martínez de Bujanda details, Mariana was influential in the preparation of the 1583–84 Index, particularly in developing the rules that prohibited entire categories of books, such as rule 7 that proscribed books of hours written in the vernacular.[462] To return to Alcalá's analysis, Mariana was asked to assess the Antwerp Polyglot Bible prepared by Benito Arias Montano (1527–98), which León de Castro (c.1505–85), a University of Salamanca professor and defender of the Vulgate, opposed. In evaluating the Bible, Mariana severely criticized Castro's assertions but also documented how Arias Montano could have used more Catholic sources and suggested some corrections. But none of these comments rose to the level of expurgations. Those colleagues disturbed by Mariana's decision about the Polyglot Bible are thus thought to have expurgated a number of passages from Mariana's *Septem tractatus* in the 1612 Index, including his often-cited observations about the dire impact that the Inquisition's prosecution of Luis de León had on intellectuals of the era.[463]

Such petty reactions may seem antithetical to men of the cloth, but as Jesuit Pineda's feuds with writers Luis de Góngora y Argote (1561–1627) and Francisco de Quevedo y Villegas (1580–1645) demonstrate, they were not. Pineda was not a minor functionary seeking to enhance his own importance in these disputes given that he exercised a considerable amount of power in the Spanish Inquisition. In 1628, Pineda was granted special powers by Inquisitor General Antonio Zapata de Mendoza (1550–1635) to inspect any library or bookstore he

---

461 Ricardo García Cárcel and Javier Burgos Rincón, "Los criterios inquisitoriales en la censura de libros en los siglos XVI y XVII," *Historia social* 14 (1992): 97–109, here 98; Ángel Alcalá, "El control inquisitorial de intelectuales en el siglo de oro: De Nebrija al 'Indice' de Sotomayor de 1640," in *Historia de la Inquisición en España y América*, ed. J. [Joaquín] Pérez Villanueva and Bartolomé Escandell Bonet (Madrid: Biblioteca de Autores Cristianos, Centro de Estudios Inquisitoriales, 2000), 3:829–956, here 3:927–28.

462 J. [Jesús] Martínez de Bujanda, "Índices de libros prohibidos del siglo XVI," in *Historia de la Inquisición*, ed. Pérez Villanueva and Escandell Bonet, 3:773–828, here 3:817–21.

463 Alcalá, "Control inquisitorial de intelectuales," 3:928.

AN OVERVIEW OF THE PRE-SUPPRESSION SOCIETY OF JESUS IN SPAIN   109

wished. So great was Pineda's influence that Alcalá sees Pineda's impact in the 1707 Index, which was published decades after his passing.[464]

Along with teaching in the Society of Jesus's *colegios*, evaluating texts for the Inquisition, and writing biblical analysis, Pineda also judged at least one poetic contest. And this was where his tensions with Góngora began. During a competition in Seville in 1610 to celebrate the beatification of Ignatius of Loyola, Góngora was displeased that his poem did not win and, in reaction, wrote a sonnet critical of Pineda. And so in 1627, when Pineda was asked to assess a posthumous edition of Góngora's poetry dedicated to Inquisitor General Zapata without his permission (and that also mistakenly omitted Góngora's name), Pineda harshly evaluated Góngora's poetry. Pineda also included a detailed list of expurgations to be made to particular poems. As Alcalá observed, subsequent editions of Góngora's works did not reflect Pineda's suggested revisions, which were dismissed as biased.[465]

Nor was Pineda's comportment in this situation an isolated incident. Pineda and the author Quevedo also feuded over Pineda's assessment of Quevedo's *Política de Dios y gobierno de Cristo* (Politics of God and governance of Christ [parts 1 and 2, 1626 and 1655]). In this case, the body for which Pineda evaluated the text is not clear. Pineda's text has not survived, but it is cited extensively in Quevedo's 1626 response.[466] In defending himself against Pineda's charges, Quevedo alleges that most of the criticized passages result from printing errors. In point of fact, Quevedo asserts that the printer made "more than two hundred" errors in the volume.[467] As Raúl A. del Piero (d.1971) observed, in a subsequent edition of his *Política*, Quevedo referenced the "calumnies" to which the text was subjected. These were not Quevedo's only responses—in del Piero's assessment, Quevedo also satirized Pineda in "La isla de monopantos" (The island of everyone [1650]).[468]

---

464   Alcalá, "Góngora y Juan de Pineda," 3:1–2.

465   Alcalá, "Góngora y Juan de Pineda," 3:3–5, 3:19. See Dámaso Alonso, "La calificación del P. Pineda," in *Obras en verso del Homero español*, ed. Dámaso Alonso (Madrid: Consejo Superior de Investigaciones Científicas, 1963), xxx–xxxvi for a transcription of Pineda's assessment.

466   R. [Raúl] A. del Piero, "Quevedo y Juan de Pineda," *Modern Philology* 56, no. 2 (November 1958): 82–91, here 82.
       Although the first part of *Política de Dios y gobierno de Cristo* was printed in 1626, like a number of Quevedo's texts, it circulated for a number of years in manuscript form prior to printing. The second part was composed some three decades before its printing.

467   Francisco de Quevedo y Villegas, "Respuesta al padre Juan de Pineda de la Compañía de Jesús," in *Obras completas*, ed. Felicidad Buendía, 4th ed. (Madrid: Aguilar, 1958), 1:377–99, here 1:381.

468   Del Piero, "Quevedo y Juan de Pineda," 85. The text was composed *c*.1635.

Personal enmities aside, and even after tightening the order's textual approval process, works by Jesuits continued to be subjected to scrutiny by the Inquisition. The case of sermons attributed to the Portuguese Jesuit António Vieira in Madrid demonstrates the difficulty that a Jesuit author might have in controlling the material that was published in his name. (Any author could have such difficulties, but by the 1660s, Jesuits were beginning to feel that their publications were subjected to particular scrutiny.)

In 1660s Madrid, Spanish-language versions of sermons by Vieira were immensely popular. But Vieira was so concerned with the large number of sermons that were either attributed erroneously to him or that, in his estimation, "corrupted and marred" his originals that he wrote to the Consejo, also known as the Suprema, about this matter. In his letter, Vieira begged the body to prohibit these works "con aduertencia y declaracion que el llamado Autor no les reconoce por suyos" (with the warning and declaration that the named author does not recognize them as his).[469] Although Vieira's letter is not dated, it was likely written in 1677 because it was marked as arriving in Madrid in November of 1677.

Because Vieira had been placed under house arrest by the Portuguese Inquisition in the past, he would be particularly wary of attention from the Inquisition in Spain. Moreover, the Portuguese Inquisition only allowed Vieira to return to preaching in 1668, so he would not have wanted this status endangered, particularly by texts that were mistakenly attributed to him.[470]

As emerges from inquisitorial investigations, Vieira's friend and fellow Jesuit Andrés Mendo assisted with the printing of Vieira's *Las cinco piedras de la honda de David* (The five rocks from the slingshot of David [c.1676 for the first Spanish translation]) in the Spanish capital. In Mendo's interviews with the inquisitorial officials who were his colleagues—Mendo was a *calificador*—he stated that he had brought the text of *Las cinco piedras* to Lorenzo de Ibarra (d.1676) for printing. Mendo himself paid for the printing and corrected the errata. When the work was finished, he brought the volumes to be sold out of the *portería* of the Colegio Imperial, but this proved too taxing for the staff. So, Mendo then charged Ibarra with their sale. After Ibarra's death, Mendo sold

---

469 AHN Inq leg. 4440 exp. 5, fol. 18^{r-v} of bound document, undated letter from António Vieira.

470 Thomas M. Cohen, *The Fire of Tongues: António Vieira and the Missionary Church in Brazil and Portugal* (Stanford, CA: Stanford University Press, 1998), 146.

AN OVERVIEW OF THE PRE-SUPPRESSION SOCIETY OF JESUS IN SPAIN   111

the remaining copies, some two thousand of the original printing of four thousand, to Madrid bookseller Gabriel de León.[471]

According to León, he purchased three thousand unsold copies of *Las cinco piedras* (the two disagreed over the number of volumes involved) because Mendo also gave him the printing privilege for Vieira's collected sermons. When questioned about the fact that the privilege did not mention that Mendo had a privilege from Vieira to print these works, León responded that any bookseller at court could get a printing license from the Council of Castile to print a work from outside of Castile without needing the permission of the author.[472]

When questioned as to whether León had added any new material to the sermons attributed to Vieira in 1662 and 1664, the bookseller admitted that he had inserted some nine other sermons. He also admitted that he had shipped those imprints as far afield as Portugal and the Indies (i.e., the Spanish colonies). It seems that León was not exaggerating their reach. In an ignominious tribute to the wide circulation of such collections, a denunciation of a later edition of Vieira's sermons arrived in Spain from the Inquisition's Mexican tribunal.[473]

In 1678, Mendo wrote to the Inquisition. He noted that word was spreading that the Inquisition was about to prohibit Vieira's works. Mendo stated that he had never been asked to evaluate any propositions from Vieira's texts in his capacity as a *calificador*. Since Mendo counseled Vieira to write to the Inquisition and then gave the letter to an inquisitorial colleague, Mendo asked that the Inquisition's proceedings not "discredit" Vieira.[474]

In order to curate his legacy, and as a defensive strategy against further problems, Vieira began to edit and publish his own sermons. Unfortunately, this editorial enterprise did not succeed in safeguarding his works. When the Spanish Inquisition published its next Index in 1707, the sermon collection underwritten by Gabriel de León that contained the works falsely attributed to Vieira was not mentioned in the required expurgations, likely because these issues were supplanted by more serious ones in subsequent editions of Vieira's sermons. Among other problems, in the 1688 Spanish-language version of Vieira's *Sermón del rosario* (Sermon on the rosary), Lucas Sanz (c.1655–96) so misrepresented Vieira's ideas on the Trinity that the 1707 Index judged them as "heretical." Due to Sanz's mistranslation, the sermon asserted that the Father

---

471   AHN Inq. leg. 4440 exp. 5, fols. 14ᵛ–15ʳ.
472   AHN Inq. leg. 4440 exp. 5, fols. 27ᵛ–28ʳ.
473   AHN Inq. leg. 4440 exp. 5, fols. 12ᵛ–13ʳ and unfoliated documents.
474   AHN Inq. leg. 4440 exp. 5, fol. 17ʳ⁻ᵛ, letter from Andrés Mendo dated May 16, 1678.

and the Son "fathered," which is to say sexually reproduced, the Holy Spirit. In the Index, readers were told to substitute the more neutral verb "produced," which Vieira employed in the Portuguese original, for Sanz's error.[475]

While the issues involved in the prohibition of Vieira's poorly translated sermon could prove embarrassing and fuel critiques of the order, the Society deemed other prohibitions as posing a more serious threat. In 1659, one Jesuit affiliated with the Inquisition worried that potential prohibitions could hamper the order's defense of their points of view against their detractors. (And such defenses would become increasingly necessary as Jansenism gained adherents.) Juan Bautista Dávila (1598–1664), a Jesuit who worked for the Inquisition inspecting bookstores in Madrid to prevent the circulation of prohibited materials, wrote to the Inquisition at the behest of his superiors in the order. As Dávila described the situation, the Society was under attack: a "war" had been declared against the order "procurando desacreditar su doctrina" (endeavoring to discredit its doctrine) and in doing so "impeding" the work the Jesuits do for the good of Catholicism. Therefore, Dávila entreated the Inquisition to allow the continued circulation of the defense that Amadeo Guimeno (the Hispanized version of the pseudonym Amadeus Guimenius Lomarensis) had made of the Jesuits' position.[476] While the direct impact of Dávila's plea is unclear, Guimeno's Latin text continued to circulate in Spain. In 1675, Mateo de Moya (1610–84), the author behind the pseudonym, wrote to the Council of the Inquisition to explain that his work did not defend any "opinions," but rather Jesuit authors who had been falsely libeled. According to Moya, he had defended his work before the Roman Sacred Congregation, but that recently "los enemigos de la Compañia" (the enemies of the Society) had succeeded in obtaining a papal bull that would prohibit his text. He asked the Inquisition to consider "el expediente que mas convenia para el servicio de las dos magestades, diuina y humana" (what was most convenient for the service of the two majesties, human and divine).[477] Since Moya was the confessor to the queen, the reference to the sovereign was not incidental. Eventually, this pseudonymous work would be prohibited by both the Roman Inquisition and a papal bull.

---

475   *Novissimus librorum prohibitorum et expurgandorum Index pro Catholicis Hispaniarum regnis Philippi V* [1707 Index], 1:777; https://babel.hathitrust.org/cgi/pt?id=gri.ark:/13960/t9k40d491&view=1up&seq=809 (accessed May 19, 2020). The 1707 Index also excised a different passage from a 1698 imprint of Vieira's *Sermón del rosario* that concerned John the Baptist. It was this passage that was first denounced to the Mexican tribunal.

476   AHN Inq. leg. 4480 exp. 10, letter from Juan Bautista Dávila dated July 30, 1659. These documents use Baptista, a form that I have modernized in my text.

477   AHN Inq. leg. 4480 exp. 10, letter from Mateo de Moya dated October 24, 1675.

AN OVERVIEW OF THE PRE-SUPPRESSION SOCIETY OF JESUS IN SPAIN 113

Although Moya maintained that he merely defended Jesuit authors, subsequent interpreters of his work, including Astrain and Hugo Hurter (1832–1914), consider that Moya was overly generous in his defense of other Jesuits who in fact had strayed from probabilism into laxism.[478]

This text was not Moya's only forceful defense of the Jesuit position on free will against the Jansenist one. Cornelius Jansen (1585–1638) and the Jansenists believed that they had returned to the purest version of Catholic ideas. Original sin, which necessitated Jesus's redemptive sacrifice, played an important role in Jansenist theology. Jansenists also believed that the divine chose those who would be saved and therefore constrained the role of free will on the part of human beings.[479]

Moya and other members of the Society were vigorous opponents of Jansenist ideas, particularly concerning free will. However, this increasingly bitter debate led to such deep factionalism within the Catholic world that Michael A. Mullett characterizes it as an "ecclesiastical civil war." Moreover, political tensions between France and Spain added fuel to this dispute. For scholars such as Ronnie Po-Chia Hsia and Bilinkoff, this caustic dispute dissolved the harmony of the Catholic world, undermined clerics' morale, and damaged laypeople's respect for the clergy. Beyond the corrosive rhetoric of the polemical texts that circulated in the course of the dispute, the need to constantly counter the opposition's latest written salvo altered the types of texts that clerics produced. In Bilinkoff's estimation, with the exception of Jansenists who praised those devoted to their cause in print, overall the Catholic clergy wrote fewer hagiographical works as they turned their intellectual energies to this polemic and thus deprived the reading public of new hagiographical *vitae*. The declining number of exemplary life stories meant that there were fewer opportunities to promote positive examples and new potential candidates for sainthood to inspire and bring Catholics together. Ultimately, the Society's fate was intimately related to this trend: "The decline in the relating of lives and *Lives* essentially coincided with the final struggles and then expulsion of the Jesuits."[480]

---

478 Astrain, *Historia de la Compañía de Jesús*, 6:150; Hugo Hurter cited in J. [José Martínez de la] Escalera, "Moya, Mateo de," in *Diccionario histórico de la Compañía de Jesús*, ed. O'Neill and Domínguez, 3:2755–56, here 2755. As Martínez de la Escalera details, Moya's complete surname was Giménez de Moya, thus explaining the use of "Guimenius" in the pseudonym that also included the demonymic "Lomarensis" (3:2755).

479 See Michel Dupuy, "Jansénisme," in *Dictionnaire de spiritualité*, 8:cols. 102–48, here 8:col. 128, 8:cols. 136–37, 8:col. 135, 8:col. 138 for more details about Jansenism.

480 Michael A. Mullett, *The Catholic Reformation* (London: Routledge, 1999), 166 and R. [Ronnie] Po-Chia Hsia, *The World of Catholic Renewal, 1540–1770* (Cambridge: Cambridge

15 Jesuit Celebrations

The order did not spend all of its time explicitly attempting to defend itself, as the Society was especially proud to recognize Jesuits' progress toward canonization. During this era, celebrations of notable events were fêted in poetic competitions. Jesuits frequently marked important occasions in their community in this fashion, as in the "poetic joust" at the Colegio de Murcia to honor Luigi Gonzaga (1568–1591) and Stanisław Kostka (1550–68). Printed compilations of poetry, like the one the archbishop of Cartagena published around 1728 of the aforementioned celebration in Murcia, as well as sermons, emblems, or shorter descriptive pamphlets, were often produced to commemorate these occasions.[481]

At the Colegio de la Encarnación in Marchena (Seville), Lozano Navarro found a distinct pattern to such celebrations. When the Ponce de León family, local nobles who had the seat for the duchy of Arcos in Marchena, contributed financially to festivities at the Jesuit *colegio*, the celebrations were quite elaborate, even "spectacular." However, without subsidies from these nobles, the festivities were much more restrained.[482]

Nobles' patronage of such events was one aspect of the complex relationships between the Society of Jesus and local elites that played out throughout Iberia. Other more permanent ostentatious displays could be misconstrued as signs of the Jesuits' wealth. In order to shore up the perilous financial situation of the Jesuit Colegio de San Gil in Toledo, the order accepted a substantial donation from royal almoner Diego de Guzmán de Haro (1566–1631), but the funds came with a number of conditions. Along with Masses to commemorate the man who specified that he must be remembered as the *colegio*'s "founder and patron," a large and expensive stone tomb for Guzmán and his nephews was built in the main chapel of the *colegio*. Moreover, the family's coat of arms decorated the walls of the chapel. Since such displays were a condition of the

---

University Press, 1998), 206–9, cited in Bilinkoff, *Related Lives*, 114, and Bilinkoff, *Related Lives*, 114. See Bilinkoff, *Related Lives*, 33–35 for the unifying goals of this genre.

481   Antonio de Rueda Marín [Rveda Marin], *Justa poetica, celebrada en el insigne Colegio de la Compañia de Jesus, de esta [...] Ciudad de Murcia, el día 17 de noviembre del año de 1727 en cvlto de S. Luis Gonzaga, estudiante, y de S. Estanislao de Kostka* (Murcia: Jayme Mesnier, [1728?]), BNE. This text is available in the BDH. See http://bdh-rd.bne.es/viewer .vm?id=0000039110&page=1 (accessed May 12, 2020). Simón Díaz's *Historia*, 1:183–506 transcribes a number of short texts that document festivities at the Colegio Imperial.

482   Lozano Navarro, "Entre jesuitas y beatas," 55–59.

AN OVERVIEW OF THE PRE-SUPPRESSION SOCIETY OF JESUS IN SPAIN   115

donation that was required in order to obtain financial solvency for the *colegio*, they did not connote the order's wealth.[483]

In Marchena, the relationship between the Ponce de León family and the Society was a mutually beneficial "symbiosis" in Lozano Navarro's analysis. On the part of the Jesuits, the relatively new religious community received economic benefits and well-placed connections. The order also gained influence through its association with the Ponce de León family. In Lozano Navarro's estimation, the Jesuits came to affect decisions about issues arising in the family's sprawling territories. On the part of the Ponce de León family, they burnished their own reputation as faithful Catholics, and in practical terms, obtained confessors for their family and a school in which offspring of their circle of retainers could be educated. (Lozano Navarro observes that the Society designated its most distinguished members as rectors of this *colegio* with the hope that they also would become confessors to the Ponce de León family.)[484]

A savvy observer of the extravagant celebrations at the *colegio* in Marchena in 1610 to mark Loyola's beatification would perceive that the three sets of symbols—the coat of arms of the noble house of Arcos; the personal one of María de Toledo (d. before 1575), the wife of the second duke of Arcos Luis Cristóbal Ponce de León (1528–73) who financed the foundation of the *colegio*; and the IHS symbol of the Society of Jesus—that alternated on the false columns erected for the festivities meant that the noble family underwrote the celebration.[485] However, others might not have parsed that the presence of the coats of arms related to the Ponce de León family telegraphed financial sponsorship. Such an individual might have come away with the impression that the Jesuits were spendthrifts with so much wealth at their disposal that they spent profligately on parties to honor their own.

Surviving evidence suggests that some were not impressed by such displays at Jesuit houses. For example, the anonymous manuscript *romance* (a poetic form with verses of eight syllables) "Descripción de las fiestas de la Compañía de Jesús: Perico y Marica" (Description of the celebrations of the Society of Jesus: Perico and Marica [manuscript copy dated to the seventeenth century by the Biblioteca Nacional de España]) offers a scathing assessment of the celebration of an unspecified new saint in Madrid. (Perico and Marica are working-class personages who critique various aspects of Spanish society in a number of anonymous poems.) Perico, in writing to his wife Marica, recounts

---

483   Bilinkoff, *Avila of Saint Teresa*, 162–63.
484   Lozano Navarro, "Entre jesuitas y beatas," 54–55.
485   Lozano Navarro, "Entre jesuitas y beatas," 53, 56.

that the Jesuits spent lavishly on decorations, like groves of pine trees, to adorn their *colegio* for the festivities. Although Perico realizes that the Jesuits did not fund these purchases themselves, he is irritated by their frivolous expenditure of others' money. More seriously in Perico's estimation, the Jesuits defiled their church by transforming it into a "corral de comedias" (a secular theater). Perico is disturbed that audience members turned their backs to the altar to search for their seats. Marica's response offers a more pointed critique of the order, which arrogantly "fear[s] no one" and possesses the grand ambition to "subjugate the world." Again according to Marica, the community initially finds humor in the many publications against it, but eventually such texts are prohibited by decree, implying that the order takes action against them.[486] These fictional characters' observations about the time and expense involved in the preparation for theatrical performances in Jesuit communities are confirmed by non-fictional sources.[487]

Conscious of this potential image problem, the Society had long urged for restraint in festivities to honor Jesuit occasions. Following the decree of the Seventh General Congregation (1615–16), which designated September 27 as a day on which Jesuits should give thanks for the founding of the Society, in 1618 Vitelleschi advised that some provinces were holding celebrations that transgressed the limits of religious modesty. The general specified that outsiders need not be invited to Jesuit houses to share this occasion. Rather, priests should say Mass, brothers should take Communion, and classes should be held as usual.[488] In 1624, Rome sent guidelines for modest celebrations honoring Saints Ignatius of Loyola and Francis Xavier: Jesuits were to take Communion and the food offered in the refectory should be "como en el dia mas solemne del año" (as on the most solemn day of the year).[489] Such concerns persisted in other generalates. In 1656, Superior General Nickel requested that Piquer plan to curtail what the general deemed were excessive celebrations in the Jesuit community in Barcelona because such expenditures were particularly inappropriate at that moment in time.[490]

Jesuit houses also marked moments of importance in the broader Christian community. *Deleitar aprovechando* (Entertaining while instructing [1635]), a collection of religiously themed prose, poetry, and plays composed by the

---

486   "Descripcion," BNE MS 12935–34, fols. 1ᵛ, 2ʳ⁻ᵛ.

487   See Kallendorf, *Conscience on Stage*, especially 19–20 for examples.

488   GC 7 d. 54, in *For Matters of Greater Moment*, ed. Padberg, O'Keefe, and McCarthy, 268; Vitelleschi to Sanz, December 12, 1618, AHN J leg. 253 doc. 72.

489   Vitelleschi to Continente, July 1, 1624, AHN J leg. 253 doc. 120.

490   Nickel to Piquer, July 29, 1656, AHN J leg. 254 doc. 153.

AN OVERVIEW OF THE PRE-SUPPRESSION SOCIETY OF JESUS IN SPAIN   117

Mercedarian friar Gabriel Téllez (c.1579–1648) (better known by his pseudonym Tirso de Molina) uses Jesuits' Carnival activities as a point of departure
for his fiction. In the frame of *Deleitar*, three noble couples wishing to avoid the
excesses of the season host social events during the last three days prior to Ash
Wednesday at which the included texts are performed. Don Luis, one of the
hosts, suggests "que contrapongamos nuestros pasatiempos a los totalmente
licenciosos del vulgo" (let us contrast our passtimes with the completely licen-
tious ones of the common people). In the ensuing conversation, don Francisco
justifies this pre-Lenten diversion by referencing men of the cloth "que, con
semejantes recreos" (who, with similar entertainments), have theatrical works
performed in their *colegios* for audiences that include distinguished guests.
Although the Jesuits are not mentioned explicitly in this passage, their houses
were known to stage plays; and the reference to *colegios* seems to point to the
Society. Moreover, their influence is more directly acknowledged in the poetic contest that follows Sunday afternoon's theatrical performance. Don Luis
concedes that the pious activities of the Society of Jesus have transformed
"Carnival" into "Holy Week." And in gratitude for the "espirituales recreos"
(spiritual recreations), which don Luis and his friends "imitate," they declaim
poetry honoring Ignatius and Xavier.[491]

According to the order's regulations, any festivities held at Jesuit institutions
were not to be ostentatious. Correspondence between Rome and the Jesuit
province of Aragon mandated that the Society's commemorations not become
excessive displays. Religious modesty was also to be kept in mind when entertaining lay guests. In 1633, Vitelleschi related to Continente that Jesuits in
Valencia had treated guests to a feast, including multiple meat courses and a
number of desserts. Vitelleschi asked Continente to investigate this "disorder"
and advised that nothing exceeding the Society's common practice should
be allowed.[492]

When participating in municipal celebrations, Jesuits were to comport
themselves in accordance with their clerical status. In 1634, Vitelleschi asked
Continente to investigate a report received in Rome that Jesuits served as judges at a poetic contest on Three Kings' Day in Barcelona in which insulting language was employed. If this was the case, the Jesuits involved should receive
penances.[493]

---

491   Tirso de Molina, *Deleitar aprovechando*, ed. Pilar Palomo Vázquez (Madrid: Turner, 1994),
       24–25, 239–40.
492   Vitelleschi to Continente, May 25, 1633, AHN J leg. 253 doc. 242.
493   Vitelleschi to Continente, June 24, 1634, ANH J leg. 253 doc. 214.

16   Domestic Life in the Society

Such attention to deportment and consumption in public was not a mere strat-agem. In 1618, Vitelleschi warned that "abuses" seemed to be growing on a daily basis and that Jesuits paid too much attention to "comfort" and "amusement." Vitelleschi reminded Sanz about Acquaviva's injunction that members avoid the overconsumption of meat. And then Vitelleschi explained that a medical license to eat meat for health reasons was not a permission to indulge, but an exemption from sin for partaking of such food on days of abstinence.[494] In 1638, in relating a number of complaints received from the province of Aragon, Vitelleschi noted the ease with which Jesuits ate meat on prohibited days.[495]

Meals at provincial congregations were subject to scrutiny. In 1629, Vitelleschi remarked that food expenditures for these events "excederse mucho los li-mites de la moderacion Religiosa" (greatly exceed[ed] the limits of religious moderation).[496] Despite this warning, in 1636 Vitelleschi also commented on the overly indulgent fare served at that provincial congregation.[497]

Yet, neglect of the alimentary needs of Jesuits could also provoke reaction from Rome. After all, there were practical motives for a certain level of creature comforts and nourishing food: they kept members healthy so that they could perform their duties. When Vitelleschi related to Provincial Pedro Fons (in of-fice 1638–41) that Rome had received reports that the food served in the refec-tory in Zaragoza was "bad," he did so because it was said that poor food had a negative impact on the health of those who were already unwell.[498]

In a similar vein, in 1618, Vitelleschi observed that inadequacies at the *colegio* in Urgell had a broad impact. According to the general's information, most of the Jesuits residing in the *colegio* in Urgell were sick with fevers due to the inadequacy of the building. Vitelleschi requested that Sanz take action on this matter because doing so was in the best interest of the Jesuit community. With better accommodation, those serving there would be more content and therefore more helpful to the order.[499]

Beyond food, the trappings of Jesuits' domestic life were also expected to be sufficiently austere. Practices that exceeded these standards were reported to

---

494   Vitelleschi to Sanz, December 12, 1618, AHN J leg. 253 doc. 74.

495   Vitelleschi to Ribas, May 28, 1638, AHN J leg. 253 doc. 329.

496   Response to a *memorial* from Francisco de Caspe (the Castilian version of Casp), procura-tor of the province of Aragon, March 4, 1629, AHN J leg. 253 doc. 124.

497   Vitelleschi to Ribas, September 13, 1636, AHN J leg. 253 doc. 278.

498   Vitelleschi to Fons, May 14, 1639, AHN J leg. 253 doc. 350.

499   Vitelleschi to Sanz, October 8, 1618, AHN J leg. 253 doc. 70.

Rome. Astrain relates the faults that Vitelleschi found in the Spanish provinces in the 1620s and 1630s. The unsuitable consumption of chocolate by Jesuits was remarked upon in several provinces over the years. One of the more unusual items deemed an inappropriate luxury was the bathtub at the Casa Profesa in Madrid.[500]

As Spanish society became increasingly interested in luxury goods, maintaining these standards became more challenging. Complaints were made to Rome about the rector of Tarazona, who, during an illness, had pillows that were not judged appropriate for a man of the cloth, a bell at the head of his bed, and a Jesuit brother in his room to attend to him.[501] Another rector, this one in Girona, was reported to have an overly comfortable bedroom.[502] Superiors were not the only ones accused of indulging in immodest comforts. In 1636, Vitelleschi related a report that ten or twelve Jesuits in Valencia were using two mattresses and two pillows without a medical need to do so.[503] In the same year, Vitelleschi approved of Valencia's plan to have some "good" mattresses made so that residents could avoid using two: this privilege was reserved for the sick.[504] Yet, a year later Rome informed the province that the number of men in Valencia using two mattresses had grown to eighteen.[505]

17 Seventeenth-Century Crises

Such attention to domestic arrangements sought to allow members to live modestly and prepare them for the challenges of their work. Martin P. Harney (1896–1976) characterized the order's second century as "a time of quiet and steady development of good works already established. If the labors of the members were not seemingly as grand as those of the first century, the heroic age, they were none the less quite as intense."[506] This was largely the case in Spain, although a series of crises—war, difficult financial conditions, and epidemic disease—upended the order's routine.

---

500   Astrain, *Historia de la Compañía de Jesús*, 5:55, 58, 59.
501   Vitelleschi to Ribas, May 24, 1636, AHN J leg. 253 doc. 267.
502   Vitelleschi to Fons, January 22, 1639, AHN J leg. 253 doc. 338.
503   Vitelleschi to Ribas, January 31, 1636, AHN J leg. 253 doc. 258.
504   Vitelleschi to Ribas, September 13, 1636, AHN J leg. 253 doc. 277.
505   Vitelleschi to Ribas, May 30, 1637, AHN J leg. 253 doc. 303.
506   Martin P. Harney, *The Jesuits in History: The Society of Jesus through Four Centuries* (New York: America Press, 1941), 259.

17.1 The Reapers' War

After the Catalonian legislative body, the Catalan Cortes, failed to provide Philip IV with either the troops he requested or funds to support Spain's military efforts in 1626, tensions surrounding the monarchy's demands on the region started to build. Once the Franco-Spanish War began in 1635, Catalans were increasingly unhappy with the actions of Spanish troops quartered in the region.[507] In this charged atmosphere, anti-monarchical comments by Jesuits, regardless of which monarch the remarks targeted, were not tolerated by superiors. After receiving information in 1634 that negative comments about the king of France were being made in a number of *colegios*, Vitelleschi requested that Continente put a stop to such talk.[508] On other occasions, Jesuits in the province of Aragon were to be disciplined for negative comments concerning the Spanish monarch and his ministers in 1635 and the count-duke of Olivares, Philip IV's closest advisor, and the king of France in 1636.[509]

As rebellion loomed in Catalonia and Portugal as Spain was at war with France, nobles approached the order for various types of assistance. In 1639, the count-duke wrote to Vitelleschi to request that Jesuits say a total of three hundred daily Masses for the king of Spain.[510] In the summer of 1640, an attack on the viceroy's palace in Barcelona began the rebellion against the crown in Catalonia. When French forces began fighting alongside the Catalans against Spanish forces, this conflict became part of the larger Franco-Spanish War. A few months after hostilities began in Catalonia, on September 11, 1640, Vitelleschi asked that the provincial advise all superiors that Jesuits should avoid saying or doing anything to foment the rebellion.[511]

Either late in 1639 or early in 1640, Francisco María Carrafa Castrioto y Gonzaga (d.1642), the duke of Nocera and viceroy of Aragon and Navarre, requested that Baltasar Gracián become his confessor. In keeping with the Society's practice of serving the religious needs of nobles when possible, Vitelleschi allowed Gracián to travel with Carrafa.[512] Accompanying the duke in Pamplona in the fall of 1640, Gracián related the devastating, and

---

507   See J. [John] H. Elliott, *The Count-Duke of Olivares: The Statesman in an Age of Decline* (New Haven: Yale University Press, 1986), 255–66 for a detailed analysis of these events.

508   Vitelleschi to Continente, March 25, 1634, AHN J leg. 253 doc. 205.

509   Vitelleschi to Continente, March 20, 1635, AHN J leg. 253 doc. 234 and to Ribas, May 24, 1636, AHN J leg. 253 doc. 267.

510   Vitelleschi to Fons, June 18, 1639, AHN J leg. 253 doc. 353.

511   Vitelleschi to Fons, September 11, 1640, AHN J leg. 253 doc. 384.

512   Vitelleschi to Fons, July 6, 1640, AHN J leg. 253 doc. 381. See Batllori, *Gracián y el barroco*, 186 for a transcription of the relevant portion of the letter. We do not know the date of Carrafa's original request. Batllori posits this timeframe (*Gracián y el barroco*, 60). Carrafa's last name is sometimes rendered as Carafa and his title as duke of Nochera.

AN OVERVIEW OF THE PRE-SUPPRESSION SOCIETY OF JESUS IN SPAIN

unsuccessful, attempt to prevent the entry of French forces into Spain. In a letter to fellow Jesuit Matienzo, Gracián recounted that the troops led by a nephew of one of the Condés had beheaded numerous Spanish soldiers, severely wounded the arm of Juan de Garay Otáñez (1586–1650), and killed the horse of another prominent Spaniard before Philip IV's troops retreated from the engagement. Although Gracián does not specify the location of this battle for his correspondent, Martínez de la Escalera identifies it as the attack at Illa.[513]

Gracián's association with Carrafa, who was eventually imprisoned for his opposition to Olivares's policy favoring war with Catalonia,[514] was not held against the Jesuit by those close to the count-duke. Like a number of other Jesuits in the region, Gracián accompanied a nobleman who commanded royal forces in Catalonia, in Gracián's case Diego Felípez de Guzmán (1582–1655), marquis of Leganés, and relative of Olivares. (Jesuits had long accompanied the Spanish military, including at the Battle of Lepanto [October 7, 1571] and on the Invincible Armada's tragic voyage.)[515] Gracián related his experiences in the area surrounding Lleida in a letter. Due to the illness or capture of the other clerics, Gracián found himself the only chaplain for the Spanish forces retaking Lleida from the French. He heard confessions "while marching all night long" and in encampments. Later, after the battle, not recognizing partisan lines among those succumbing to their wounds, Gracián ministered to the dying on both sides. But he admitted that some refused the services of a Catholic priest.[516] In addition to serving as chaplains to nobles commanding royal forces, Jesuits also made missions to minister to Catalan and French troops.[517]

In terms of the Jesuits' relationship with the Spanish monarchy, this conflict involving the French and Spanish in Catalonia followed an especially difficult period. In 1630, Spanish diplomats informed Philip IV that the Jesuit confessors of the Catholic delegates at the Diet of Regensburg were collaborating to thwart Spanish influence in the Germanic territories. As Fernando Negredo del Cerro and Enrique Villalba Pérez assert, an analysis of Spanish governmental documents provides a new perspective on the 1631 crisis between

---

513 Baltasar Gracián to Sebastián de Matienzo, October 20, 1640 transcribed in Martínez de la Escalera, "Baltasar Gracián desde Pamplona," 151, 151n35.

514 Adolphe Coster, *Baltasar Gracián*, trans. Ricardo del Arco (Zaragoza: Institución Fernando el Católico, 1947), 33, 37n16.

515 Maryks, *Jesuit Order as a Synagogue of Jews*, 101.

516 Baltasar Gracián, November 24, 1646 from subsequent correspondence between two Jesuits, in *Obras completas*, ed. E. [Evaristo] Correa Calderón (Madrid: M. Aguilar, 1944), 929–34, here 934, 930, 933.

517 Miguel Batllori, "Los jesuitas y la guerra de Cataluña (1640–1659)," in Batllori and Peralta, *Baltasar Gracián*, 189–223, here 196.

Philip IV and Vitelleschi. According to Negredo del Cerro and Villalba Pérez's research, it was not Wilhelm Lamormaini's (1570–1648) actions as confessor of Ferdinand II (1578–1637, r.1619–37) but another incident that most seriously damaged the relationship between the Spanish sovereign and Jesuit superior general. In a meeting with Cardinal Gaspar de Borja (1580–1645), Vitelleschi expressed a desire to help improve the fractured relationship between the Spanish king and Ferdinand II to the cardinal, an emissary of Philip IV. Following this meeting, however, Spanish governmental officials soon learned that Vitelleschi had written to Ferdinand II to inform him that Philip IV had asked that Lamormaini be removed as the Holy Roman emperor's confessor. Although various blustering reactions against the Society of Jesus were assuaged, in Negredo del Cerro and Villalba Pérez's estimation, this incident motivated Vitelleschi to strengthen the Society's relationship with France. Moreover, Negredo del Cerro and Villalba Pérez signal that this incident had long-lasting negative consequences for the prestige of the Society at the court of Philip IV: the number of Jesuits who were appointed to positions as "predicadores reales" (royal preachers) declined precipitously between 1637 and 1665.[518]

This was only one source of resentment on the part of the Spanish monarchy. Philip IV was also displeased with the Jesuits' actions in Portugal during the rebellion against Spanish control, but that conflict lies outside the scope of this essay. Nonetheless, Jesuits in the province of Aragon attempted to assuage royal pique. According to Batllori's research, delegates to the 1642 provincial congregation, which was not attended by representatives of the six Jesuit houses in areas of Catalonia then controlled by French forces, noted that Philip IV felt slighted by the order. (The monarch felt that some Jesuits had not given their full-throated support to the Spanish crown.) The body discussed whether the group should ask Vitelleschi to express the province's support for the Spanish monarch but ultimately decided to ask the their own provincial to do so. As Batllori indicates, the general could not afford to alienate the king of France, and therefore would have had less interest in expressing support for Philip IV.[519]

Despite Vitelleschi's advice to avoid fomenting anti-Spanish feeling, three Jesuits gained reputations as partial to French rule during the uprising in

---

518   Fernando Negredo del Cerro and Enrique Villalba Pérez, "Los jesuitas y la monarquía hispánica en el contexto de la Guerra de los treinta años 1625–1635," *Hispania sacra* 67 (2015): 635–72, here 655, 657–61, 665.

519   Miguel Batllori, "Entre la corte y Cataluña en armas," in Batllori and Peralta, *Baltasar Gracián*, 77–97, here 85. See Batllori, *Gracián y el barroco*, 186 for a transcription of this deliberation.

AN OVERVIEW OF THE PRE-SUPPRESSION SOCIETY OF JESUS IN SPAIN 123

Catalonia. After the rebellion ended, Nickel suggested that the three should be reassigned out of the area.[520] Since Philip IV's government in the person of Juan José de Austria (1629–79), member of the victorious military forces and later viceroy, offered amnesty to partisans of the French, these Jesuits' departure was not required by the monarchy. Instead, Nickel's desire to treat Jesuits who supported the French more severely than royal officials required likely represented an overt attempt to appease the Spanish monarchy. Ultimately, however, Alastuey left the three Jesuits in place in Catalonia. Batllori interprets the differing opinions of the two superiors in terms of their personalities and also Rome's lack of understanding of Philip IV and Juan José de Austria's "pacifying and conciliatory attitude" toward the Catalan populace.[521] While both these factors likely influenced Alastuey's and Nickel's decision-making process, this incident also illustrates an under-appreciated aspect of Jesuit governance.

Loyola's dictates on obeying instructions from superiors are very well known; however, other Ignatian sources privilege the abilities of local superiors to make decisions.[522] Locals' detailed knowledge of particular situations gives them an advantage over distant superiors less familiar with the salient details.[523] In this case, Alastuey trusted his own assessment, both of the political and societal context and of the three individuals, and acted accordingly. As Batllori signals, the provincial's instincts proved sound. One of the Jesuits whom Nickel wanted to deport, Joseph de Olzina (1607–67), became so friendly with Juan José de Austria that the viceroy helped Olzina print a treatise on the immaculate conception.[524]

As a result of the Peace of the Pyrenees (1659), several territories, including what had been the most northeasterly portion of Spanish Catalonia before the conflict, passed to French control. According to Batllori's research, the preference for the use of French over Catalan on the part of the French Jesuits who came to staff these houses helped "assimilate" the region into France.[525]

---

520 Nickel to Alastuey, August 30, 1653, AHN J leg. 254 doc. 82.
521 Batllori, "Jesuitas y la guerra de Cataluña," 208–9. Such disputes concerning politics were not unique to the Jesuits located in the province of Aragon. Batllori observes that even Jesuits in Madrid were divided into pro- and anti-Olivares factions ("Jesuitas y la guerra de Cataluña," 190–91).
522 See the most well-known example in Ignatius, Sociis lusitanis, 26 martii 1553, epist. 3304, in *Epp. Ign.* 4, 669–81.
523 See, for example, Ignatius to Simon Rodrigues, Patri Simoni Roderico, medio anno 1542, epist. 44, *Epp. Ign.* 1, 211–12.
524 Batllori, "Jesuitas y la guerra de Cataluña," 209.
525 Batllori, "Jesuitas y la guerra de Cataluña," 221.

17.2 *Financial Crises*

Beginning in the 1620s, royal monetary policy created inflation. In an attempt to remedy the problem, the currency was devalued in 1628, which led to significant losses. And wars in Italy and then Catalonia put further strains on the fiscal situation.[526] Under these conditions, the order became more cautious about the financial resources needed to support *colegios*. In 1637, Vitelleschi informed Ribas that the general planned to decline the offer of a Jesuit *colegio* in Orihuela because the unspecified conditions that would be imposed by the potential founder would be a burden. Moreover, there seemed to have been myriad problems with the location, not least that the order did not want to establish another small *colegio* in an under-resourced area.[527] Early in 1638, Vitelleschi stood firm, even as the city of Orihuela and Tomás Pedro (*fl.* seventeenth century), presumably the aforementioned patron, wrote to Rome to ask that the Society establish a presence in this locale. In lieu of a *colegio*, Vitelleschi asked that Orihuiela be included in the order's missions, and specifically requested a Jesuit presence there during Advent and Lent.[528]

The challenging fiscal situation even caused the order to close established *colegios*. Vitelleschi shared details about the closing of the Colegio de Bellimar in the province of Castile. In this case, Vitelleschi observed that the small yearly benefit (eighty *ducados* per annum) that the *colegio* received at its foundation was not sufficient. Beyond stretched finances, the community in which the institution was located was small, some thirty houses, and therefore offered few opportunities to Jesuits "del exercicio de los ministerios, los pocos nuestros que alli estan viuan amargados, y con no pequeño riesgo de la disciplina religiosa" (for the exercise of their ministries, the few of ours who are there live embittered, and not with small risk to religious discipline).[529] Thus, an inappropriately placed institution posed dangers beyond fiscal risks.

Economic conditions worsened following the crown's bankruptcies in 1647 and 1653. England's alliance with France blockaded Spain's ports and disrupted the arrival of the treasure fleet from the Americas.[530] Correspondence between Rome and the province of Aragon indicates that by 1639 the economic health of the province had suffered, as had that of individual houses in the 1640s and 50s. There was no facile remedy for these situations. In responding

---

526 Elliott, *Imperial Spain*, 334–35.
527 Vitelleschi to Ribas, August 30, 1637, AHN J leg. 253 doc. 307.
528 Vitelleschi to Ribas, January 25, 1638, AHN J leg. 253 doc. 317.
529 Vitelleschi to Continente, July 31, 1634, AHN J leg. 253 doc. 219.
530 Elliott, *Imperial Spain*, 356–57.

AN OVERVIEW OF THE PRE-SUPPRESSION SOCIETY OF JESUS IN SPAIN 125

to a complaint from the house in Girona that there was not sufficient food or clothing, Vitelleschi acknowledged that it had been a difficult year in that area and requested that everything possible be done so that Jesuits did not lack the basic necessities.[531] In 1652, the *colegio* in Valencia was "reduced to misery and poverty."[532] In 1654, Zaragoza suffered after several years in which the olive crops were lost to freezes.[533]

17.3 Ministerial Consequences of Upheavals and Epidemics

Financial challenges were not the only issues facing Spanish Jesuit communities. War and disease inevitably altered the nature of Jesuits' ministry. Due to the province of Aragon's proximity to the fighting, the impact of the Reapers' War was greatest on it. In some cases, these challenges merely altered established routines. In 1652, in response to the rector of Girona's explanation that his men did not minister in hospitals because of epidemics nor make pilgrimages because of the war, Nickel asked that the Jesuits perform "more external mortifications" until circumstances could allow them to return to their normal practices.[534]

Other changes were more dramatic. When plague broke out in a city, after the 1550s Jesuit policy generally followed the counsel of medical authorities like Girolamo Fracastoro (c.1478–1553), who advocated for departure from the affected area.[535] According to A. Lynn Martin's research, the "death of twenty Jesuits" in a 1559 outbreak of plague in the province of Aragon was decisive— after that loss, the order sought to limit the number of Jesuits who ministered to the stricken.[536] When plague threatened cities in which Jesuits resided, generals routinely asked most members and students to evacuate, leaving behind a skeleton staff to look after the property and minister to the ill in the area. Nickel made such requests to Provincials Fons and Francisco Franco (d.1675) respectively in 1651 and 1652 when plague endangered the Jesuit communities in Barcelona and Zaragoza.[537]

---

531   Vitelleschi to Provincial Crespin López, May 18, 1631, AHN J leg. 253 doc. 131.
532   Nickel to Piquer, July 10, 1652, AHN J leg. 254 doc. 62.
533   Nickel to Alastuey, August 24, 1654, AHN J leg. 254 doc. 108.
534   Nickel to Fons, April 8, 1652, AHN J leg. 254 doc. 46.
535   Martin, *Plague?*, 125.
536   Martin, *Plague?*, 120–21.
537   Nickel to Fons, July 27, 1651, AHN J leg. 254 doc. 27 and to Provincial Francisco Franco, September 26, 1652, AHN J leg. 254 doc. 67. (The date in July is difficult to read in the first letter.)

18   Controlling Chocolate and Tobacco Usage in the Society

After the war ended and the plague abated, correspondence between Rome and Spanish Jesuit provinces resumed more familiar routines, including attempts on the part of generals to restrain Jesuits' participation in two highly popular fads: the consumption of chocolate and tobacco. A 1660 letter from Oliva to Provincial Domingo Langa (in office 1662–65) specified that members could only use tobacco, with the permission of the provincial, if they had a medical need for it. The process for licensing the consumption of chocolate was more stringent: use of cacao products required the explicit permission of the general.[538] In evaluating requests, if Oliva found them credible, he requested that they then be evaluated at the provincial level where the "edad, trabajos y meritos" (age, works, and merits) of potential chocolate consumers were well known.[539] If Jesuits were granted a license to take chocolate, they were supposed to do so in secret, presumably to avoid normalizing the behavior in the community or motivating others to seek permission.[540]

Despite this rigorous process, by 1663 Oliva remarked to Langa that both tobacco use and chocolate consumption were spreading in the order. In fact, in Oliva's estimation, Jesuits' desire to consume chocolate was spurring their interest in saying Mass early. Since the general had only issued a few licenses to use cacao products, he surmised that these individuals were indulging without the requisite permission. Oliva ordered that Langa use "efficacious remedies" to rein in these indulgences.[541] Two years later, Oliva again warned Langa about the "el uso, ò el abuso del Tabaco, y chocolate" (use, or abuse of tobacco, and chocolate), asked him to correct these behaviors, and once again remarked that he had issued a very small number of licenses to consume chocolate.[542]

Beyond Jesuits' regulations for members, issues relating to chocolate were a broader point of concern for the Catholic Church. The question of whether or not chocolate could be consumed without breaking the ecclesiastical fast became the subject of debate among Catholic theologians. In Sophie D. Coe (1933–94) and Michael D. Coe's (1929–2019) assessment, Dominicans argued that one could not drink chocolate during periods of fasting whereas Jesuits maintained that doing so was permissible. Coe and Coe also observe that the Jesuits "were far from uninterested parties" in this argument because of

---

538   Oliva to Provincial Domingo Langa, January 30, 1660, AHN J leg. 255 doc. 135 positive microfilm 1360.

539   Oliva to Piquer, August 22, 1667, AHN J leg. 255 doc. 148 positive microfilm 1360.

540   Oliva to Langa, January 30, 1660, AHN J leg. 255 doc. 135 positive microfilm 1360.

541   Oliva to Langa, November 18, 1663, AHN J leg. 255 doc. 76 positive microfilm 1360.

542   Oliva to Langa, July 30, 1665, AHN J leg. 255 doc. 125 positive microfilm 1360.

AN OVERVIEW OF THE PRE-SUPPRESSION SOCIETY OF JESUS IN SPAIN   127

their role in the cacao trade.[543] Cacao was harvested on Jesuit *reducciones* (settlements of indigenous peoples created through forced relocations by European monarchs and/or ecclesiastical authorities in what is now Latin America). In 1632, a group of professors of theology from various religious orders, including Jesuits, discussed whether the consumption of chocolate broke the fast at the University of Salamanca.[544] A number of treatises were composed on the question, with men of the cloth such as the Dominican Agustín Dávila y Padilla (1562–1604) arguing that drinking chocolate did not break one's fast. Jurist Antonio de León Pinelo (1590/91–1660) specified that, in order not to incur mortal sin, chocolate could be consumed one time during the period of fasting, and only then provided that no other substance was added to the liquid cacao.[545] Eventually, this controversy found its way into non-theological texts, like José Pellicer de Ossau y Salas y Tovar's (1602–79) *El fénix y su historia natural* [...] (The phoenix and its natural history [...] [1630]). In 1670, the Inquisition suppressed Pellicer's comment that drinking chocolate did not break the fast in the Indies.[546]

19   The Immaculate Conception, Part 2: The Seventeenth and
        Eighteenth Centuries

The debate over chocolate and fasting was not the only controversy during the era. The Spanish crown continued to be invested in the promotion of the immaculate conception. Philip IV was not satisfied with Gregory XV's 1622 bull on the immaculate conception. As a result, the members of Philip IV's Junta de la Concepción (Temporary Royal Council on the Immaculate Conception) published on Marian theology and the immaculate conception. Nieremberg served on this commission and, in Hendrickson's count, composed "some ten Marian treatises."[547] Another Jesuit, the queen's confessor, Johann Eberhard Nithard (1607–81), better known in the Spanish-speaking world by the Hispanized version of his name Juan Everardo Nithard, also served on the junta

---

543   Sophie D. Coe and Michael D. Coe, *The True History of Chocolate*, 3rd ed. (London: Thames & Hudson, 2013), 148.

544   Marcy Norton, *Sacred Gifts, Profane Pleasures: A History of Tobacco and Chocolate in the Atlantic World* (Ithaca, NY: Cornell University Press, 2008), 234–35.

545   Beth Marie Forrest and April L. Najjaj, "Is Sipping Sin Breaking Fast? The Catholic Chocolate Controversy and the Changing World of Early Modern Spain," *Food & Foodways* 15, nos. 1–2 (2007): 31–52, here 42, 44; Coe and Coe, *True History of Chocolate*, 148–50.

546   December 20, 1670, AHN Inq. leg. 4444 exp. 43.

547   Hendrickson, *Jesuit Polymath of Madrid*, 14.

at the behest of the king. (The Austrian Jesuit had been Queen Mariana de Austria's [1634–96] confessor since her youth and came to Spain with her from the imperial court when she married Philip IV.) Nithard wrote a number of works, including on the immaculate conception; however, an anonymous letter from a Jesuit from Zaragoza maintained that Nithard only claimed authorship of texts that the aforementioned unnamed Jesuit actually composed.[548] Regardless of the authorship question, these works figure among the roughly 450 Marian texts authored by Jesuits.[549]

There was movement on the question of the immaculate conception during Philip IV's reign. In 1661, Pope Alexander VII declared that Mary was conceived without sin and prohibited discussion of the contrary position.[550] From the Spanish point of view, the matter continued to be of such concern that the Spanish Inquisition became involved. Surviving documentation from this body indicates that it maintained a special file for texts relating to the immaculate conception. (This file notation is written on several sets of documents.)[551]

Nithard was not the first Jesuit confessor brought to the Spanish court by a royal bride from the Austrian branch of the Habsburgs, who tended to have Jesuit confessors. Margaret of Austria (1584–1611), wife of Philip III, brought her Jesuit confessor Richard Haller (1550–1612) with her to Spain. Nonetheless, the Franciscan Mateo de Burgos (c.1548–1611) was appointed to serve as the new queen's confessor. In fact, the duke of Lerma Francisco Gómez de Sandoval y Rojas (c.1553–1625), Philip III's *privado* (the king's favorite advisor), "attempted to substitute" Burgos for Haller, but the queen informed her new husband that she needed to confess in her native language. Philip III allowed Haller to stay in place, but the relationship between Haller and the duke of Lerma never recovered. Haller often arranged for the delivery of messages, including money, to Margaret's family. And the duke of Lerma did not approve of Haller's involvement. As a result, Haller had to counter accusations that Jesuits did not respect the seal of the confessional and revealed the content of confessions to their superiors. According to Magdalena Sánchez's study of a manuscript letter in which Haller defended himself, the Jesuit specified that he could participate in non-religious tasks provided that he cleared the matter with his

---

548   J. [Joaquín] Pérez Villanueva, "La crisis del Santo Oficio (1621–1700)," in *Historia de la Inquisición*, ed. Pérez Villanueva and Escandell Bonet, 1:996–1203, here 1:1082, 1:1087.

549   Hendrickson, *Jesuit Polymath of Madrid*, 14.

550   Holweck, "Immaculate Conception."

551   See AHN Inq. leg. 4452 exp. 15 and leg. 4453 exp. 5.

AN OVERVIEW OF THE PRE-SUPPRESSION SOCIETY OF JESUS IN SPAIN   129

superiors.[552] In the longer term, Haller might have had to defend himself further, but Margaret of Austria died in 1611 and Haller in the following year.

Nithard's situation was different given that he was in a position to have far greater influence over the queen and Spanish governance. After Philip IV's death, the widowed Mariana de Austria came to depend even more on the counsel of her confessor as she served as regent to her young son, the future Charles II. As Nithard came to serve in official capacities beyond the Junta de la Concepción, opposition to him grew substantially. Dominicans objected to the Jesuit because of his support for the immaculate conception, and Franciscans opposed Nithard's usurpation of their order's traditional role as confessor to the queen. In Rafaella Pilo's assessment, Franciscans collaborated with pamphlet writers to blame Nithard for the monarchy's problems.[553] There was also resistance beyond religious orders, as the bankers who financed the realm were not confident in Nithard's grasp of economic policy.[554]

This disapproval became most vehement as it became clear that Nithard would be appointed inquisitor general. Not only was Nithard not Spanish, and therefore would have to be naturalized in order to take up this position, but also significant concerns were raised relating to Nithard's membership in the Society of Jesus. As Joaquín Pérez Villanueva (1910–94) relates, one manuscript pamphlet, "Dudas políticas teológicas que consultan los señores de España y sus mayores ministros [...]" (Political [and] theological doubts that Spain's distinguished men and principal ministers examine [...] [c.1666]), expressed fears that a Jesuit inquisitor general would incorporate more members of his order into the Inquisition. Given Jesuits' vows of obedience to their superiors, there were worries that a Jesuit inquisitor general would have no choice but to violate the Inquisition's policy of secrecy at the behest of a superior. Beyond opposition to Nithard's potential elevation to inquisitor general, this text more broadly critiqued the order for, among other issues, its "relaxed doctrines." As attested to by the notable number of surviving copies, this pamphlet enjoyed broad circulation.[555]

---

552   Magdalena S. Sánchez, *The Empress, the Queen, and the Nun: Women and Power at the Court of Philip III of Spain* (Baltimore: Johns Hopkins University Press, 1998), 21–22, 50.

553   Rafaella Pilo, *Juan Everardo Nithard y sus causas no causas: Razones y pretextos para el fin de un valimiento* (Madrid: Sílex, CajaSur, 2010), 22–23. See also Miguel Córdoba Salmerón, "A Failed Politician, a Disputed Jesuit: Cardinal Johann Eberhard Nithard (1607–81)," *Journal of Jesuit Studies* 7, no. 4 (2020): 545–69, https://doi.org/10.1163/22141332-00704003 (accessed November 4, 2020).

554   Pérez Villanueva, "Crisis del Santo Oficio," 1:1082.

555   "Dudas políticas teológicas que consultan los señores de España, y sus mayores ministros a las Universidades de Salamanca, Alcalá en el Estado en que se haya la Monarquía," cited in Pérez Villanueva, "Crisis del Santo Oficio," 1:1086–87.

130 MANNING

Despite these concerns, Nithard did become inquisitor general in the fall of 1666. After Juan José de Austria raised an army and marched on Madrid in 1669, Nithard departed.[556] Once Nithard left Spain, he produced a lengthy memoir, one volume of which chronicled the opposition that he faced there.[557]

When Juan José de Austria came to form part of Charles II's administration, he made a number of changes, including exiling Queen Mariana, Charles's mother and regent, to Toledo. Eventually, Juan José de Austria took action against several Jesuits still at court. In 1671, Charles II's administration expanded the number of designated royal preachers and appointed three Jesuits new to the rank. In 1677, the king's half-brother decided to reduce the expenses at the royal chapel and therefore cut the number of preachers. A number of Jesuits lost their positions and had to leave court, including the by then elderly Manuel de Nájera, who had been appointed by Philip IV. By severing ties with certain royal preachers, Juan José de Austria also fulfilled non-fiscal goals, such as eliminating those preachers who had been most critical of him in their sermonizing. Jesuits looked unfavorably on Juan José de Austria for a variety of reasons, including his role in forcing Nithard into exile and the order's support of Queen Mariana whom Juan José sent to Toledo.[558]

In 1700, Charles II died childless; his will made Philip of Anjou (1683–1746) the king of Spain (r.1700–24; 1724–46). But the future Holy Roman emperor Archduke Charles of Austria (1685–1740, r.1711–40) also had a claim to the throne. And other nations had interests in Spanish territory and those of its empire; these factors touched off the War of the Spanish Succession (1701–14).

During the war, the Jesuits firmly supported Philip V. The sermons they delivered supported their point of view. According to Fernando Martínez Gil's research, Philip V continued to advocate for the immaculate conception to the pope, and his military victory in Brihuega on the feast of the immaculate conception was interpreted as a sign of divine favor. The list of sermons compiled by Martínez Gil demonstrates that Jesuits, along with other clergy loyal to the Bourbon cause, often gave sermons of thanksgiving for Philip V's military victories.[559] In 1707, at Madrid's Colegio Imperial, Jesuit Gutierre Alfonso Hurtado (1667–1721) said a "funerary prayer" for those soldiers who lost their lives during Philip V's victory in the Battle of Almansa (April 25, 1707). Lest anyone wonder why the Jesuits chose to dwell on the grim

---

556 Francisco José García Pérez, "La oratoria sagrada como arma política: Los predicadores reales de Juan José de Austria," *Obradoiro de historia moderna* 26 (2017): 237–65, here 244.

557 See Pilo, *Juan Everardo Nithard*, 103–257 for a transcription.

558 García Pérez, "Oratoria sagrada como arma," 245–46, 251–53.

559 Fernando Martínez Gil, "Los sermones como cauce de propaganda política: La Guerra de sucesión," *Obradoiro de historia moderna* 20 (2011): 303–36, here 306, 326, 330–36.

AN OVERVIEW OF THE PRE-SUPPRESSION SOCIETY OF JESUS IN SPAIN   131

reality that brought about the victory, the title of the printed version of this discourse emphasized the fact that they did so at the behest of Philip v.[560]

As Astrain observes, with the arrival of the Bourbon dynasty in Spain, Jesuits became confessors to the king between 1700 and 1755.[561] The Dominicans and Franciscans, seeing themselves increasingly displaced from their positions as confessors to the king and queen, were not pleased by this turn of events. Other religious orders were perturbed by their negative depictions in satirical texts authored by Jesuits or perceived to have been written by members of the order. (Pedro Rodríguez Campomanes y Pérez de Sorriba [1723–1802] raised the issue of these satires in his *Dictamen fiscal de la expulsión de los jesuitas de España* [Prosecutor's opinion on the expulsion of the Jesuits from Spain] [1766–67].)[562] Despite their closeness to the monarchs in these years, the question of the Jesuits' loyalty to a superior in Rome, and ultimately to the pope, became increasingly problematic as regalism, which granted the highest ecclesiastical authority to the state, gained ground. As Haliczer relates, following the 1753 concordat, the state's power over the church grew to such an extent that bishops who did not endorse royal policies were removed from their posts. The perception of "the Jesuit order, which was seen as a major supporter of the papacy in its struggle with the secular state" played an important role in its expulsion in 1759 from Portugal and in 1764 from France. Jesuits' opposition to Charles III's (1716–88, r.1759–88) "regalist measures" did not help their cause in Spain.[563]

20   Publications Unfavorable to the Order

As Juan José de Austria made his displeasure with the Jesuits at court known and regalism gained momentum, negative feelings toward the Society of Jesus became increasingly evident in texts published in Spain in the years leading up

---

560   Gutierre Alfonso Hurtado [Gvtierre Alphonso Hvrtado], "Oracion funebre en las exeqvias qve el Rey N[uestro] Señor Phelipe V (qve Dios gvarde) mandò celebrar en la iglesia de el Colegio Imperial [...]" (Madrid: Juan Garcia Infançon, 1707), *portada*. BNE. The text is available in the BDH. See http://bdh-rd.bne.es/viewer.vm?id=0000048202&page=1 (accessed May 19, 2020).

561   Astrain, *Historia de la Compañía de Jesús*, 7:147.

562   Pedro Rodríguez de Campomanes, *Dictamen fiscal de expulsión de los jesuitas de España (1766–1767)*, ed. Jorge Cejudo López and Teófanes Egido (Madrid: Fundación Universitaria Española, 1977), 156. See Cejudo López and Egido's "Introducción," 34–37 for more information about the poor state of the Jesuits' relationship with other religious orders in Spain before the expulsion.

563   Haliczer, *Sexuality in the Confessional*, 205–6.

to the 1767 expulsion. Before considering the republication of Palafox's work, we will first turn to a text published in France that purported to offer Arias Montano's negative opinions on the Society. The "Lettre du célèbre docteur Arias Montanus" (Letter from the famous doctor Arias Montano [dated 1571 in 1692 pamphlet]) reprints a 1571 supposed letter from Arias Montano to the Spanish king in three languages, Latin, French, and Spanish, in order to make these opinions on the matter more widely available. Admittedly, the preliminaries and notes in French and the reference at the end of the "avertisement" (foreword) that refers to those readers who do not read Spanish, suggest a primarily French audience.[564] However, there is some evidence that the text did circulate in Spain. Antonio Pérez Goyena (1863–1962) references a manuscript copy in the Biblioteca Nacional in Madrid.[565]

Clearly, this particular piece of propaganda was effective since it was reprinted in 1701. The translation of negative assessments of the Jesuit order from outside of France was a strategy that the Jansenists' employed in their dispute with the Society. According to David Anthony Brading's research, Jansenists also translated and often referenced Palafox's critique of the Jesuit community.[566] But the French-language version of Arias Montano's letter was not a simple translation; many scholars correctly consider it a fabrication. Yet it is a tribute to its plausibility that some apparently continue to believe it is authentic.[567] Nonetheless, the strategy and intellectual effort involved in creating such a false letter demonstrates the strength of the opposition to the Jesuits.

Whereas the previously mentioned French pamphlet purported to resurrect Arias Montano's negative assertions about the Society of Jesus, authentic critiques of the order from the past reemerged in Spain in various forms, including those by Palafox.

When Palafox died in 1659, he left his literary works to the Carmelites, who produced an edition of his collected works, along with a favorable biography

---

564 "Lettre du celebre docteur Arias Montanus Chevalier de l'Ordre de S. Jacques Bibliothecaire de S. M. C. au Roy d'Espagne Philippe II" (n.p.: n.p., 1692), 6. Newberry Library, hereafter Newberry, available online. See https://archive.org/details/lettreduclebredoooaria (accessed May 19, 2020). The 1701 version is available online through Gallica at the Bibliothèque Nationale de France. See https://gallica.bnf.fr/ark:/12148/bpt6k5608589d/f2.image.texteImage (accessed May 19, 2020).

565 Pérez Goyena, "Arias Montano y los jesuítas," 309.

566 Brading, First America, 250.

567 Van Kley seems to believe the text is authentic. Van Kley, Reform Catholicism, 59–61. For the opposing point of view, in addition to Pérez Goyena's "Arias Montano y los jesuítas," see also Roberto Giammanco, "Sull'inautenticità' del memoriale antigesuitico attribuito a Benito Arias Montano," Archivum historicum Societatis Iesu 26 (1957): 276–84.

AN OVERVIEW OF THE PRE-SUPPRESSION SOCIETY OF JESUS IN SPAIN   133

of the deceased bishop.[568] In the years following Palafox's death, a number of bishops and other men of the cloth in Spain supported his beatification, no doubt aided by several hagiographical biographies. The Society of Jesus, however, did not share this enthusiasm. Jesuit Paolo Segneri (1624–94) criticized Palafox's *Vida interior* (Inner life [1682]). Ultimately, Superior General González officially expressed his opposition to Palafox's beatification. A number of other Jesuits publicly opposed Palafox's case; and other anonymous anti-Palafox satirical materials were attributed to the Jesuits. The Society's dissent became so vehement that the pope admonished the order in 1758 and urged its members to cease their publications against Palafox.[569]

Several Spanish monarchs expressed interest in supporting Palafox's beatification, but it was ultimately Charles III who formally submitted the case in 1760.[570] In Palafox, regalists found "both a precursor and an inspiration" to regalism.[571] Moreover, as Gregorio Bartolomé Martínez suggests, Palafox's proceedings were unquestionably used, and perhaps abused, as a means to attack the Jesuits. At times, the Jesuits resorted to questionable means to oppose them.[572]

In 1761, the Roman Congregation approved Palafox's works. After that decision, Palafox's writings that had been prohibited in Spain were removed from the Spanish Inquisition's Index. The 1762 luxury edition of Palafox's texts underwritten by Charles III's government signaled the monarchy's loyalties.[573] A number of new editions of the former bishop of Puebla's texts followed, many at price points lower than the state-sponsored imprint. Several imprints expressed negative feelings about the Jesuits. And the works likely fueled such sentiments in their consumers. A 1766 Spanish-language edition of Palafox's letter to Pope Innocent X (1574–1655, r.1644–55) contains an introduction to this missive in which the unidentified first-person editorial voice affirms that Palafox sought to curtail the Society's negative qualities, including its "excessive self-love." Following the translation of Palafox's Latin letter, this imprint details the manner in which the Jesuits continued to defend their position.[574]

---

568   Brading, *First America*, 250.
569   Bartolomé Martínez, *Jaque mate al obispo virrey*, 115–16.
570   Teófanes Egido, "El siglo XVIII: Del poder a la extinción," in Egido, Burrieza Sánchez, and Revuelta González, *Jesuitas en España*, 225–78, here 250–51.
571   Brading, *First America*, 250.
572   Bartolomé Martínez, *Jaque mate al obispo virrey*, 118–19.
573   Egido, "Siglo XVIII," 251.
574   [Juan de Palafox y Mendoza], *Carta del V. siervo de Dios D. Juan de Palafox y Mendoza* (Madrid: n.p., 1766), no pagination and 167–69. Newberry.

134 MANNING

A 1768 edition of the *Cartas del venerable siervo de Dios D. Juan de Palafox y Mendoza* [...] (Letters of the venerable servant of God Juan de Palafox y Mendoza [...]) revisited the nature of the dispute between the bishop and the Society of Jesus in the volume's introduction. Palafox's correspondence did not appear on its own. This edition also included other materials that portrayed the Society in a negative light: a *memorial* concerning the financial difficulties at the Jesuit Colegio de San Hermenegildo de Sevilla, another treating a fraud committed by this same *colegio* in Seville against Rodrigo Barba Cabeza de Vaca (*fl.* seventeenth century), and "La verdad desnuda" (The naked truth [1659]), a letter that took Palafox's burial as an occasion to offer an extended reproof of the Society of Jesus.[575]

21   The Expulsion

During Holy Week in 1766, Madrid residents took to the streets to protest in what would come to be known as the *motín de Esquilache*. (The marquis of Esquilache Leopoldo de Gregorio y Masnata [*c.*1700–85] was the royal minister whose reforms led to the uproar.) Whatever inspired these street protests, whether the rising costs of staple commodities, the prohibition of popular sartorial items, or plans regarding lighting in Madrid's streets, the Jesuits were rumored to have incited the demonstrations. The secret investigations to find the instigators of the riot, led by the count of Aranda Pedro Pablo Abarca de Bolea y Ximénez de Urrea (1719–98) and the count of Campomanes, both of whom had anti-Jesuit sympathies, led to the compilation of a wide variety of denunciations against the order.

Judging by the reasons mentioned in the *Dictamen*, international, domestic, and religious concerns brought about the expulsion of the Society from Spain. Campomanes mentioned the Jesuits' role in planning and inciting the populace to participate in the *motín de Esquilache*. The Jesuits' perceived role in the attempted regicide in Portugal also concerned the minister. Back in Spain, Jesuits circulated satires against the government and other Catholic religious orders and fomented negative feelings against their satirical targets. The Society's espousal of probabilism also received detailed criticism.[576] For

---

575   [Palafox y Mendoza], *Cartas del venerable siervo de Dios D. Juan de Palafox y Mendoza* (Madrid: Manuel Martin, 1768). Newberry. The text renders Rodrigo Barba Cabeza de Vaca's final surname as Baca. This "La verdad desnuda" is a letter dated 1659. This same title was used for at least one other short text.

576   Rodríguez de Campomanes, *Dictamen fiscal*, 43–65, 156, 167, 141–46.

AN OVERVIEW OF THE PRE-SUPPRESSION SOCIETY OF JESUS IN SPAIN

Van Kley, the presence of language critiquing the order in terms similar to those used by Jansenists points toward a large-scale international network that conspired against the Jesuits.[577] Perhaps more archival evidence may come to light to substantiate this opinion, but such language could have been inspired by domestic sources in Spain. Even Mariana used similar terms to criticize the Society's governance.

On the designated mornings in the first days of April 1767, Jesuits in Spain awoke to find their institutions surrounded—and eventually entered—by armed forces. Once all the resident Jesuits were grouped together in the house, judicial authorities read them Charles III's pragmatic.[578] Although the pragmatic alluded to "urgent," "very grave causes" for the expulsion, the monarch also stated that he would not share them publicly. In Teófanes Egido and Isidoro Pinedo's (1929–2018) analysis, in so doing, the Spanish monarch sought to avoid the "polemics" that surrounded the order's expulsion from Portugal and France.[579]

The expulsion order made its way to Spain's overseas territories, where Jesuits were deported with varying degrees of speed. Many Jesuits sailed from Mexico in 1767, but others from California, Sinaloa, and Sonora departed in 1769. Transportation difficulties delayed members' departure from the Philippines until 1770.[580]

22   The Aftermath

Charles III's pragmatic ordered silence on the topic of the Jesuits' expulsion. If Jesuits broke this provision, their pensions would be frozen.[581] Yet, as Egido and Pinedo observe, anti-Jesuit positions were published.[582] In point of fact, as Egido details, publications concerning the expulsion could circulate with a special license. Naturally, authorized publications favored the government's point

---

577   Dale K. Van Kley, "Plots and Rumors of Plots: The Role of Conspiracy in the International Campaign against the Society of Jesus, 1758–1768," in *Jesuit Suppression in Global Context*, ed. Burson and Wright, 13–39, here 32–33.

578   Egido, "Siglo XVIII," 262.

579   Pragmatic cited in Teófanes Egido and Isidoro Pinedo, *Las causas "gravísimas" y secretas de la expulsión de los jesuitas por Carlos III* (Madrid: Fundación Universitaria Española, 1994), 9, 11.

580   Egido, "Siglo XVIII," 266.

581   Emanuele Colombo and Niccolò Guasti, "The Expulsion and Suppression in Portugal and Spain: An Overview," in *Jesuit Suppression in Global Context*, ed. Burson and Wright, 117–38, here 132.

582   Egido and Pinedo, *Causas "gravísimas" y secretas*, 9–10.

of view. Bishops and superiors of religious orders in Spain circulated letters endorsing the monarch's decision.[583] In 1768, Mariana's critique of the order's governance structure was once again retitled and printed as *Discurso de las enfermedades de la Compañía de Jesús* (Discourse on the diseases of the Society of Jesus).[584] Between 1768 and 1770, Madrid's Imprenta de la Gaceta published four volumes of "anti-jesuitical libels" that Francisco Mateos (1896–1975) asserted were printed to "justify the expulsion." Moreover, in Mateos's estimation, it was a group of Charles III's advisors, including Abarca de Bolea, the count of Aranda, who urged for the printing of this series of imprints.[585] (It is not at all incidental that a number of the documents related to the expulsion bear the count of Aranda's title.)[586] While these volumes served to explain these officials' decision to expel the order as well as to encourage its suppression, evidence suggests that this imprint was read outside of courtly circles. Two sets of handwritten comments, dated 1816 and 1821, on the title page of the fourth volume indicate that two different readers with differing perspectives found the text "useful." The 1816 note writer was a cleric; the 1821 note taker specified that the work was "useful" to "guerrilleros" (guerillas). Although the 1821 comment specified that it was made in Madrid, the volume deals with the Jesuits' territories in Paraguay.[587] The comment seems most likely to reference the 1821 attempt to oust José Gaspar Rodríguez de Francia (1766–1840) from power in Paraguay.

In another move against the order after its expulsion from Spain, a 1768 royal decree from Charles III eliminated university courses dedicated to Suárez's works. It also banned the use of any texts composed by Jesuit authors in pedagogical settings.[588]

---

583 Egido, "Siglo XVIII," 268.

584 García Cárcel, "Crisis de la Compañía de Jesús," 387.

585 Francisco Mateos, "Papeles secuestrados a los jesuítas en el siglo XVIII, reunidos en Madrid," *Razón y fe* 175 (1967): 527–40, here 538.

586 For example, see the decree and instructions ("Real decreto" and "Instruccion") in the Consejo's *Instruccion* in the Newberry in which the title "conde de Aranda" (count of Aranda) is written by hand at the end of the printed documents.

587 José de Antequera y Castro, *Coleccion general de documentos, tocantes a la persecucion, que los regulares de la Compañia suscitaron y siguieron tenázmente por medio de sus jueces conservadores, y ganando algunos ministros seculares desde 1644 hasta 1660* (Madrid: Imprenta de la Gaceta, 1768–70). Handwritten comments on 4:unpaginated page. The work is available in the BDH. See http://bdh-rd.bne.es/viewer.vm?id=0000030327&page=1 (accessed May 12, 2020), pane number 1566.

588 Antonio Pérez Goyena, "Francisco Suárez," in *The Catholic Encyclopedia*, vol. 14 (New York: Robert Appleton Company, 1912); http://www.newadvent.org/cathen/14319a.htm (accessed April 28, 2020).

AN OVERVIEW OF THE PRE-SUPPRESSION SOCIETY OF JESUS IN SPAIN 137

At least in the area of Latin teaching materials, the plagiarism of pedagogical matter prepared by Jesuits meant that texts written by Jesuits might have made their way surreptitiously into post-expulsion classrooms. Menéndez Pelayo specifies that José Goya y Muniain's (1756–1807) 1798 commentaries on Julius Caesar (100 BCE–44 BCE) were actually composed by the Jesuit José Petisco (1724–1800). Another case, according to Bernabé Bartolomé Martínez's research, involved the director of the Real Academia Latina Matritense. Around 1772, the director, Alfonso Gómez Zapata (*fl.* eighteenth century) appropriated the work of the Jesuit Francisco Javier de Idiáquez (1711–90).[589]

Even after the Jesuits left Spain, several historical works composed by members continued to be very popular. Although Mariana's *Historia general de España* was originally published in the seventeenth century, in Kamen's assessment, Mariana's text was the historical work "most consulted by Spaniards" for some three hundred years.[590] And Mariana's was not the only historical text by a Jesuit to continue to be read widely after the order's expulsion from Spain. Isla's *Compendio de la historia de España*, a translation of Jean-Baptiste Philippoteau Duchesne's (1682–1755) French-language work, was reissued in a number of cities in Europe, among them Madrid in the 1770s after the order left Spain and in the 1780s after the suppression, and continuing into the 1840s.[591]

Despite the royal order for silence on the matter, after the Society was expelled from Spain, at least one Jesuit attempted to change the king's mind. Isla used his skills as a historian to compose a *memorial* to Charles III, which as Íñigo Arranz Roa and Fernando del Ser Pérez signal, employed historical data to measure the Jesuits' importance. This text enumerated the communities that were left without schools as a result of the expulsion.[592]

Others outside the Jesuit community concurred about the dire impact of the order's departure on the educational landscape. As Bernabé Bartolomé Martínez details, the Society, particularly the press at the *colegio* in Villagarcía de Campos, published a significant number of texts for the teaching of classical languages in the years before the expulsion. In 1771, the University of Valladolid lamented that the dictionaries that were sold at the Jesuit *colegios* in Villagarcía and Valladolid were no longer available. They asked that any such

---

589 Miguel Cascón, *Los jesuitas en Menéndez Pelayo* (Santiago: Librería Santarén, 1940), 145, cited in Bartolomé Martínez, "Cátedras [...] Castilla," 490 and Bartolomé Martínez, "Cátedras [...] Castilla," 490.

590 Kamen, *Imagining Spain*, 13.

591 See Sommervogel, *Bibliothèque*, 4:cols. 657–58 for a detailed listing.

592 Íñigo Arranz Roa and Fernando del Ser Pérez, "Aproximación a las fuentes para el estudio de la provincia jesuítica de Castilla (ss. XVI–XVIII)," *Hispania sacra* 52 (2000): 73–98, here 79.

138 MANNING

volumes as well as any works related to the teaching of Latin grammar found in the Jesuits' buildings be given to the university.[593]

As some missed the Jesuit presence in education, the patterns of circulation of certain texts demonstrate ongoing sympathy for the order. According to Juan Carrete Parrondo's research, engravings of the sacred heart and Our Lady of the Light, devotions that the order promoted, continued to be popular. Eventually, such images were withdrawn from circulation due to their relationship to the Society of Jesus.[594]

Moreover, as Carrete Parrondo demonstrates, other satirical images implicitly favored the expelled Jesuits. Beginning in 1767, authorities in Spain and the Spanish Empire regularly prohibited engravings that satirized Charles III's expulsion of the Jesuits. In 1769, a satirical engraving entitled "Saint Ignatius of Loyola," which criticized the decision to deport the Jesuits, was prohibited. The prohibition decree threatened the death penalty and confiscation of one's possessions as punishment for anyone trafficking in images relating to the expulsion—or potential return—of the Jesuits. But this was not the most controversial of the images that criticized Charles III's decision. According to Carrete Parrondo and Javier Antón Pelayo, that distinction belonged to the engraving "Judicium universale: El juicio universal" (The last judgment [c.1772]), which was denounced in 1772 in Rome and in Popayán in Nueva Granada (in present-day Colombia). This image included Spain's coat of arms and the monarch's name next to a scale and doors leading to hell, purgatory, and heaven, implying that the monarch would face divine justice for his decision to expel the Society.[595] As Antón Pelayo indicates, this inflammatory engraving, and the investigations to discover who circulated it, caused diplomatic tensions between Spain, Italy, and Venice.[596]

---

593 Bartolomé Martínez, "Cátedras [...] Castilla," 488, 494.

594 Juan Carrete Parrondo, "Más allá del poder: Imágenes prohibidas; Humanidades digitales;" https://sites.google.com/site/masalladelpoderporjuancarrete/ (accessed April 28, 2020). The electronic version of the article is not paginated. See Astrain, *Historia de la Compañía de Jesús*, 7:118–46 for the Jesuits' role in the dissemination of devotions to the sacred heart in Spain.

595 Carrete Parrondo, "Más allá," no pagination. The web-based article contains a high-quality version of the image concerning the judgment of King Charles III. See Javier Antón Pelayo, "La 'causa di Spagna': Antijesutismo, comercio de estampas y relaciones diplomáticas entre España y Venecia durante el reinado de Carlos III," *Estudis: Revista de historia moderna* 35 (2009): 221–58, here 240–45, 250–55 for details about the production of this engraving.

596 Antón Pelayo, "'Causa di Spagna,'" 222.

23   Conclusion

In many ways, the treatment that Ignatius and a number of early Jesuits received in Spain proved the biblical adage that no one is a prophet in his or her own land.[597] Once the Society overcame royal suspicions, its expansion provoked rivalries among other religious orders, both in theological matters and in terms of Jesuits' perceived infringement on other orders' traditional responsibilities. As the order's detractors became more vocal elsewhere in the world, old attacks against the order were revived in Spain through new printings. And the order's connection to a superior general in Rome and avowed loyalty to the pope became increasingly problematic in a regalistic era. By attributing the responsibility for the *motín de Esquilache* to the order, Charles III's government hit upon a pretext to expel the order from Spain and the Spanish Empire. In 1773, exiled Jesuit Manuel Luengo (1735–1816) admitted in his diary that he clung to a prophecy by Escobar that the expulsion would be temporary. Escobar's deep connections to the Society of Jesus likely gave this spurious prediction more credibility.[598] But greater tribulations would follow with the papal suppression of the order in 1773. It would be decades before Escobar's supposed vision would be proven correct. And once the order was restored in Spain, it would be suppressed on a number of occasions in the nineteenth century and dissolved during the Second Republic.[599]

These post-restoration suppressions by non-monarchical governments demonstrate that regalism was not the only political philosophy that caused friction between the Society of Jesus and the Spanish state. As we have seen, a detailed analysis of the Spanish Society defies the facile characterization of Spain as the nurturing birthplace of the order. In lieu of this maternal image, the relationship vis-à-vis Spain and the order also encompassed initial suspicions about Ignatius of Loyola's orthodoxy, rivalries between other religious orders, and tensions between the Jesuits and the king and the nobles who served as administrators in royal governance structures.

In the early years of his religious journey, Ignatius and his beliefs were subjected to scrutiny by various religious tribunals, both in Spain and beyond. Moreover, on a number of occasions, such as Philip II's lobbying for a fourth Spanish superior general, the question of Spanish influence within the

---

597   Luke 4:24.
598   Burrieza Sánchez, "Percepción jesuítica," 103.
599   See Manuel Revuelta González, "Los jesuitas durante la Segunda República y la Guerra Civil (1931–39)," in Egido, Burrieza Sánchez, and Revuelta González, *Jesuitas en España*, 343–64 for more about the Society during the Second Republic.

religious community caused conflicts with the sovereign and within the order. Iberian concerns eventually prompted the Society to ban the admission of *conversos*. Shortly thereafter, a number of Spanish Jesuits from *converso* families were removed from prominent positions. For some *memorialistas*, these exclusionary decisions motivated their complaints; however, others protested a top-down governance structure rooted in Spain's approach to its empire. But the integration of the Society of Jesus into mainstream Spanish society fomented negative reactions to the Jesuit community. There are many motives for the vehemence of the reaction against the Society in 1766–67, among them the Jesuits' incursion into the spheres of influence of older religious orders, like the Dominicans' authority in the Inquisition and the Franciscans' traditional position as confessors to the Spanish queen. The Society's notable influence on the educational system, particularly in the teaching of Latin, was a point of contention for other religious institutions and, eventually, for those who favored different pedagogical approaches. As became evident in the wake of the expulsion, however, the Society's role in pedagogy—both in terms of teaching and producing materials for the teaching of Latin—was difficult to replace.

Yet it would be overly simplistic to understand the order's expulsion from Spain as solely the result of jealousies over the community's power. Jesuits were active participants in the impassioned theological debates of the era. Although the immaculist position favored by the Jesuits and Franciscans eventually became doctrine, the Society's position on free will and its willingness to consider the circumstances in which sins were committed resulted in continued accusations of laxism. Whereas some deemed the Jesuits' theatrical religious displays to be excessive, the continued circulation of devotional images associated with the order—like the sacred heart—after the expulsion demonstrates the public's continued interest in these devotions. In order to quell these practices, authorities eventually banned the circulation of these printed images.

As well as zealously protecting the order by seeking to prohibit texts that criticized it, some members of the Society were equally fervent in criticizing those who did not favor the order. The Jesuits' critiques of Palafox as well as satires of him and other religious figures did not endear the Society to certain consumers of these works. Although the heated reactions against these texts by men of the cloth and nobles have been well documented, the impact of shorter texts, particularly manuscripts in the style of Perico and Marica's *romance* against the order, remains less clear. (Until the advent of search engines and digital library catalogs, these works could be difficult to locate, let alone analyze.) Particularly as digitization efforts accelerate, and this body of texts becomes more readily available, such works will no doubt provide further insights into the relationship between the Society and the Spanish populace and the sentiments that favored the order's expulsion.

Bibliography

Manuscripts

Biblioteca Nacional de España (BNE), Madrid

"Copia de la carta de Diego de Acuña a Felipe III" and "Memorial sumario de los veynte y quatro informaciones que el Arçobispo de Seuilla mandò hazer cerca de las contradiciones que los religiosos de Santo Domingo [...]." BNE MS 9956.

"Descripcion de las fiestas de la Compañia de Jesus—Perico y Marica—Romance—Hermosa Marica." BNE MS 12935–34.

Relacion de la variedad que ha avido en la comunicacion de disputas con los padres de la Compañia en la prouincia de España, de la Orden de Predicadores. In Papeles de Gil *González Dávila.* BNE MS 18174. This manuscript is available in the BNE's Biblioteca Digital Hispánica: http://bdh-rd.bne.es/viewer.vm?id=0000135516&page=1 (accessed May 19, 2020).

Salazar Mardones, Cristóbal de to Juan Francisco Andrés de Uztarroz, June 28, 1642 and Ataide, Jerónimo de to Andrés de Uztarroz, April 20, 1646, BNE MS 8391.

Rare Books

Biblioteca Nacional de España, Madrid

Alcázar, Bartolomé de [Bartholome Alcazar]. *Chrono-historia de la Compañia de Jesvs, en la provincia de Toledo: Y elogios de sus varones illustres, fundadores, bienhechores, [f]autores, é hijos espirituales.* Madrid: Juan Garcia Infançon, 1710. This imprint is available in the BNE's Biblioteca Digital Hispánica: http://bdh-rd.bne.es/viewer .vm?id=0000016699&page=1 (accessed May 19, 2020).

Antequera y Castro, José de. *Coleccion general de documentos, tocantes a la persecucion, que los regulares de la Compañia suscitaron y siguieron tenázmente por medio de sus jueces conservadores, y ganando algunos ministros seculares desde 1644 hasta 1660.* 4 Vols. Madrid: Imprenta de la Gaceta, 1768–70. This text is available in the BNE's BDH: http://bdh-rd.bne.es/viewer.vm?id=0000030327&page=1 (accessed May 19, 2020).

Avisos para la mverte: Escritos por algunos Ingenios de España. Zaragoza: Iuan de Larrumbe, 1640. R 31911.

Esquex, Pedro Francisco. *Sermon en las exeqvias, qve se celebraron el colegio Imperial de la Compañia de Iesvs, al Excelentissimo señor D. Luis Crespi de Borja, del Consejo de su Magestad, y su embaxador extraordinario a nuestro muy santo Padre Alexandro Septimo, por el santo negocio de la Concepcion.* Madrid: Ioseph Fernandez de Buendia, 1663.

González, Jacinto [Iacinto Gonzalez]. *Panegyrico fvneral en las honras de D. Felipe IIII el grande, nvestro rey, y señor.* Madrid: Ioseph Fernandez de Buendia, 1666.

Hurtado, Gutierre Alfonso [Gvtierre Alphonso Hvrtado]. "Oracion funebre en las exeqvias qve el Rey N[uestro] Señor Phelipe V (qve Dios gvarde) mandò celebrar en la iglesia de el Colegio Imperial [...]." Madrid: Juan Garcia Infançon, 1707. The text is availableintheBNE'sBDH:http://bdh-rd.bne.es/viewer.vm?id=0000048202&page=1 (accessed May 19, 2020).

León, Gabriel de [Gabriel de Leon]. "A Antonio Farfan de los Godos, tesorero, iuez, y oficial por su magestad de la ciudad de Cartagena de las Indias, y su prouincia, y familiar del Santo Oficio de la Inquisicion &." In Juan Bautista Poza, *Practica de ayvdar a bien morir*. Madrid: Melchor Sanchez, n.d. [license dated 1657], no pagination.

[Martín Redondo, Santiago]. "Al Ilvstrissimo señor don Antonio Manrique de Guzman, patriarca de las Indias [...]." Partial dedication to Antonio Manrique de Guzmán between the folios of the dedication to García de Velasco in *Obras de Lorenzo Gracian: Tomo primero qve contiene* El criticon, primera, segunda y tercera parte; El oraculo; *Y* El heroe. Madrid: Pablo de Val, 1664. BNE R 17585.

Nájera, Manuel de [Manvel de Naxera]. "Sermon qve predico el padre Manvel de Naxera predicador de sv magestad en las piadosas exeqvias, que consagrò a la memoria del P. Ivan Evsebio Nieremberg el Ilvstrissimo señor Don Christoval Crespi de Baldavra, vicecanciller del Svpremo y Real Consejo de Aragon." Madrid: Andres Garcia de la Iglesia, 1658.

Poza, Juan Bautista [Ivan Bavtista Poça]. *Practica de ayvdar a bien morir.* Madrid: Melchor Sanchez, n.d. [license dated 1657].

Rueda Marín, Antonio de [Rveda Marin]. *Justa poetica, celebrada en el insigne Colegio de la Compañia de Jesus, de esta [...] Ciudad de Murcia, el día 17 de noviembre del año de 1727 en cvlto de S. Luis Gonzaga, estudiante, y de S. Estanislao de Kostka.* Murcia: Jayme Mesnier, [1728?]. This text is available in the BNE's BDH: http://bdh-rd.bne .es/viewer.vm?id=0000039110&page=1 (accessed May 19, 2020).

Vega, Lope de. *Fiestas del Santissimo Sacramento, repartidos en doze avtos sacramentales, con sus loas, y entremeses.* Zaragoza: Pedro Verges, 1644.

Newberry Library, Chicago

Consejo Real en extraordinario. *Instruccion de lo que deberan executar los comisionados para el estrañamiento, y ocupacion de bienes y haciendas de los jesuitas en España è islas adjacentes.* No place of publication or printer, but the end of the text dates the document March 1, 1767.

"Lettre du celebre docteur Arias Montanus Chevalier de l'Ordre de S. Jacques Bibliothecaire de S. M. C. au Roy d'Espagne Philippe II." n.p.: n.p., 1692. Available in electronic form: https://archive.org/details/lettreduclebredoooaria (accessed May 19, 2020).

[Palafox y Mendoza, Juan de]. *Carta del V. Siervo de Dios D. Juan de Palafox y Mendoza al sumo Pontifice Inocencio X.* Madrid: n.p., 1766.

[Palafox y Mendoza, Juan de]. *Cartas del venerable siervo de Dios D. Juan de Palafox y Mendoza.* Madrid: Manuel Martin, 1768.

AN OVERVIEW OF THE PRE-SUPPRESSION SOCIETY OF JESUS IN SPAIN 143

Real decreto ... He venido en mandar se estrañen de todos mis dominios de España, é Indias, islas Filipinas, y demás adyacentes à los religiosos de la Compañia de Jesus. n.p. [Madrid?]: n.p., n.d. [1767?].

Spencer Research Library, University of Kansas, Lawrence, Kansas

Mendo, Andrés. "Censvra de el Reverendissimo Padre Maestro Andrès Mendo [...]." In María de Jesús de Ágreda [Maria de Jesus], *Mystica ciudad de Dios, milagro de sv omnipotencia, y abismo de la gracia.* 3 Vols. Madrid: Manvel Rviz de Mvrga, 1701.

Internet Copies of Rare Books

Alegambe, Philippe [Philippo]. *Bibliotheca scriptorvm Societatis Iesv.* Antwerp: Ioannem Mevrsivm, 1643. https://books.google.com/books?id=3YVLAAAAcAAJ& printsec=frontcover&source=gbs_ge_summary_r&cad=0#v=onepage&q&f=false (accessed May 19, 2020).

"Lettre du celebre docteur Arias Montanus Chevalier de l'Ordre de S. Jacques Bibliothecaire de S. M. C. au Roy d'Espagne Philippe II." n.p.: n.p., 1701. https://gallica .bnf.fr/ark:/12148/bpt6k560858gd/f2.image.texteImage (accessed May 19, 2020).

Novissimus librorum prohibitorum et expvrgandorvm Index pro Catholicis Hispaniarum regnis Philippi IIII. n.p.: n.p., 1640. https://books.google.com/books?id=M1UrC4D VZd4C&printsec=frontcover&source=gbs_ge_summary_r&cad=0#v=onepage&q= Poza&f=false (accessed May 19, 2020).

Novissimus librorum prohibitorum et expurgandorum Index pro Catholicis Hispaniarum regnis Philippi V. 2 Vols. Madrid: Ex Typographia Musicae, 1707. https://babel.ha -thitrust.org/cgi/pt?id=gri.ark:/13960/t9k40d491&view=1up&seq=809; https://books .google.com/books?id=f9lQAAAAcAAJ&printsec=frontcover&source=gbs_ge_sum mary_r&cad=0#v=onepage&q&f=false (accessed May 19, 2020).

Poza, Juan Bautista [Ivan Bavtista Poça]. *Practica de ayvdar a bien morir.* Madrid: Domingo Garcia y Morràs, 1648. https://books.google.com/books?id=J2ab_sXcGT EC&printsec=frontcover&source=gbs_ge_summary_r&cad=0#v=onepage&q&f=fal se (accessed May 19, 2020).

Puente, Luis de la. *Vida maravillosa de la venerable virgen doña Marina de Escobar, natural de Valladolid.* Madrid: Joachin Ibarra, 1766. https://archive.org/details/bub _gb_Fjk5hAOyg4EC/page/n6/mode/2up (accessed May 19, 2020).

Painting

Museo de Historia de Madrid

Valpuesta, Pedro de. *Felipe IV jurando defender la doctrina de la inmaculada concepción.* c.1634–66.

Modern Printed Texts

Abad, Camilo María. "Escobar (Marine de)." In *Dictionnaire de spiritualité: Ascétique et mystique, doctrine et histoire*, edited by Marcel Viller, Charles Baumgartner, and André Rayez, 4.1:cols. 1083–86. 17 Vols. Paris: G. Beauchesne et ses fils, 1932–95.

Abad, Camilo María. *Vida y escritos del V. P. Luis de la Puente de la Compañía de Jesús (1554–1624)*. Santander: Universidad Pontificia Comillas, 1957.

Ahlgren, Gillian T. W. *Teresa of Avila and the Politics of Sanctity*. Ithaca, NY: Cornell University Press, 1996.

Alcalá, Ángel. "El control inquisitorial de intelectuales en el siglo de oro: De Nebrija al 'Índice' de Sotomayor de 1640." In *Historia de la Inquisición en España y América*, edited by J. [Joaquín] Pérez Villanueva and Bartolomé Escandell Bonet, 3:829–956. 3 Vols. Madrid: Biblioteca de Autores Cristianos, Centro de Estudios Inquisitoriales, 1984–2000.

Alcalá, Ángel. "Góngora y Juan de Pineda: Escaramuzas entre el poeta y el inquisidor." In *Homenaje a Pedro Sáinz Rodríguez*, 3:1–19. 4 Vols. Madrid: Fundación Universitaria Española, 1986.

Alonso, Dámaso. "Las 'Obras en verso del Homero español'." In *Obras en verso del Homero español*, edited by Dámaso Alonso, xiii–lxxix. Madrid: Consejo Superior de Investigaciones Científicas, 1963.

Andrade, Alonso de. "P. Estéban Fabro." In Juan Eusebio Nieremberg, *Varones ilustres de la Compañía de Jesús*, 2:105–27. 2nd ed. 9 Vols. Bilbao: Administración del Mensajero del Corazón de Dios, 1887–92. https://archive.org/details/varonesilus-tresooniergoog/page/n133/mode/2up (accessed April 28, 2020).

Antón Pelayo, Javier. "La 'causa di Spagna': Antijesutismo, comercio de estampas y relaciones diplomáticas entre España y Venecia durante el reinado de Carlos III." *Estudis: Revista de historia moderna* 35 (2009): 221–58.

Arranz Roa, Íñigo, and Fernando del Ser Pérez. "Aproximación a las fuentes para el estudio de la provincia jesuítica de Castilla (ss. XVI–XVIII)." *Hispania sacra* 52 (2000): 73–98.

Astrain, Antonio. "Congregatio de Auxiliis." In *The Catholic Encyclopedia*. Vol. 4. New York: Robert Appleton Company, 1908. http://www.newadvent.org/cathen/04238a.htm (accessed April 28, 2020).

Astrain, Antonio. *Historia de la Compañía de Jesús en la asistencia de España*. 7 Vols. Madrid: Administración de Razón y Fe, 1912–25. BNE. Biblioteca Digital Hispánica. http://bdh-rd.bne.es/viewer.vm?id=0000010528&page=1 (accessed April 28, 2020).

Atienza López, Ángela. "De beaterios a conventos: Nuevas perspectivas sobre el mundo de las beatas en la España moderna." *Historia social* 57 (2007): 145–68.

Bailey, Gauvin Alexander. "'Le style jésuite n'existe pas': Jesuit Corporate Culture and the Visual Arts." In *The Jesuits: Cultures, Sciences, and the Arts, 1540–1773*, edited by

AN OVERVIEW OF THE PRE-SUPPRESSION SOCIETY OF JESUS IN SPAIN 145

John W. O'Malley, Gauvin Alexander Bailey, Steven J. Harris, and T. Frank Kennedy, 38–89. Toronto: University of Toronto Press, 1999.

Bangert, William V. *A History of the Society of Jesus*. 2nd ed. St. Louis, MO: Institute of Jesuit Sources, 1986.

Bartolomé Martínez, B. [Bernabé]. "Las cátedras de gramática de los jesuitas en las universidades de Aragón." *Hispania sacra* 34 (1982): 389–448.

Bartolomé Martínez, B. [Bernabé]. "Las cátedras de gramática de los jesuitas en las universidades de su provincia de Castilla." *Hispania sacra* 35 (1983): 449–97.

Bartolomé Martínez, B. [Bernabé]. "Las librerías e imprentas de los jesuitas (1540–1767): Una aportación notable a la cultura española." *Hispania sacra* 40 (1988): 315–88.

Bartolomé Martínez, Gregorio. *Jaque mate al obispo virrey: Siglo y medio de sátiras y libelos contra don Juan de Palafox y Mendoza*. Mexico: Fondo de Cultura Económica, 1991.

Batllori, Miguel. "Entre la corte y Cataluña en armas," and "Los jesuitas y la guerra de Cataluña (1640–1659)." In Miguel Batllori and Ceferino Peralta, *Baltasar Gracián en su vida y en sus obras*, 77–97 and 189–223. Zaragoza: Institución Fernando el Católico, Diputación Provincial de Zaragoza, 1969.

Batllori, Miguel, and Ceferino Peralta. "La época de *El Criticón* y *El Comulgatorio*." In Miguel Batllori and Ceferino Peralta, *Baltasar Gracián en su vida y en sus obras*, 157–69. Zaragoza: Institución Fernando el Católico, Diputación Provincial de Zaragoza, 1969.

Batllori, Miguel. *Gracián y el barroco*. Rome: Edizioni di Storia e Letteratura, 1958.

Bilinkoff, Jodi. *The Avila of Saint Teresa: Religious Reform in a Sixteenth-Century City*. Ithaca, NY: Cornell University Press, 1989.

Bilinkoff, Jodi. "The Many 'Lives' of Pedro de Ribadeneyra." *Renaissance Quarterly* 52, no. 1 (1999): 180–96.

Bilinkoff, Jodi. *Related Lives: Confessors and Their Female Penitents, 1450–1750*. Ithaca, NY: Cornell University Press, 2005.

Bilinkoff, Jodi. "A Saint for a City: Mariana de Jesús and Madrid, 1565–1624." *Archive for Reformation History* 88 (1997): 322–37.

Boloqui, Belén. "Niñez y adolescencia de Baltasar Gracián." In *Baltasar Gracián: Selección de estudios, investigación actual y documentación*, edited by Jorge M. Ayala, 5–62. Barcelona: Anthropos, 1993.

Bouza, Fernando. *Corre manuscrito: Una historia cultural del Siglo de Oro*. Madrid: Marcial Pons Historia, 2001.

Brading, D. A. [David Anthony]. *The First America: The Spanish Monarchy, Creole Patriots, and the Liberal State, 1492–1867*. Cambridge: Cambridge University Press, 1991.

Burrieza Sánchez, Javier. "La Compañía de Jesús y la defensa de la monarquía hispánica." *Hispania sacra* 60 (2008): 181–229.

Burrieza Sánchez, Javier. "Establecimiento, fundación y oposición de la Compañía de Jesús en España (siglo XVI)," "Los ministerios de la Compañía," and "'Las glorias del segundo siglo' (1622–1700)." In Teófanes Egido, Javier Burrieza Sánchez, and Manuel Revuelta González, *Los jesuitas en España y en el mundo hispánico*, 49–106, 107–50, and 151–78. Madrid: Fundación Carolina, Centro de Estudios Hispánicos e Iberoamericanos, Marcial Pons, 2004.

Burrieza Sánchez, Javier. "La percepción jesuítica de la mujer." *Investigaciones históricas, época moderna y contemporánea* 25 (2005): 85–116.

Burson, Jeffrey D., and Jonathan Wright, eds. *The Jesuit Suppression in Global Context: Causes, Events, and Consequences*. Cambridge: Cambridge University Press, 2015.

Callado Estela, Emilio. "El confesor regio fray Luis Aliaga y la controversia inmaculista." *Hispania sacra* 68 (2016): 317–26.

Calzada, Gabriel. "Facing Inflation Alone: Juan de Mariana and His Struggle against Monetary Chaos." Translated by Eric Clifford Graf. *Quarterly Journal of Austrian Economics* 21, no. 2 (Summer 2018): 110–36.

Carrete Parrondo, Juan. "Más allá del poder: Imágenes prohibidas; Humanidades digitales." https://sites.google.com/site/masalladelpoderporjuancarrete/ (accessed April 28, 2020).

Casalini, Cristiano. "Discerning Skills: Psychological Insight at the Core of Jesuit Identity." In *Exploring Jesuit Distinctiveness: Interdisciplinary Perspectives on Ways of Proceeding within the Society of Jesus*, edited by Robert Aleksander Maryks, 189–211. Leiden: Brill, 2016.

Cejudo López, Jorge, and Teófanes Egido. "Introducción." In Pedro Rodríguez de Campomanes, *Dictamen fiscal de expulsión de los jesuitas de España (1766–1767)*, edited by Jorge Cejudo López and Teófanes Egido, 1–40. Madrid: Fundación Universitaria Española, 1977.

Civil, Pierre. "Iconografía y relaciones en pliegos: La exaltación de la Inmaculada en la Sevilla de principios del siglo XVII." In *Las relaciones de sucesos en España (1500–1750): Actas del primer coloquio internacional (Alcalá de Henares, 8, 9 y 10 de junio de 1995)*, edited by María Cruz García de Enterría et al., 65–77. Paris and Alcalá de Henares: Publicaciones de la Sorbonne and Servicio de Publicaciones de la Universidad de Alcalá, 1996.

Coe, Sophie D., and Michael D. Coe. *The True History of Chocolate*. 3rd ed. London: Thames & Hudson, 2013.

Cohen, Thomas M. *The Fire of Tongues: António Vieira and the Missionary Church in Brazil and Portugal*. Stanford, CA: Stanford University Press, 1998.

Colombo, Emanuele, and Niccolò Guasti. "The Expulsion and Suppression in Portugal and Spain: An Overview." In *The Jesuit Suppression in Global Context: Causes, Events, and Consequences*, edited by Jeffrey D. Burson and Jonathan Wright, 117–38. Cambridge: Cambridge University Press, 2015.

Córdoba Salmerón, Miguel. "A Failed Politician, a Disputed Jesuit: Cardinal Johann Eberhard Nithard (1607–81)." *Journal of Jesuit Studies* 7, no. 4 (2020): 545–69. https://doi.org/10.1163/22141332-00704003 (accessed November 4, 2020).

Coster, Adolphe. *Baltasar Gracián*. Translated by Ricardo del Arco. Zaragoza: Institución Fernando el Católico, 1947.

Cruz, Anne J. "Introduction." In *The Life and Writings of Luisa de Carvajal y Mendoza*, edited and translated by Anne J. Cruz, 1–109. Toronto: Iter, Centre for Reformation and Renaissance Studies, 2014.

Cruz, Anne J., ed. and trans. *The Life and Writings of Luisa de Carvajal y Mendoza*. Toronto: Iter, Centre for Reformation and Renaissance Studies, 2014.

Cruz, Anne J. "Willing Desire: Luisa de Carvajal y Mendoza and Female Subjectivity." In *Power and Gender in Renaissance Spain: Eight Women of the Mendoza Family, 1450–1650*, edited by Helen Nader, 177–93. Urbana: University of Illinois Press, 2004.

Dalmases, Cándido de. *Francis Borgia: Grandee of Spain, Jesuit, Saint*. Translated by Cornelius Michael Buckley. St. Louis, MO: Institute of Jesuit Sources, 1991.

Dalmases, Cándido de. *El padre Francisco de Borja*. Madrid: Biblioteca de Autores Cristianos, 1983.

Dalmases, Cándido de. "San Francisco de Borja y la Inquisición española 1559–1561." *Archivum historicum Societatis Iesu* 41 (1972): 48–135.

Del Piero, R. [Raúl] A. "Quevedo y Juan de Pineda." *Modern Philology* 56, no. 2 (November 1958): 82–91.

Donahue, Darcy. "The Mysticism of Saint Ignatius of Loyola." In *A New Companion to Hispanic Mysticism*, edited by Hilaire Kallendorf, 201–29. Leiden: Brill, 2010.

Dupuy, Michel. "Jansénisme." In *Dictionnaire de spiritualité: Ascétique et mystique, doctrine et histoire*, edited by Marcel Viller, Charles Baumgartner, and André Rayez, 8:cols. 102–48. 17 Vols. Paris: G. Beauchesne et ses fils, 1932–95.

Echarte, I. [Ignacio]. "Comisario" in "Gobierno: Sumario." In *Diccionario histórico de la Compañía de Jesús: Biográfico—temático*, edited by Charles E. O'Neill and Joaquín María Domínguez, 2:1749–50. 4 Vols. Madrid and Rome: Universidad Pontificia Comillas and Institutum Historicum S.I., 2001.

Egido, Teófanes. "El siglo XVIII: Del poder a la extinción." In Teófanes Egido, Javier Burrieza Sánchez, and Manuel Revuelta González, *Los jesuitas en España y en el mundo hispánico*, 225–78. Madrid: Fundación Carolina, Centro de Estudios Hispánicos e Iberoamericanos, Marcial Pons, 2004.

Egido, Teófanes, and Isidoro Pinedo. *Las causas "gravísimas" y secretas de la expulsión de los jesuitas por Carlos III*. Madrid: Fundación Universitaria Española, 1994.

Egido, Teófanes, Javier Burrieza Sánchez, and Manuel Revuelta González. *Los jesuitas en España y en el mundo hispánico*. Madrid: Fundación Carolina, Centro de Estudios Hispánicos e Iberoamericanos, Marcial Pons, 2004.

Elliott, J. [John] H. *The Count-Duke of Olivares: The Statesman in an Age of Decline*. New Haven: Yale University Press, 1986.

Elliott, J. [John] H. *Imperial Spain 1469–1716*. London: Penguin, 2002 [1963].

Endean, Philip. "The Strange Style of Prayer: Mercurian, Cordeses, and Álvarez." In *The Mercurian Project: Forming Jesuit Culture 1573–1580*, edited by Thomas M. McCoog, 351–97. St. Louis, MO, and Rome: Institute of Jesuit Sources and Institutum Historicum Societatis Iesu, 2004.

Escalera, J. [José Martínez de la]. "Moya, Mateo de." In *Diccionario histórico de la Compañía de Jesús: Biográfico—temático*, edited by Charles E. O'Neill and Joaquín María Domínguez, 3:2755–56. 4 Vols. Madrid and Rome: Universidad Pontificia Comillas and Institutum Historicum S.I., 2001.

Escalera, J. [José Martínez de la]. "Poza, Juan Bautista." In *Diccionario histórico de la Compañía de Jesús: Biográfico—temático*, edited by Charles E. O'Neill and Joaquín María Domínguez, 4:3029. 4 Vols. Madrid and Rome: Universidad Pontificia Comillas and Institutum Historicum S.I., 2001.

Fejér, Joseph [Josephus]. *Defuncti secundi saeculi Societatis Jesu 1641–1740*. 5 Vols. Rome: Curia Generalitia S.J., Institutum Historicum S.J., 1985–90. http://www.sjweb.info/arsi/documents/Defuncti_1640–1740_vol_IIII_N_R.pdf (accessed July 27, 2020).

Fernández, Luis. "Íñigo de Loyola y los alumbrados." *Hispania sacra* 35 (1983): 585–680.

Fois, Mario. "Everard Mercurian." In *The Mercurian Project: Forming Jesuit Culture 1573–1580*, edited by Thomas M. McCoog, 1–33. St. Louis, MO, and Rome: Institute of Jesuit Sources and Institutum Historicum Societatis Iesu, 2004.

Forrest, Beth Marie, and April L. Najjaj. "Is Sipping Sin Breaking Fast? The Catholic Chocolate Controversy and the Changing World of Early Modern Spain." *Food & Foodways* 15, nos. 1–2 (2007): 31–52.

Fraschina, Alicia. *Mujeres consagradas en el Buenos Aires colonial*. Buenos Aires: Eudeba, 2010.

Fullam, Lisa. "Juana, S.J.: The Past (and Future?) Status of Women in the Society of Jesus." *Studies in the Spirituality of Jesuits* 31 (November 1999): 1–39.

Garcés, María Antonia. *Cervantes in Algiers: A Captive's Tale*. Nashville: Vanderbilt University Press, 2002.

García Cárcel, Ricardo. "La crisis de la Compañía de Jesús en los últimos años del reinado de Felipe II (1585–1598)." In *La monarquía de Felipe II a debate*, edited by Luis Antonio Ribot García, 383–404. Madrid: Sociedad Estatal para la Conmemoración de los Centenarios de Felipe II y Carlos V, 2000.

García Cárcel, Ricardo, and Javier Burgos Rincón. "Los criterios inquisitoriales en la censura de libros en los siglos XVI y XVII." *Historia social* 14 (1992): 97–109.

García Hernán, Enrique. *Ignacio de Loyola*. Madrid: Taurus, Fundación Juan March, 2013.

AN OVERVIEW OF THE PRE-SUPPRESSION SOCIETY OF JESUS IN SPAIN 149

García Oro, José. "Conventualismo y observancia: La reforma de las órdenes religiosas en los siglos XV y XVI." In *La iglesia en la España de los siglos XV y XVI*, edited by José Luis González Novalín, 3.1:211–350. Vol. 3.1 of *Historia de la iglesia en España*, edited by Ricardo García Villoslada. 7 Vols. Madrid: Biblioteca de Autores Cristianos, 1979–82.

García Pérez, Francisco José. "La oratoria sagrada como arma política: Los predicadores reales de Juan José de Austria." *Obradoiro de historia moderna* 26 (2017): 237–65.

Garmendia Larrañaga, Juan. "El Señor de Loyola, patrono de la iglesia de San Sebastián de Soreasu y sus filiales: Las seroras S. XVI." *Boletín de la Real Sociedad Bascongada de los Amigos del País* 63, no. 2 (2007): 471–81. Reproduced with different pagination from Eusko Ikaskuntza, 2010: http://www.euskomedia.org/PDFAnlt/jgl/70223232.pdf (accessed April 28, 2020).

Gayangos, Pascual de, ed. *Cartas de algunos PP. de la Compañía de Jesús: Sobre los sucesos de la monarquía entre los años 1634 y 1648*. 7 Vols. Madrid: Imprenta Nacional, 1861–65.

Giammanco, Roberto. "Sull'inautenticità' del memoriale antigesuitico attribuito a Benito Arias Montano." *Archivum historicum Societatis Iesu* 26 (1957): 276–84.

Giles, Mary E. "Glossary." In *Women in the Inquisition: Spain and the New World*, edited by Mary E. Giles, 377–79. Baltimore: Johns Hopkins University Press, 1999.

Giordano, Maria Laura. "Al borde del abismo: 'Falsas santas' e 'ilusas' madrileñas en la vigilia de 1640." Translated by Josep Monter. *Historia social* 57 (2007): 75–97.

Giordano, Maria Laura. "Historicizing the Beatas: The Figures behind Reformation and Counter-Reformation Conflicts." Translated by Silvia Dupont and Alison Weber. In *Devout Laywomen in the Early Modern World*, edited by Alison Weber, 91–111. London: Routledge, 2016.

Gonçalves, Nuno da Silva. "Jesuits in Portugal." In *The Mercurian Project: Forming Jesuit Culture 1573–1580*, edited by Thomas M. McCoog, 705–44. St. Louis, MO, and Rome: Institute of Jesuit Sources and Institutum Historicum Societatis Iesu, 2004.

González Novalín, José Luis. "La Inquisición y la Compañía de Jesús." *Anthologica annua* 37 (1990): 11–56.

Gracián, Baltasar. *Obras completas*. Edited by E. [Evaristo] Correa Calderón. Madrid: M. Aguilar, 1944.

Guibert, Joseph de. *The Jesuits: Their Spiritual Doctrine and Practice; A Historical Study*. Translated by William J. Young. St. Louis, MO: Institute of Jesuit Sources, 1986.

Guibovich Pérez, Pedro M. *Censura, libros e inquisición en el Perú colonial, 1570–1754*. Seville: Consejo Superior de Investigaciones Científicas, Escuela de Estudios Hispano-Americanos, Universidad de Sevilla, Diputación de Sevilla, 2003.

Haliczer, Stephen. *Sexuality in the Confessional: A Sacrament Profaned*. New York: Oxford University Press, 1996.

Harney, Martin P. *The Jesuits in History: The Society of Jesus through Four Centuries*. New York: America Press, 1941.

Harty, John. "Probabilism." In *The Catholic Encyclopedia*. Vol. 12. New York: Robert Appleton, 1911. http://www.newadvent.org/cathen/12441a.htm (accessed April 28, 2020).

Hendrickson, D. Scott. *Jesuit Polymath of Madrid: The Literary Enterprise of Juan Eusebio Nieremberg (1595–1658)*. Leiden: Brill, 2015.

Holweck, Frederick. "Immaculate Conception." In *The Catholic Encyclopedia*. Vol. 7. New York: Robert Appleton Company, 1910. http://www.newadvent.org/cathen/07674d.htm (accessed April 28, 2020).

Ignatius of Loyola. *The Constitutions of the Society of Jesus and Their Complementary Norms*. Translated by George E. Ganss. St. Louis, MO: Institute of Jesuit Sources, 1996.

Ignatius of Loyola. *Epistolae et instructiones*. Vol. 1. Monumenta Historica Societatis Iesu 22. Madrid: Typis Gabrielis Lopez de Horno, 1903.

Ignatius of Loyola. *Epistolae et instructiones*. Vol. 4. Monumenta Historica Societatis Iesu 29. Madrid: Typis Gabrielis Lopez de Horno, 1906.

Ignatius of Loyola. *Fontes narrativi de S. Ignatio de Loyola et de Societatis Iesu initiis*. Vol. 1. Monumenta Historica Societatis Iesu 66. Rome: Apud Monumenta Historica Societatis Iesu, 1943.

Jiménez Pablo, Esther. "El final de la hegemonía hispana en la Compañía de Jesús: Los memorialistas italianos (1585–1593)." *Hispania sacra* 69 (2017): 619–37.

Johnson, Trevor. "Blood, Tears, and Xavier-Water: Jesuit Missionaries and Popular Religion in the Eighteenth-Century Upper Palatinate." In *Popular Religion in Germany and Central Europe, 1400–1800*, edited by Bob Scribner and Trevor Johnson, 183–202. New York: St. Martin's Press, 1996.

Kagan, Richard L. *Students and Society in Early Modern Spain*. Baltimore: Johns Hopkins University Press, 1974.

Kallendorf, Hilaire. *Conscience on Stage: The* Comedia *as Casuistry in Early Modern Spain*. Toronto: University of Toronto Press, 2007.

Kallendorf, Hilaire, ed. *A New Companion to Hispanic Mysticism*. Leiden: Brill, 2010.

Kamen, Henry. *Imagining Spain: Historical Myth and National Identity*. New Haven: Yale University Press, 2008.

Kamen, Henry. *The Phoenix and the Flame: Catalonia and the Counter-Reformation*. New Haven: Yale University Press, 1993.

Kamen, Henry. *The Spanish Inquisition: A Historical Revision*. 4th ed. New Haven: Yale University Press, 2014.

Keenan, James F. "The Birth of Jesuit Casuistry: *Summa casuum conscientiae, sive de instructione sacerdotum, libri septem* by Francisco de Toledo (1532–1596)." In *The Mercurian Project: Forming Jesuit Culture 1573–1580*, edited by Thomas M. McCoog,

461–82. St. Louis, MO, and Rome: Institute of Jesuit Sources and Institutum Historicum Societatis Iesu, 2004.

Laburu, J. A. [José Antonio] de. *La salud corporal y san Ignacio de Loyola.* Montevideo: Editorial Mosca Hermanos, 1938.

Lacouture, Jean. *Jésuites: Une multibiographie,* vol. 1, *Les conquérants.* 2 Vols. Paris: Éditions du Seuil, 1991.

Lara Martínez, Laura. "Enfermedades y remedios de la Compañía: El diagnóstico del padre Mariana y otros pensadores jesuitas." In *La actualidad del padre Juan de Mariana: Congreso internacional 22, 23 y 24 de marzo de 2017, Talavera de la Reina,* edited by Jacinto Rivera de Rosales and Francisco Javier Gómez Díez, 87–95. Pozuelo de Alarcón: Editorial UFV, Universidad Francisco de Vitoria, 2018.

Lavenia, Vincenzo. "La scienza dell'Immacolata: Invenzione teologica, politica e censura romana nella vicenda di Juan Bautista Poza." *Roma moderna e contemporanea* 18, nos. 1–2 (2010): 179–211.

Le Brun, Jacques. "Quiétisme." In *Dictionnaire de spiritualité: Ascétique et mystique, doctrine et histoire,* edited by Marcel Viller, Charles Baumgartner, and André Rayez, 12:cols. 2756–842. 17 Vols. Paris: G. Beauchesne et ses fils, 1932–95.

Lehfeldt, Elizabeth A. *Religious Women in Golden Age Spain: The Permeable Cloister.* Aldershot, England: Ashgate, 2005.

L'Heureux, John. "From St. Ignatius Loyola, Founder of the Jesuits: His Autobiography." In *No Place for Hiding: New Poems,* 35–43. Garden City, NY: Doubleday, 1971.

López Arandia, María Amparo. "La forja de la leyenda blanca: La imagen de la Compañía de Jesús a través de sus crónicas." *Historia social* 65 (2009): 125–46.

Lozano Navarro, Julián J. *La Compañía de Jesús y el poder en la España de los Austrias.* Madrid: Cátedra, 2005.

Lozano Navarro, Julián J. "Entre jesuitas y beatas: La percepción de la santidad en el colegio de la Compañía de Jesús en Marchena (siglos XVII y XVIII)." In *Subir a los altares: Modelos de santidad en la Monarquía Hispánica (siglos XVI—XVIII),* edited by Inmaculada Arias de Saavedra, Esther Jiménez Pablo, and Miguel Luis López-Guadalupe Muñoz, 51–77. Granada: Universidad de Granada, 2018.

Malaxechevarría, José. *La Compañía de Jesús por la instrucción del pueblo vasco en los siglos XVII y XVIII: Ensayo histórico.* San Sebastián: Imprenta y librería san Ignacio, 1926. http://www.liburuklik.euskadi.eus/handle/10771/25046 (accessed April 28, 2020).

Marín Barriguete, Fermín. "Los jesuitas y el culto mariano: La Congregación de la Natividad en la Casa Profesa de Madrid." *Tiempos modernos* 9 (2003–4): 1–20.

Márquez, Antonio. *Los alumbrados: Orígenes y filosofía (1525–1559).* 2nd ed. Madrid: Taurus, 1980.

Marsá, María. *La imprenta en los siglos de oro (1520–1700).* Madrid: Ediciones del Laberinto, 2001.

Martin, A. Lynn. "Jesuits and Their Families: The Experience in Sixteenth-Century France." *Sixteenth Century Journal* 13, no. 1 (1982): 3–24.

Martin, A. Lynn. *Plague? Jesuit Accounts of Epidemic Disease in the Sixteenth Century.* Kirksville, MO: Sixteenth Century Journal Publishers, 1996.

Martín López, David, and Francisco José Aranda Pérez. "La conformación de la provincia jesuítica de Toledo en torno al generalato de Diego Laínez (1556–1565)." *Hispania sacra* 66, extra 2 (2014): 357–96.

Martínez de Bujanda, J. [Jesús]. "Índices de libros prohibidos del siglo XVI." In *Historia de la Inquisición en España y América*, edited by J. [Joaquín] Pérez Villanueva and Bartolomé Escandell Bonet, 3:773–828. 3 Vols. Madrid: Biblioteca de Autores Cristianos, Centro de Estudios Inquisitoriales, 1984–2000.

Martínez de la Escalera, José. "Baltasar Gracián desde Pamplona (1640)." *Archivum historicum Societatis Iesu* 55 (1986): 145–53.

Martínez Gil, Fernando. "Los sermones como cauce de propaganda política: La Guerra de sucesión." *Obradoiro de historia moderna* 20 (2011): 303–36.

Martínez Millán, José, and Teresa Sánchez Rivilla. "El Consejo de Inquisición (1483–1700)." *Hispania sacra* 36 (1984): 71–193.

Martínez Millán, José. "Transformación y crisis de la Compañía de Jesús (1578–1594)." In *I religiosi a corte: Teologia, politica e diplomazia in antico regime; Atti del seminario di studi, Georgetown University a Villa Le Balze, Fiesole 20 ottobre 1995*, edited by Flavio Rurale, 101–29. Rome: Bulzoni, 1998.

Maryks, Robert Aleksander. "Census of the Books Written by Jesuits on Sacramental Confession (1554–1650)." *Annali di storia moderna e contemporanea* 10 (2004): [415]–519.

Maryks, Robert Aleksander, ed. *A Companion to Ignatius of Loyola: Life, Writings, Spirituality, Influence.* Leiden: Brill, 2014.

Maryks, Robert Aleksander. *The Jesuit Order as a Synagogue of Jews: Jesuits of Jewish Ancestry and Purity-of-Blood Laws in the Early Society of Jesus.* Leiden: Brill, 2010.

Mateos, Francisco. "Papeles secuestrados a los jesuítas en el siglo XVIII, reunidos en Madrid." *Razón y fe* 175 (1967): 527–40.

McCoog, Thomas M., ed. *The Mercurian Project: Forming Jesuit Culture 1573–1580.* St. Louis, MO, and Rome: Institute of Jesuit Sources and Institutum Historicum Societatis Iesu, 2004.

Medina, Francisco de Borja. "Everard Mercurian and Spain: Some Burning Issues." Translated by Walter P. Krolikowski. In *The Mercurian Project: Forming Jesuit Culture 1573–1580*, edited by Thomas M. McCoog, 945–66. St. Louis, MO, and Rome: Institute of Jesuit Sources and Institutum Historicum Societatis Iesu, 2004.

Medina, F. B. [Francisco de Borja]. "López, Gaspar." In *Diccionario histórico de la Compañía de Jesús: Biográfico—temático*, edited by Charles E. O'Neill and Joaquín María Domínguez, 3:2414. 4 Vols. Madrid and Rome: Universidad Pontificia Comillas and Institutum Historicum S.I., 2001.

Medina, F. B. [Francisco de Borja]. "Puerto, Gabriel Baptista del." In *Diccionario histórico de la Compañía de Jesús: Biográfico—temático*, edited by Charles E. O'Neill and Joaquín María Domínguez, 4:3257–58. 4 Vols. Madrid and Rome: Universidad Pontificia Comillas and Institutum Historicum S.I., 2001.

Meissner, W. [William] W. *Ignatius of Loyola: The Psychology of a Saint*. New Haven: Yale University Press, 1992.

Menéndez Pelayo, Marcelino. *Historia de los heterodoxos españoles*. 3 Vols. Madrid: Librería Católica de San José, 1880–81.

Molina, J. Michelle, and Ulrike Strasser. "Missionary Men and the Global Currency of Female Sanctity." In *Women, Religion, and the Atlantic World (1600–1800)*, edited by Daniella Kostroun and Lisa Vollendorf, 156–79. Toronto: University of Toronto Press, UCLA Center for Seventeenth- and Eighteenth-Century Studies, and the William Andrews Clark Memorial Library, 2009.

Molina, Tirso de. *Deleitar aprovechando*. Edited by Pilar Palomo Vázquez. Madrid: Turner, 1994.

Moreno, Doris. "Francisco de Borja y la Inquisición." In *Francesc de Borja (1510–1572), home del Renaixement, sant del barroc: Actes del Simposi Internacional (Gandia, 25–27 d'oct.–València, 4–5 nov. de 2010)*, edited by Santiago La Parra, 351–75. Gandía: CEIC Alfons el Vell, 2012.

Moreno, Doris. "Los jesuitas, la Inquisición y la frontera espiritual de 1559." *Bulletin of Spanish Studies* 92, no. 5 (2015): 655–75.

Moreno Martínez, Doris, and Manuel Peña Díaz. "El jesuita Juan Bautista Poza y la censura." In *Per Adriano Prosperi*, vol. 3, *Riti di passaggio, storie di giustizia*, edited by Vincenzo Lavenia and Giovanna Paolin, 3:159–70. 3 Vols. Pisa: Edizioni della Normale, 2011.

Muller, Jeffrey. "Historiography of the Art and Architecture of the Jesuits." *Jesuit Historiography Online*. Edited by Robert Aleksander Maryks. https://reference works.brillonline.com/entries/jesuit-historiography-online/historiography-of-the -art-and-architecture-of-the-jesuits-SIM_192594 (accessed April 28, 2020).

Navarro Brotóns, Víctor. "Los jesuitas y la renovación científica en la España del siglo XVII." *Studia historica: Historia moderna* 14 (1996): 15–44.

Negredo del Cerro, Fernando, and Enrique Villalba Pérez. "Los jesuitas y la monarquía hispánica en el contexto de la Guerra de los treinta años 1625–1635." *Hispania sacra* 67 (2015): 635–72.

Nieremberg, Juan Eusebio. "P. Francisco de Villanueva." In *Varones ilustres de la Compañía de Jesús*, 8:5–69. 2nd ed. 9 Vols. Bilbao: Administración del Mensajero del Corazón de Dios, 1887–92. https://archive.org/details/varonesilustreso1niergoog/ page/n81/mode/2up (accessed April 28, 2020).

Nieremberg, Juan Eusebio. *Varones ilustres de la Compañía de Jesús*. 2nd ed. 9 Vols. Bilbao: Administración del Mensajero del Corazón de Dios, 1887–92.

Norton, Marcy. *Sacred Gifts, Profane Pleasures: A History of Tobacco and Chocolate in the Atlantic World*. Ithaca, NY: Cornell University Press, 2008.

Nyberg, Tore. "The Prophetic Call of St. Birgitta and of Her Order." *Hispania sacra* 52 (2000): 367–76.

O'Banion, Patrick J. *The Sacrament of Penance and Religious Life in Golden Age Spain*. University Park, PA: Pennsylvania State University Press, 2012.

O'Malley, John W. *The First Jesuits*. Cambridge, MA: Harvard University Press, 1993.

O'Malley, John W. "The Historiography of the Society of Jesus: Where Does It Stand Today?" In *The Jesuits: Cultures, Sciences, and the Arts, 1540–1773*, edited by John W. O'Malley, Gauvin Alexander Bailey, Steven J. Harris, and T. Frank Kennedy, 3–37. Toronto: University of Toronto Press, 1999.

O'Malley, John W. "Some Distinctive Characteristics of Jesuit Spirituality in the Sixteenth Century" and "Renaissance Humanism and the Religious Culture of the First Jesuits." Reprinted in John W. O'Malley, *Saints or Devils Incarnate? Studies in Jesuit History*, 165–80 and 181–98. Leiden: Brill, 2013.

O'Malley, John W., Gauvin Alexander Bailey, Steven J. Harris, and T. Frank Kennedy, eds. *The Jesuits: Cultures, Sciences, and the Arts, 1540–1773*. Toronto: University of Toronto Press, 1999.

O'Neill, Charles E., and Joaquín María Domínguez, eds. *Diccionario histórico de la Compañía de Jesús: Biográfico—temático*. 4 Vols. Madrid and Rome: Universidad Pontificia Comillas and Institutum Historicum S.I., 2001.

O'Reilly, Terence. "Early Printed Books in Spain and the *Exercicios* of Ignatius of Loyola." *Bulletin of Spanish Studies* 89, no. 4 (2012): 635–64.

Padberg, John W. "The Third General Congregation April 12–June 16, 1573." In *The Mercurian Project: Forming Jesuit Culture 1573–1580*, edited by Thomas M. McCoog, 49–75. St. Louis, MO, and Rome: Institute of Jesuit Sources and Institutum Historicum Societatis Iesu, 2004.

Padberg, John W., Martin D. O'Keefe, and John L. McCarthy, eds. *For Matters of Greater Moment: The First Thirty Jesuit General Congregations*. St. Louis, MO: Institute of Jesuit Sources, 1994.

Page, Carlos A. "De beatas y beaterios jesuitas de la provincia del Paraguay, siglos XVII–XVIII." *Región y sociedad* 30, no. 73 (2018): 1–22.

Palomo, Federico. "La doctrine mise en scène: Catéchèse et missions intérieures dans la Péninsule Ibérique à l'époque moderne." *Archivum historicum Societatis Iesu* 74 (2005): 23–55.

Palomo, Federico. *Fazer dos campos escolas excelentes: Os jesuítas de Évora e as missões do interior em Portugal (1551–1630)*. Lisbon: FCG-FCT/MCES, 2003.

Palomo, Federico. "Limosnas impresas: Escritos e imágenes en las prácticas misioneras de interior en la península Ibérica (siglos XVI–XVIII)." *Manuscrits* 25 (2007): 239–65.

AN OVERVIEW OF THE PRE-SUPPRESSION SOCIETY OF JESUS IN SPAIN 155

Pando-Canteli, María J. "Letters, Books, and Relics: Material and Spiritual Networks in the Life of Luisa de Carvajal y Mendoza (1564–1614)." In *Devout Laywomen in the Early Modern World*, edited by Alison Weber, 294–311. London: Routledge, 2016.

Pardo Tomás, José. *Ciencia y censura: La Inquisición española y los libros científicos en los siglos XVI y XVII*. Madrid: Consejo Superior de Investigaciones Científicas, 1991.

Pastore, Stefania. "La 'svolta antimistica' di Mercuriano: I retroscena spagnoli." *Dimensioni e problemi della ricerca storica* 1 (2005): 81–93.

Pastore, Stefania. "Unwise Paths: Ignatius of Loyola and the Years of Alcalá de Henares." Translated by John Tedeschi. In *A Companion to Ignatius of Loyola: Life, Writings, Spirituality, Influence*, edited by Robert Aleksander Maryks, 25–44. Leiden: Brill, 2014.

Pastore, Stefania. *Il vangelo e la spada: L'inquisizione di Castiglia e i suoi critici (1460–1598)*. Rome: Edizioni di Storia e Letteratura, 2003.

Pavone, Sabina. *The Wily Jesuits and the* Monita Secreta: *The Forged Secret Instructions of the Jesuits; Myth and Reality*. Translated by John P. Murphy. St. Louis, MO: Institute of Jesuit Sources, 2005.

Peña Díaz, Manuel. "El castellano en la Cataluña de los siglos XVI y XVII." *Manuscrits* 15 (1997): 149–55.

Pérez, Joseph. *The Spanish Inquisition: A History*. Translated by Janet Lloyd. New Haven: Yale University Press, 2005.

Pérez Goyena, Antonio. "Arias Montano y los jesuítas." *Estudios eclesiásticos* 7 (1928): 273–317.

Pérez Goyena, Antonio. "Francisco Suárez." In *The Catholic Encyclopedia*. Vol. 14. New York: Robert Appleton Company, 1912. http://www.newadvent.org/cathen/14319a.htm (accessed April 28, 2020).

Pérez Villanueva, J. [Joaquín]. "La crisis del Santo Oficio (1621–1700)." In *Historia de la Inquisición en España y América*, edited by J. [Joaquín] Pérez Villanueva and Bartolomé Escandell Bonet, 1:996–1203. 3 Vols. Madrid: Biblioteca de Autores Cristianos, Centro de Estudios Inquisitoriales, 1984–2000.

Pérez Villanueva, J. [Joaquín], and Bartolomé Escandell Bonet, eds. *Historia de la Inquisición en España y América*. 3 Vols. Madrid: Biblioteca de Autores Cristianos, Centro de Estudios Inquisitoriales, 1984–2000.

Perry, Mary Elizabeth. *Gender and Disorder in Early Modern Seville*. Princeton: Princeton University Press, 1990.

Pilo, Rafaella. *Juan Everardo Nithard y sus causas no causas: Razones y pretextos para el fin de un valimiento*. Madrid: Sílex, CajaSur, 2010.

Pohle, Joseph. "Controversies on Grace." In *The Catholic Encyclopedia*. Vol. 6. New York: Robert Appleton Company, 1909. http://www.newadvent.org/cathen/06710a.htm (accessed April 28, 2020).

Pohle, Joseph. "Luis de Molina." In *The Catholic Encyclopedia*. Vol. 10. New York: Robert Appleton Company, 1911. http://www.newadvent.org/cathen/10436a.htm (accessed April 28, 2020).

Poutrin, Isabelle. "Una lección de teología moderna: La vida maravillosa de doña Marina de Escobar (1665)." *Historia social* 57 (2007): 127–43.

Prosperi, Adriano. "L'immaculée conception à Séville et la fondation sacrée de la monarchie espagnole." *Revue d'histoire et de philosophie religieuses* 87, no. 4 (2007): 435–67.

Quevedo y Villegas, Francisco de. "Respuesta al padre Juan de Pineda de la Compañía de Jesús." In *Obras completas*, edited by Felicidad Buendía, 1:377–99. 4th ed. 2 Vols. Madrid: Aguilar, 1958–60.

Real Academia de la Historia. *DB~e*. Online version of the *Diccionario biográfico español*. http://dbe.rah.es/ (accessed July 17, 2020).

Redworth, Glyn. "A New Way of Living? Luisa de Carvajal and the Limits of Mysticism." In *A New Companion to Hispanic Mysticism*, edited by Hilaire Kallendorf, 273–95. Leiden: Brill, 2010.

Redworth, Glyn. *The She-Apostle: The Extraordinary Life and Death of Luisa de Carvajal*. Oxford: Oxford University Press, 2008.

Revuelta González, Manuel. "Ignacio de Loyola: El fundador de la Compañía." *Historia* 16, no. 191 (1992): 37–48.

Revuelta González, Manuel. "Los jesuitas durante la Segunda República y la Guerra Civil (1931–39)." In Teófanes Egido, Javier Burrieza Sánchez, and Manuel Revuelta González, *Los jesuitas en España y en el mundo hispánico*, 343–64. Madrid: Fundación Carolina, Centro de Estudios Hispánicos e Iberamericanos, Marcial Pons, 2004.

Rhodes, Elizabeth. "About Luisa de Carvajal y Mendoza, 1566–1614." In *This Tight Embrace: Luisa de Carvajal y Mendoza (1566–1614)*, edited and translated by Elizabeth Rhodes, 1–37. Milwaukee, WI: Marquette University Press, 2000.

Rhodes, Elizabeth. "Ignatius, Women, and the *Leyenda de los santos*." In *A Companion to Ignatius of Loyola: Life, Writings, Spirituality, Influence*, edited by Robert Aleksander Maryks, 7–23. Leiden: Brill, 2014.

Rhodes, Elizabeth. "Join the Jesuits, See the World: Early Modern Women in Spain and the Society of Jesus." In *The Jesuits II: Cultures, Sciences, and the Arts, 1540–1773*, edited by John W. O'Malley, Gauvin Alexander Bailey, Steven J. Harris, and T. Frank Kennedy, 33–49. Toronto: University of Toronto Press, 2006.

Rhodes, Elizabeth. "Luisa de Carvajal's Counter-Reformation Journey to Selfhood (1566–1614)." *Renaissance Quarterly* 51, no. 3 (1998): 887–911.

Rhodes, Elizabeth, ed. and trans. *This Tight Embrace: Luisa de Carvajal y Mendoza (1566–1614)*. Milwaukee, WI: Marquette University Press, 2000.

Rico Callado, Francisco Luis. "Las misiones interiores en la España postridentina." *Hispania sacra* 55 (2003): 109–29.

Río Parra, Elena del. *Cartografías de la conciencia española en la Edad de Oro*. Mexico City: Fondo de Cultura Económica, 2008.

AN OVERVIEW OF THE PRE-SUPPRESSION SOCIETY OF JESUS IN SPAIN   157

Rodríguez de Campomanes, Pedro. *Dictamen fiscal de expulsión de los jesuitas de España (1766–1767).* Edited by Jorge Cejudo López and Teófanes Egido. Madrid: Fundación Universitaria Española, 1977.

Royal English College of St. Alban/Real Colegio de los Ingleses. http://www.sanalbano .org/ (accessed July 17, 2020).

Rurale, Flavio. "Carlo Borromeo and the Society of Jesus in the 1570s." In *The Mercurian Project: Forming Jesuit Culture 1573–1580,* edited by Thomas M. McCoog, 559–605. St. Louis, MO, and Rome: Institute of Jesuit Sources and Institutum Historicum Societatis Iesu, 2004.

Ryan, María del Pilar. *El jesuita secreto: San Francisco de Borja.* Valencia: Biblioteca Valenciana, Generalitat Valenciana, 2008.

Sánchez, Magdalena S. *The Empress, the Queen, and the Nun: Women and Power at the Court of Philip III of Spain.* Baltimore: Johns Hopkins University Press, 1998.

Schlau, Stacey. "Flying in Formation: Subjectivity and Collectivity in Luisa Melgarejo de Soto's Mystical Practices." In *Devout Laywomen in the Early Modern World,* edited by Alison Weber, 133–51. London: Routledge, 2016.

Scott, Amanda L. "*Seroras* and Local Religious Life in the Basque Country and Navarre, 1550–1769." *Church History* 85, no. 1 (March 2016): 40–64.

Scott, Amanda L. "St. Ignatius of Loyola, María Beltrán de Loyola, and the Seroras of Azpeitia." Talk at the Sixteenth Century Society Conference, Albuquerque, NM. November 3, 2018.

Scully, Robert E. "The Lives of Anne Line: Vowed Laywoman, Recusant Martyr, and Elizabethan Saint." In *Devout Laywomen in the Early Modern World,* edited by Alison Weber, 276–93. London: Routledge, 2016.

Sicroff, Albert A. *Los estatutos de limpieza de sangre: Controversias entre los siglos XV y XVII.* Translated by Mauro Armiño. Madrid: Taurus, 1985.

Simmonds, Gemma. "Women Jesuits?" In *The Cambridge Companion to the Jesuits,* edited by Thomas Worcester, 120–35. Cambridge: Cambridge University Press, 2008.

Simón Díaz, José. *La bibliografía: Conceptos y aplicaciones.* Barcelona: Planeta, 1971.

Simón Díaz, José. *Historia del Colegio Imperial de Madrid.* 2 Vols. Madrid: Consejo Superior de Investigaciones Científicas, Instituto de Estudios Madrileños, 1952–59.

Simón Díaz, José. *El libro español antiguo: Análisis de su estructura.* Kassel: Edition Reichenberger, 1983.

Sommervogel, Carlos. *Bibliothèque de la Compagnie de Jésus.* 11 Vols. Brussels and Paris: Oscar Schepens and Alphonse Picard, 1890–1909.

Soto Artuñedo, Wenceslao. "Juana de Austria, ¿de la compañía de Jesús?" In *V Reunión científica asociación española de historia moderna,* vol. 1, *Felipe II y su tiempo,* edited by José Luis Pereira Iglesias and Jesús Manuel González Beltrán, 1:579–88. 2 Vols. Cádiz: Servicio de Publicaciones de la Universidad de Cádiz, Asociación Española de Historia Moderna, 1999.

Strasser, Ulrike. "'The First Form and Grace': Ignatius of Loyola and the Reformation of Masculinity." In *Masculinity in the Reformation Era*, edited by Scott H. Hendrix and Susan C. Karant-Nunn, 45–70. Kirksville, MO: Truman State University Press, 2008.

Stratton, Suzanne L. *The Immaculate Conception in Spanish Art*. Cambridge: Cambridge University Press, 1994.

Van Kley, Dale K. "Plots and Rumors of Plots: The Role of Conspiracy in the International Campaign against the Society of Jesus, 1758–1768." In *The Jesuit Suppression in Global Context: Causes, Events, and Consequences*, edited by Jeffrey D. Burson and Jonathan Wright, 13–39. Cambridge: Cambridge University Press, 2015.

Van Kley, Dale K. *Reform Catholicism and the International Suppression of the Jesuits in Enlightenment Europe*. New Haven: Yale University Press, 2018.

Viller, Marcel, Charles Baumgartner, and André Rayez, eds. *Dictionnaire de spiritualité: Ascétique et mystique, doctrine et histoire*. 17 Vols. Paris: G. Beauchesne et ses fils, 1932–95.

Weber, Alison. "Demonizing Ecstasy: Alonso de la Fuente and the *Alumbrados* of Extremadura." In *The Mystical Gesture: Essays on Medieval and Early Modern Spiritual Culture in Honor of Mary E. Giles*, edited by Robert Boenig, 141–58. Aldershot, UK: Ashgate, 2000.

Weber, Alison, ed. *Devout Laywomen in the Early Modern World*. London: Routledge, 2016.

Weber, Alison. "Introduction: Devout Laywomen in the Early Modern World; The Historiographical Challenge." In *Devout Laywomen in the Early Modern World*, edited by Alison Weber, 1–28. London: Routledge, 2016.

Weber, Alison. "Jesuit Apologias for Laywomen's Spirituality." In *Devout Laywomen in the Early Modern World*, edited by Alison Weber, 331–52. London: Routledge, 2016.

Weber, Alison. "Los jesuitas y las carmelitas descalzas en tiempos de san Francisco de Borja: Amistad, rivalidad y recelos." In *Francisco de Borja y su tiempo: Política, religión y cultura en la edad moderna*, edited by Enrique García Hernán and María del Pilar Ryan, 103–13. Valencia and Rome: Albatros Ediciones and Institutum Historicum Societatis Iesu, 2011.

Weber, Alison. "Spiritual Administration: Gender and Discernment in the Carmelite Reform." *Sixteenth Century Journal* 31, no. 1 (Spring 2000): 123–46.

Wright, Anthony D. "The Jesuits and the Older Religious Orders in Spain." In *The Mercurian Project: Forming Jesuit Culture 1573–1580*, edited by Thomas M. McCoog, 913–44. St. Louis, MO, and Rome: Institute of Jesuit Sources and Institutum Historicum Societatis Iesu, 2004.

Wright, Jonathan, and Jeffrey D. Burson. "Introduction: Towards A New History of the Eighteenth-Century Suppression in Global Context." In *The Jesuit Suppression in Global Context: Causes, Events, and Consequences*, edited by Jeffrey D. Burson and Jonathan Wright, 1–10. Cambridge: Cambridge University Press, 2015.

Printed in the United States
By Bookmasters